The Farm Book by Thomas Jefferson

With light notes and annotations by Sam Sloan

Ishi Press International

This is a facsimile reproduction of the original Farm Book, hand written by Thomas Jefferson from 1774 to 1826.

ISBN 0-923891-80-3

Ishi Press International
1664 Davidson Avenue, Suite 1B
Bronx NY 10453

917-507-7226

Printed in the United States of America

The Farm Book of Thomas Jefferson

Introduction and Analysis by Sam Sloan

Thomas Jefferson has left to posterity a wonderful source document which provides details about his life on the Monticello estate near to Charlottesville, Virginia. To those who have never been there, Monticello is a grand palatial estate situated on a mountain-top. It is the closest thing America has to the Taj Mahal. The building is shown on the "tails" side of the American five-cent coin. No other president in American history ever owned anything approaching Monticello. Thomas Jefferson was almost certainly the richest man of his day to become President. He got his money the old fashioned way: He inherited it

The Farm Book contains a complete list of all slaves at various times, how many blankets each was given and how much food. It shows to which farm each slave was assigned. It also records the births and deaths of slaves.

The Farm Book is also a log containing information about the planting of crops and other items. However, it mostly deals with slaves, including how much food, blankets and clothing each slave was to be given. It also records births and deaths of slaves as well as the loans and leases of slaves. It contains long inventories of the names of slaves for various years. However, it does not record the purchase and sale of slaves.

Unfortunately, there is no complete record of the purchase and sale of slaves. In some cases, documents, such as bills of sale, have survived elsewhere, but they are not in the Farm Book.

There are only a few instances where Jefferson actually bought slaves. Instead, he bred his own. On June 20,1820, in a letter to his son-in-law John Eppes, he wrote:

> ***"I consider a woman who brings a child every two years as more profitable than the best man on the farm. What she produces is an addition to the capital, while his labors disappear in mere consumption."***

Almost all of the purchases of slaves by Thomas Jefferson were of pregnant women with children. One of the purchases of slaves took place while Thomas Jefferson was President. In the account book dated August 21, 1805, there is the entry:

> ***bought a Negro woman, Lucretia, James wife and her two sons John and Randall and the child of which she is pregnant, when born, for 180 pounds, of which 100 pounds to be paid before departure and the residue twelve months hence.***

Thomas Jefferson had several slaves named Sally. One died in 1781, during the American Revolution. Next to her name on page 29 of the Farm Book is the entry, "Cumberland .... fled to the enemy and died." A total of eight names are included in this category. Below is another entry with five more names of slaves who caught smallpox from the enemy and died and five more who caught camp fever from Negroes who returned and died. Altogether, there seems to have been 30 slaves who died in 1781 during the American Revolution.

Thomas Jefferson claimed that British General Cornwallis was personally responsible for their deaths. This was not mainly because the British attacked both Richmond and Monticello during the American Revolution in the hopes of capturing Jefferson, who was then the Governor of Virginia at the time. Rather, most of the deaths involved slaves on another plantation belonging to Jefferson named *"Elk Hill"*, which Lord Cornwallis occupied, using Jefferson's house as his office.

During the Revolution, the British rounded up many slaves as prisoners, not only the slaves of Thomas Jefferson, and kept them at Yorktown, where many of them died of various diseases due to the unsanitary conditions. This is reported by many sources, including Isaac Jefferson, one of the captured slaves, in ***Jefferson at Monticello***, p. 10, edited by James A. Bear, Jr. There, Isaac Jefferson states, "great many colored people died there.

The Americans have often been accused of treating their slaves badly, but the British treated them far worse. This subject is treated in greater detail in **Benjamin Quarles, *The Negro in the American Revolution***, Chapel Hill, North Carolina, 1961.

Although the Farm Book lists slaves who "fled with the enemy and died", the ***Memoirs of Isaac Jefferson***, p. 10, makes it clear that actually those slaves were taken as prisoners. Isaac Jefferson, then six years old, after being captured by the British along with his parents, was given the nickname "Sambo" by the British soldiers and allowed to beat the drum during the forced march to Yorktown. Isaac further states that after the fighting was over, General George Washington helped Isaac, along with his parents, Great George and Ursula, get back with their master, Thomas Jefferson.

Those slaves who died dearly did not include the Sally about whom history is primarily concerned. She is listed as ***"Sally 73"***, with 73 being her year of birth. This is the reason that the historians mention Sally as being 16 when she was with Jefferson in 1789 in France.

There is also a ***Sally 80***, who was too young to be of concern to us. However, as will be seen, this causes a lot of confusion, because both Sallys produced many children. The other Sally apparently was pure black and spent her life as a field hand in Bedford.

The Farm Book begins with a listing of all of the slaves of Thomas Jefferson and from where obtained on January 14, 1774 Page 5 of the Farm Book has a "Roll of the proper slaves of Thomas Jefferson", with

29 slaves listed at Monticello, four at Lego and eight at Shadwell. Lego and Shadwell were other farms owned by Thomas Jefferson. On page 6 of the Farm Book is a listing of `Slaves conveyed by my mother to me under the power given her in my father's will upon indemnification for the debts I had paid for her". Eleven slaves are listed: one at Lego, ten at Shadwell.

After that, on pages 7-9 is, A Roll of the slaves of John Wayles which were allotted to T.J. in right of his wife on a division of the estate Jan. 14 1774." This is a listing showing the whereabouts of all of the slaves in January, 1774, at the time that they were inherited from John Wayles. John Wayles had owned the impressive total of 11 different farms when he died. These were: Poplar Forest, Wingo's, Judith Creek, Crank's, Elk Hill, Indian Camp, Angola, Guinea, Bridge Quarter, Liggon's and Forest. Many of these farms were sold by Thomas Jefferson promptly after he inherited them. There were 135 slaves in all originally belonging to John Wayles, including the slaves on each farm.

This shows the importance of the Farm Book. We can see that at the beginning, in January, 1774, Thomas Jefferson owned exactly 187 slaves. Through the pages of the Farm Book, we can track the movements and the whereabouts of these slaves. Coincidentally, in the last inventory in the Farm Book, taken in 1824, just before he died in 1826, Thomas Jefferson also owned exactly 187 slaves.

This gives us a recorded history over the length of 50 years from 1774 to 1824 of the births and deaths and the comings and goings of these 187 slaves. No other slave owner during this period kept such a detailed record.

The entries in the Farm Book regarding ***Sally 73***, to the extent that they are legible, along with some other relevant entries, are as follows:

Page 9. Sally 73, Guinea. Below the name of Betty Hemings (Betty being short for Elizabeth) are the names of six children and one grandchild. The children are: Nancy, 1761; Jimmy, 1765; Thenia, 1767; Critta, 1769; Peter, Aug. 1770; and Sally, 1773. The grandson is Daniel, 1772. All are listed under the heading of Guinea. Guinea was not the country but rather the name of the farm in Cumberland County belonging to John Wayles where Sally had presumably been born. (Another farm was named Angola, also the name of a country, adding to the confusion). The name of Betty's mother, who was from Africa, but probably not from Angola, does not seem to have been mentioned by any source. Martin, 1756, and Bob, 1762, two other children of Betty Hemings, are listed separately on page 9 of the Farm Book as being at `Forest", the official residence of John Wayles, which was in Charles City County, near Richmond.

Page 18. Under Elk Hill (the farm where they were assigned to work in 1774) is the same list of names, except that Jimmy 1765 is missing. At the bottom is the notation "187 [slaves] in all". From other sources, we know that Jimmy", or James Hemings, the son of Betty Hemings, was taken to France by Thomas Jefferson in 1784, and later returned. James Hemings worked as a chef in the house of Thomas Jefferson at what is now 287 Market Street in Philadelphia, while Thomas Jefferson was Secretary of State. Finally, he was given his freedom on February 5, 1796. He and his brother, Robert Hemings, were the only slaves ever to be officially freed by Thomas Jefferson in his lifetime.

Page 21. Under Deaths in 1774 is listed "Betty (Sue's Elk Hill) November 15". However, this Betty who died on November 15, 1774 was another Betty, not the mother of Sally.

At this point, there is a 20-year gap. During this period, Thomas Jefferson went to France and upon his return became Secretary of State. Sally apparently stayed with him and did not return to the farm until 1794. However, there is no proof of this, but it is reported by Gore Vidal, author of ***Burr,*** that Aaron Burr in his diary noted the presence of Sally in Philadelphia in March, 1797, to attend the inauguration of Thomas Jefferson as Vice-President. Because of the distance involved, the daughters of Jefferson did not attend that inauguration.

Page 30. "Roll of the Negroes Nov. 1794 and where to be settled for the year 1795. Monticello Sally 73."

Page 31. Squeezed in at the bottom of the page there is an illegible entry under births which says, `H-, Sally's, October 5, 1795".

Page 39. Sally along with her sisters, Critta and Nancy, are mentioned as having received a blanket in various years.

Page 41. Sally, Critta and others were given clothing in December 1794.

Page 42. Sally was given 2 yards of linen and other items in 1794.

Page 43. Both "Betty Hem" and several Sallys are on the bread fist for 1795.

Page 46. One Sally is mentioned as a gatherer at Shadwell. Another Sally is on the list of eight women who "would remain to keep half the ploughs a going".

Page 49. Sally is on the list as receiving various items of clothing in 1795

Page 50. Bread list for 1796. Perhaps the first important entry. Sally is listed as being at Monticello and below her is the name "Edy". They are to receive two loaves of bread per week. It appears that Edy is a child of Sally's. Sally 80 is listed under Shadwell. That must have been the Sally who is listed as a gatherer on page 46 above.

Page 51. Ration list for 1796. Sally and Edy are to receive 8 fish.

Page 52. Col. 2. Cloths list 1796. Sally and Harriet are to receive one bed.

Page 52. Col. 3. Bread list 1797. Sally, Harriet and Aggy are to receive 3 bread.

Page 53. Sally and Harriet get 8 fish.

Page 55. 1799 Oct Sally and Beverly 98 get 1 1/2 of something illegible.

Page 56. Sally and Beverly get 8 fish and one bread. Below them are Betty Hem., John Hem. and Peter Hem. They each get 4 fish and 1/2 bread.

Page 57. Roll of the Negroes in the Winter of 1798-9. Listed below Sally is Beverly, who was born on April 1, 1798. Sally and Beverly get 8 fish and 1 bread.

Page 58a. Sally and Beverly are on the ration list for 1800.

Page 60. There is a list of 46 "Negroes leased to J. H. Craven" in 1801. There is another list of "Negroes retained". Sally and Beverly are on the list of Negroes retained, along with "Betty Hemings 35 & 07". This is the only indication of the possible actual birth and death dates of Betty. This shows that Betty was born in 1735 and died in 1807. This would make Betty 26 when she first gave birth to a child of John Wayles, and would make John Wayles only 20 when he bought her. Both seem unlikely.

However, other sources indicate that the reason for this discrepancy is that Madison Hemings, who, as will be seen, was the source for much of the information about the Hemings family history, was wrong when he said that his grandmother had been purchased directly off the slave ship by John Wayles. According to James A. Bear, Jr., the mother of Betty Hemings had first been owned by Col. Francis Eppes IV, who resided in what was then Henrico County, in a place now near to Hopewell, which is south of Richmond. Even recently, there were people named Hemings in that area, before they all changed their names. In 1746, Betty Hemings was deeded to John Wayles as part of the dowry he received in consideration of his marriage to Martha Eppes.

The reason that Betty Hemings did not become the mistress of John Wayles until age 26, after she had already given birth to six children by a slave husband who had died, was that she did not become the mistress of John Wayles until after his third wife, Elizabeth Lomax, had died in 1761. Betty produced her first child from John Wayles in 1762.

All of this may or may not be true. There is no mention of any of this in the Farm Book, other than the birth and death dates of Betty Hemings of 1735 and 1807.

The only persons with the name given as Hemings listed in the Farm Book are Betty Hemings, Peter Hemings, sometimes Sally Hemings and John Hemings. John Hemings was a son of Betty Hemings who was born long after the death of John Wayles. His father was said to be a carpenter named John Neilson who had worked for Thomas Jefferson.

We know from other correspondence by Thomas Jefferson that there was a James Hemings and a Robert Hemings. Robert Hemings almost never lived on the farm and traveled freely, almost like a white man. He was able to do so easily, being 75% white. He was eventually freed by Thomas Jefferson and settled in Richmond, Virginia, where he had a wife named Dolly and lived in a house on the corner of 7th and Grace Streets, which is now in downtown Richmond and is occupied by a skyscraper. His descendants live in the area of Richmond to this day. In addition, there are still people in the area of Charlottesville, Bedford and Lynchburg, Virginia named Hemmings (note the "mm). All of them are undoubtedly descended from Betty Hemings.

After the 1801 entry, this there is a nine-year gap in the Farm Book.

This apparently reflects the fact that Thomas Jefferson was President during the years 1801 to 1809.

Page 128. Contains an entry of great importance. This is the roll of Negroes 1810 Feb. in Albemarle, the county were Monticello was located. Under Monticello is listed `house ... Sally 73" and below her Harriet 01 May, Madison 05 Jan. and Eston 08 May 21. This means that during the eight years when Thomas Jefferson was in the White House, Sally Hemings produced three children. Harriet was born in 1801, Madison in 1805 and Eston on May 21, 1808. Also there is Edy 87 and three children, James, Jan. 7,1805; Maria, October 27, 1807 and Patsy, May 11, 1810. Under Tradesmen is listed John Hemings 75 and Beverly April 1, 1798.

From this it appears that Sally at age 37 already had possibly six children, of whom one had died. Harriet, who perhaps was also called Edy, who was born in 1795, must have died, but now Sally had a new daughter, also named Harriet. Her child Beverly at age 12 is already an emancipated person with a separate place on this list. However, it is important to note that Beverly was a boy, not a girl. Usually, Beverly is a girl's name, but occasionally it is a boy's, as was the case here.

Page 130. Roll of the Negroes according to their ages at Albemarle. Betty (the mother) is not on the list and presumably has died. Peter Hemings 1770, Sally 73 and John Hemings 75 are listed. There is also 1758 Beverly run away 22; 1801 Harriet (Sally's) run 22,; Madison (Sally's) 1805; Eston (Sally's) 1808; Peter (Edy's) June 5, 1815; Innet Sally's July 1816; Loranan Sally's 1818; Isabella Edy's Jan 7,1819; [blank] Sally's May 1821; William Edy's May 1821; Gilly Aggy's Dec. 1822;,1sabella, Sally's Cha wife, May 1823.

The above entry is of great importance, because most agree that the notation "run 22" next to the names of Beverly and Harriet indicates that they ran away in 1822,

Page 131. Roll of the Negroes in Bedford according to-their ages. This list shows at least three children born to Sally, but this is apparently Sally 80, who was a field hand, not Sally Hemings.

Page 134. Under bread list Feb. 1810 is listed Sally, followed by Beverly, Harriet, Madison and Eston.

Page 135. Under Monticello House is listed Sally grown-2 children-3. Unlike some of the other women on the list, Sally has no husband. Beverly is apparently considered grown. There are a total of 25 adults and 28 children on the house list.

Page 136. Dec. 1810. Again Sally is listed with her four children.

Page 137. Sally gets a blanket in 1808. Harriet, Madison and Eston each get a blanket in 1809.

Page 139. Again Sally is listed with four children.

Page 142. Distribution of blankets, 1812. Sally and four children get blankets.

Page 145. December 1813 clothing list Sally has three children. Beverly has his own place on the list

Page 147. December 14,1814. No change from above.

Page 148. Bread lists for 1815. Sally has all four children again.

Page 151. Dec. 1815. Sally back to three children. Beverly has his own spot on the list

Page 155. 1816. Same as above.

Page 156. Bread list Again all four children listed under Sally.

Page 159. There are now a total of 140 slaves. Sally listed with three children.

Page 160. Negroes leased to Thos. Randolph. 29 adults and 31 children, for a total of 60. Sally and her four children are all on the list of "Negroes retained", of which there are 80.

Page 162. 1818. Sally and three children plus Beverly are on the ration list Page 169.1819-182Q. Same as above.

Page 165. Blanket list Sally and four children are on the list, but lines are drawn through the names of Beverly and Harriet There is no explanation for this, but it has been explained that at about this time, Beverly and Harriet were allowed to run away and later took up residence in Washington, D.C.

Page 169. Dec 1823. Sally Hem. is on the list but no mention of the children.

Page 171. Sally and all four children are on the house list

Page 172. Sally, Madison and Eston only are on the list for 1821-2.

Page 174. 1822. Again the same. No more mention of Beverly and Harriet

Page 175. December 1823. No change.

Page 176. December 1824. No change. There are now 23 children, 21 men and 16 women on the Monticello house list.

The End of the Farm Book

Although the ration list of Thomas Jefferson of 8 fish and one bread per week for each slave does not appear to be particularly sumptuous, it shows that, unlike some other masters, Thomas Jefferson did at least feed his slaves. It is often forgotten that some slave owners did not feed their slaves at all. Instead, after a hard days work in the fields, the slaves were left to forage in the woods for whatever food they could find. Slaves ate dandelions, weeds, wild plants and roots, plus the occasional rabbit if they could catch one. They also ate chitlins and other undesirable animal parts which were leftovers the white people were not willing to eat. From this, we have the "soul food", which is still eaten in fine restaurants in places such as Harlem. Among the best known soul food is "collard greens".

Strangely, at least among the slaves mentioned in this book, it appears that they, more often than not, outlived their masters. It is possible that the unusual diet which the slaves were forced to eat was more healthy in the long run. A television documentary entitled **The Civil War** has talked about the deplorable condition of the slaves, stating that they rarely lived to be more than forty or fifty years old. However, this documentary forgot to mention that in those days, the life expectancy of white people was even less than that. Of course, this is not an apology for slavery. It merely means that a person who lives by foraging for weeds in the woods might live a longer life than one who is waited on by servants at the dinner table.

From reading the Farm Book, it does not appear that Sally was given special treatment. Nothing in the book identifies her as the President's personal concubine. When the others got eight fish and one bread, she also got the same.

However, other documents show that Sally was different from the other girls. The other women on the Monticello house list had various duties, such as cleaning and cooking. Only Sally, her mother, Betty, and her sister, Critta, had no other job. They were the personal attendants to Thomas Jefferson. Sally is occasionally listed as a seamstress.

Whenever a child was born, Jefferson noted not only the name of the mother but also the name of the father. All of the children produced by field hands at Poplar Forest in Bedford County had the names of their fathers on the lists in the Farm Book. However, no father is given for the children of Sally or for many of the other children born at Monticello. This does not, however, mean to imply that Jefferson might have been the father of all of these many children.

Sally is consistently listed as having four children. However, there may have been as many as six or even seven. Tom, the one who was claimed by Callender to have been conceived in France, probably did not exist, but if he did exist, possibly never lived on the farm. Harriet, born in 1795, died in 1797.

The 1796 entry shows a child named Edy. That name never appears again. It seems possible that Edy is the same child as Harriet, who died in 1797. It has been suggested by Fawn Brodie that these were different children, and that both died at about the same time. However, from a careful examination of the Farm Book, the statement by Fawn Brodie that Sally Hemings had a child named Edy who died has now been virtually disproven by ***Jack McLaughlin*** in his 1988 book ***Jefferson and Monticello***, page 406, note 119.

There is another Edy, the daughter of Isabella and the mother of James, Maria, Patsy, Betsy and Peter. She was born in 1787 and is clearly a different person. McLaughlin points out that when the name "Edy" appears under the name of Sally on page 50 of the Farm Book, it disappears under the name of Isabel, the mother of Edy 87. This means, according to McLaughlin, that this Edy was not the child of Sally at all but rather that she had been assigned to Sally to act as a nursemaid to care for the infant, Harriet. Later, on page 52, the name of Aggy appears below the name of Sally. Aggy 89 was another child of Isabel. This means that Aggy is now helping Sally to take care of Harriet.

This explanation is almost convincing. However, there is one small problem. Edy and Harriet are not listed together; as they presumably would have been had Edy been the nursemaid of Harriet. At the same time, on page 52 of the Farm Book, right hand columns, the names of

Sally, Harriet and Aggy appear together. Edy is back under the name of Isabel, her mother. This would seem to indicate that now Aggy has been assigned as a nursemaid to care for Harriet

Thus, McLaughlin's basic point appears to be correct. From checking several thousand entries in the Farm Book, we can see that Thomas Jefferson never made a mistake. His accuracy was almost super-human. Since we exclude the possibility of a mistake, McLaughlin's explanation is the only one which is plausible.

This provides strong evidence that there was something special about Harriet and that she actually was the daughter of Thomas Jefferson. There is no other instance in which anyone besides the mother was assigned as a nursemaid to care for an infant slave child.

It is refreshing to learn that there is one author, Jack McLaughlin, who does bother to check these small but extremely important facts and details in the Farm Book. This is in contrast to the sloppy work done by so many other writers on this subject, especially ***Virginius Dabney***. Incidentally, this Edy is the same person who later served as a cook in the White House and who became the wife of Joe Fossett. Also, just to remind the reader; the Harriet in question here is the one who died as an infant in 1797, not the second Harriet who was born in 1801.

Many other women at Monticello produced multiple children. One of the most prolific was Ursula, born in 1787, who had seven. These were Joe, Anna, Dolly, Cornelius, Thomas, Louisa, and Caroline.

Critta only bore one child. However, another woman on the house list with a similar name, Cretia, had seven children. This was apparently the same person as Lucretia, who was purchased while pregnant in 1805.

The allegation that Jefferson had children by at least one of his slaves seems likely. However; the allegation that he actually sold his children into slavery was clearly without foundation when made. Jefferson sold no slaves during that period. However, in just the last few years of his life, when Thomas Jefferson was desperately broke and short of cash, he started selling his slaves. There is one especially pathetic instance regarding this.

On November 30, 1815, when Thomas Jefferson was 72 years old, he entered into a contract to sell a three year old girl, coincidentally named Sally, daughter of Aggy, for the sum of one hundred fifty dollars, to a Mr. Jeremiah Goodman of Bedford County.

After making that contract, an addendum was added stating that the child would remain in the possession of her mother until either Mr. Goodman or Thomas Jefferson desired that she be taken into his possession.

Two years later, on July 20,1817, Thomas Jefferson must have realized that he had done a terrible thing, because he wrote a letter to Mr. Goodman stating that he wanted the contract to be annulled. He said, however, that he did not have the money to pay back the 150 dollars. He therefore requested that he be given two years credit to repay this sum.

This is truly a pathetic specter. Here is a former President of the United States, in the waning years of his life, who actually does not have $150 which he needs to rescue a by this time five-year-old girl.

One of the last entries of his life, when he was 81 years old, shows that by that time Thomas Jefferson was so desperately broke that he just wanted to sell his slaves for any money he could get for them. This was the first time he had reached that level of desperation.

A letter dated January 5, 1824 to Bernard Payton states:

> ***'Jefferson returned last night from a sale of some Negroes in Bedford. He could make no hand off selling for any portion of ready money. He sold therefore at one***

and two years credit"

Jefferson died completely insolvent on July 4,1826, when he was 83 years old. His debts amounted to $107,000, a huge amount in that time. It is said that it took fifty years before they were completely paid oft

On January 15, 1827, after the death of Thomas Jefferson, there was an auction advertised in the Richmond Enquirer. That notice, published in the Richmond Enquirer dated November 7,1826, said:

EXECUTOR'S SALE

On the fifteenth of January, at Monticello, in the county of Albemarle, the whole of the residue of the personal property of Thomas Jefferson, dec., consisting of valuable negroes, stock, crops, etc, household and kitchen furniture. The attention of the public is earnestly invited to this property. The negroes are believed to be the most valuable for their number ever offered in the state of Virginia.

As a result of this ad, all of the personal property and effects of Thomas Jefferson at Monticello were sold at this auction in an attempt to pay his debts. Included in the sale were almost all of his slaves at Monticello. A second slave auction took place in January, 1829, regarding the slaves in Bedford County.

However, in his will he had decreed freedom for five of his slaves. All five of them were males who had white fathers. The five were Burwell Colburn, John Hemings, Joe Fossett (the son of Mary, who was the first-born child of Betty Hemings and a slave father), Madison Hemings and Eston Hemings. The name of Sally Hemings, was not on the list, but apparently there was a private understanding that she would not be sold. All the rest of the slaves were sold. Nobody knows this for certain, however There is no absolute proof that the terms of the will of Thomas Jefferson were carried out, but the descendants of these five claim that this was done. Also, there was apparently a special act passed by the Virginia legislature in 1827 which decreed that the five slaves freed in the will of Thomas Jefferson were allowed to remain in the State of Virginia. Otherwise, all freed slaves were required to go north, under the law of Virginia at that time.

Sally Hemings continued to live at Monticello after the death of Thomas Jefferson, along with her sons, Madison and Eston, but all the other slaves were dispersed to various parts of the South. Sally Hemings died at Monticello in 1835. When she died, she and her two sons were the only former slaves of Thomas Jefferson still living at Monticello. Of course, they did not live in the `big house", but in a nearby cabin. By that time, the big house at Monticello had a new owner. After Sally Hemings died, her sons, Madison and Eston, moved to the area of Chillicothe, Ohio.

Sam Sloan

Uncle Jeff's Cabin and Judith's Creek

Uncle Jeff was an elderly Black man who lived in a cabin just past the bridge on Trent's Ferry Road in Lynchburg, Virginia that crossed Judith's Creek, which now marks the border between the City of Lynchburg and Bedford County. To reach the cabin, one needed to cross the bridge and then turn right onto Fox Hill Road. The cabin would be on a hillock to the immediate right.

Uncle Jeff had been born into slavery and he had lots of children, grandchildren, great-grandchildren and great-great-grandchildren, more than a hundred in all, who could always be seen around the cabin every time I drove past.

The cabin has since been demolished. I believe that his descendants still live on the land or in the immediate vicinity, which is now a wealthy high-class area where the rich people live.

I never got to meet Uncle Jeff, because he was already more than one hundred years old when I lived near there and he never left the house. I do not know when he died but he was still alive in 1962 when I went off to college.

In researching the lives of the slaves of Thomas Jefferson, it has occurred to me that Uncle Jeff might have had something to do with Thomas Jefferson, hence the name Uncle Jeff.

Also, Thomas Jefferson kept some of his slaves at a place named Judith's Creek. This is mentioned on page 7 of the Farm Book by Thomas Jefferson as Judith's Creek or Dunlora. Thomas Jefferson had nine slaves there.

However, the Judith's Creek is several miles long. It empties into the James River less than a mile from Uncle Jeff's former cabin. It is not clear exactly where Thomas Jefferson kept those nine slaves. Does anybody know?

Just explain this a little better: Thomas Jefferson kept nine slaves in a place he called "Judith's Creek", which was in Bedford County, Virginia.

During the years I lived in Bedford County, Virginia, there was an elderly Black man named "Uncle Jeff" who lived next to Judith's Creek and just off of Fox Hill Road.

Uncle Jeff had been born as a slave and he lived to be more than one hundred years old. I do not know when Uncle Jeff died, but it was after 1962, when I went off to college.

Due to the coincidence in name and place, I am wondering if Uncle Jeff's parents might have been slaves of Thomas Jefferson.

Sam Sloan

NOTES ON THE PAGINATION OF THE FARM BOOK

The folios in type, which duplicate Jefferson's own where visible, represent the numbering of the original Farm Book.

Pages 3, 4, 11, 12, 13, 14, 121, 122 are blank and are therefore omitted.

Pages 10, 20, 34, 58-b, 98, 99, 101, 112, 115, 118, 120, 126, 141, 170 are blank but are retained in order to keep the recto-verso relationship of the book itself.

Pages 25, 26, 35, 36, 49, 50, 73, 74, 151$_{1}$ 152, 169, 170, 175, 176 are missing from the original Farm Book. Of these, pages 49 and 50 have been restored to their proper places from the Alderman Library, University of Virginia; pages 73, -74, 151, 152, 169, 170, 175, 176 from the former Barren collection,

Between pages 54 and 59 there are missing two sheets. A loose Unnumbered sheet was found inserted here and since the dates follow chronologically those of the preceding ones it has been numbered 55, 56. One loose sheet from the Barren collection was numbered 57, 58 by Jefferson. It has been inserted in its original place. Also at this gap it appears that an unnumbered sheet has been pasted in. This has been numbered 58-a, 58-b.

NOTES ON THE FARM BOOK

The illustration on the facing page is of Jefferson's original ***Farm Book***, 1774-1826, now in the possession of the **Massachusetts Historical Society**. It is a memorandum book with leather strip board covers, 20.2 cm by 16 cm. It originally contained 379 pages of which Jefferson's plantation notes cover most of the first 177 pages. There are 202 blank pages after Jefferson's notes. The pages are not numbered after 147. The marginal words, set in type, are to help clarify the obscure words.

NOTES: This is the actual original Farm Book, now in the possession of the Massachusetts Historical Society.

NOTES: Inside cover of the Farm Book. As you can see, "Farm Book" is what Jefferson called this book, from whence it derives its name. At the top of this page is the genealogy of Thomas Jefferson's favorite horse, Caractacus.

NOTES to Page 1: This page has more information about his horse, Caractacus

NOTES to Page 2: More about horses of Thomas Jefferson

NOTES to Page 5: First inventory of the Slaves of Thomas Jefferson: "A Roll of the proper slaves of Thomas Jefferson, Jan. 14. 1774." There are 29 slaves listed here.

NOTES to Page 6: `Slaves conveyed by my mother to me under the power given her in my father's will upon indemnification for the debts I had paid for her".

NOTES to Page 7: A Roll of the slaves of John Wayles which were allotted to T.J. in right of his wife on a division of the estate Jan. 14 1774
NOTES to Page 8: Continuation of the Roll of the slaves of John Wayles

NOTES to Page 9: Continuation of the Roll of the slaves of John Wayles

NOTES to Page 10: Blank page retained in order to keep the left-right relationship of the book.

NOTES to Page 15: Location of Slaves in 1774, Monticello

NOTES to Page 16: Location of Slaves in 1774, Lego, Shadwell, Poplar Forest and Wingo's

NOTES to Page 17: Location of Slaves in 1774, Dunlora and Elk Hill

NOTES to Page 18: Location of Slaves in 1774, Elk Hill

NOTES to Page 19: Blankets Bed given to slaves in 1774

NOTES to Page 20: Blank page retained in order to keep the left-right relationship of the book.

NOTES to Page 21: Births and Deaths in 1774

NOTES to Page 22: Births and Deaths in 1775

NOTES to Page 23: Blankets Beds etc. given to slaves in 1775.

NOTES to Page 24: Roll of the Negroes taken in 1783

NOTES to Page 27: Blankets Beds etc. given to slaves in 1776.

NOTES to Page 28: Births and Deaths in 1777

NOTES to Page 29: Births and Deaths from 1779 to 1781 inclusive.

NOTES to Page 30: "Roll of the Negroes Nov. 1794 and where to be settled for the year 1795. Monticello Sally 73."

NOTES to Page 31: Register of births Bdemotis Bedford. Squeezed in at the bottom of the page there is an illegible entry under births which says, `H-, Sally's, October 5, 1795".

NOTES to Page 32: Land Roll in 1794.

NOTES to Page 33: Inventory of livestock on Monticello, Tufton, Shadwell, Lego, Poplar Forest

NOTES to Page 34: Blank page retained in order to keep the left-right relationship of the book.

NOTES to Page 37: Rates of estimating builders work.

NOTES to Page 38: Peach trees planted Dec. 1794

NOTES to Page 39: Distribution of blankets: Sally along with her sisters, Critta and Nancy, are mentioned as having received a blanket in various years.

NOTES to Page 40: Logs killed Dec. 94, Monticello, Shadwell

NOTES to Page 41: Sally, Critta and others were given clothing in December 1794.

NOTES to Page 42: Sally was given 2 yards of linen and other items in 1794.

NOTES to Page 43: Both "Betty Hem" and several Sallys are on the bread fist for 1795.

NOTES to Page 44: Estimate of the issues of the corn on hand Dec. 15, 1794.

NOTES to Page 45: Dairy for 1795.

NOTES to Page 46: One Sally is mentioned as a gatherer at Shadwell. Another Sally is on the list of eight women who "would remain to keep half the ploughs a going".

NOTES to Page 47: Dairy continued

NOTES to Page 48: Hogs killed Dec. 1795

NOTES to Page 49. Clothes 1795: Sally is on the list as receiving various items of clothing in 1795.

NOTES to Page 50: Bread Lists for 1796 per week

NOTES to Page 51: Ration lists for 1796

NOTES to Page 52: Clothes 1796, Bread List May 1797

NOTES to Page 53: Ration list of fish for each slave

NOTES to Page 54: Dairy 1796

NOTES to Page 55: Beds, Shoes Oct. 1799

NOTES to Page 56: Plantation. Sally has a line through Thenia.

NOTES to Page 57: Roll of the Negroes in the Winter of 1798.9

NOTES to Page 58: 1799 June 27 arrangement of the harvest.

NOTES to Page 58a: 1800 beds and shoes

NOTES to Page 58b: Blank page retained in order to keep the left-right relationship of the book.

NOTES to Page 59: 1805 Nov. blankets were given as follows.

NOTES to Page 60: 1801 Negroes leased to J.H. Craven, Negroes retained, Negroes in Bedford

NOTES to Page 61: Aphonoms, Observations, facts in husbandry

NOTES to Page 62: Implements in husbandry, the plough

NOTES to Page 63: Harrow. Roller.

NOTES to Page 64: Hoes, Axes

NOTES to Page 65: Waggons, Carts

NOTES to Page 66: Slides, Wheel barrows

NOTES to Page 67: Farm Buildings and conveniences, threshing machines, houses for laborers

NOTES to Page 68: Treading floor, granaries

NOTES to Page 69: Roads & Fords

NOTES to Page 70: Fences, Roads continued from page 69.

NOTES to Page 71: Fuel and light, timber

NOTES to Page 72: Animals, Horses, Mules, Cattle

NOTES to Page 73: Oxen, Cattle

NOTES to Page 74: Sheep
NOTES to Page 75: Goats, Hogs

NOTES to Page 76: Contracts for Persons

NOTES to Page 77: Labourers

NOTES to Page 78: Provisions

NOTES to Page 79: Preparation of Ground Fallow

NOTES to Page 98: Blank page retained in order to keep the left-right relationship of the book.

NOTES to Page 99: Blank page retained in order to keep the left-right relationship of the book.

NOTES to Page 100: Calendar of Work

NOTES to Page 101: Blank page retained in order to keep the left-right relationship of the book.

NOTES to Page 102: Building Brickwork

NOTES to Page 103: Stone, Stonework, paving or other stone cut

NOTES to Page 104: Wood, Paint, Venetian Blinds

NOTES to Page 105: Lime, Fresco painting, Bohemian glass

NOTES to Page 106: Mill

NOTES to Page 107: Movement of the millworks, Threshing Machine

NOTES to Page 108: Still to make beer

NOTES to Page 109: Smith's shops

NOTES to Page 110: Nails

NOTES to Page 111: Estimate on the actual work of the autumn of 1792

NOTES to Page 112: Blank page retained in order to keep the left-right relationship of the book.

NOTES to Page 113: Coal

NOTES to Page 114: Carpenters, Wheelwrights, coopers

NOTES to Page 115: Blank page retained in order to keep the left-right relationship of the book.

NOTES to Page 116: Spinning, Weaving

NOTES to Page 117: Pot-ash, Pearl-ash

NOTES to Page 118: Blank page retained in order to keep the left-right relationship of the book.

NOTES to Page 119: Tenants

NOTES to Page 120: Blank page retained in order to keep the left-right relationship of the book.

NOTES to Page 123: Miscellaneous

NOTES to Page 124: 1809 Monticello

NOTES to Page 125: Lego plan for the crop of 1810

NOTES to Page 126: Blank page retained in order to keep the left-right relationship of the book.

NOTES to Page 127: Land Roll 1810

NOTES to Page 128: Roll of Negroes 1810 Feb. in Albemarle

NOTES to Page 129: Roll of Negroes in Bedford 1810

NOTES to Page 130: Roll of the negroes according to their ages Albemarle

NOTES to Page 131: Roll of the Negroes in Bedford, according to their ages

NOTES to Page 132: Lego, Tufton, Monticello plantation

NOTES to Page 133: Bear creek, Poplar Forest

NOTES to Page 134: Bread list, Feb. 1810

NOTES to Page 135: 1810 harvest at Monticello

NOTES to Page 136: 1810 slaves list

NOTES to Page 137: Blankets 1808-1810

NOTES to Page 138: Estimate of corn from Monticello

NOTES to Page 139: 1812 slave list

NOTES to Page 140: continuation of slave list

NOTES to Page 141: Blank page retained in order to keep the left-right relationship of the book.

NOTES to Page 142: Distribution of Blankets

NOTES to Page 143: Slaves 1810 to 1812

NOTES to Page 144: Slaves 1813 Dec.

NOTES to Page 145: Slaves continued

NOTES to Page 146: Slaves 1814 December

NOTES to Page 147: Slaves list continued 1814

NOTES to Page 148: Bread lists for 1815

NOTES to Page 149: Wheat harvest in1815 and slave workers.

NOTES to Page 150: Slave list 1815 Dec.

NOTES to Page 151: Continuation of Slave list

NOTES to Page 152: Slaves and wool 1816-1822

NOTES to Page 153: Crop of 1816

NOTES to Page 154: Slaves 1815 and 1816

NOTES to Page 155: Slaves list continued read list 1817 Monticello

NOTES to Page 156: Slaves list continued read list 1817 Monticello

NOTES to Page 157: 1817 Dec. & Jan. 1818 hogs killed

NOTES to Page 158: 1817 slave list

NOTES to Page 159: 1817 slave list continued, Sally has three children

NOTES to Page 160: Negroes leased to Tho. Randolph - Negroes Retained

NOTES to Page 161: 17-18 Summer clothes for slaves spun cotton

NOTES to Page 162: Slave list for 1818

NOTES to Page 163: Estimates of corn from Jan 1 1817

NOTES to Page 164: Slaves 1819-22

NOTES to Page 165: Blankets, roll beds

NOTES to Page 166: Slaves Woolen shirts blankets

NOTES to Page 167: Bear cv Woolen Shirting blankets beds

NOTES to Page 168: Distribution of blankets at Poplar Forest 1819 1820 1821

NOTES to Page 169: Blankets 1822 Dec. 1825 1823 Dec. 1826 1824 Dec. 1827

NOTES to Page 170: Blank page retained in order to keep the left-right relationship of the book. Doodle

NOTES to Page 171: Outer clothing house slaves resources

NOTES to Page 172: Slave list 1821-2

NOTES to Page 173: Mont hogs

NOTES to Page 174: Slave list 1822

NOTES to Page 175: 1823 Decomb Woolen Shirting blankets beds

NOTES to Page 176: Slave list 1825 Dec. Woolen Shirting blankets beds Sally Hem. Is listed with her two remaining children below her.

NOTES to Page 177: Blank page

NOTES to Page 178: Blank page

NOTES: This is the actual original Farm Book, now in the possession of the Massachusetts Historical Society.

NOTES: Inside cover of the Farm Book. As you can see, "Farm Book" is what Jefferson called this book, from whence it derives its name.

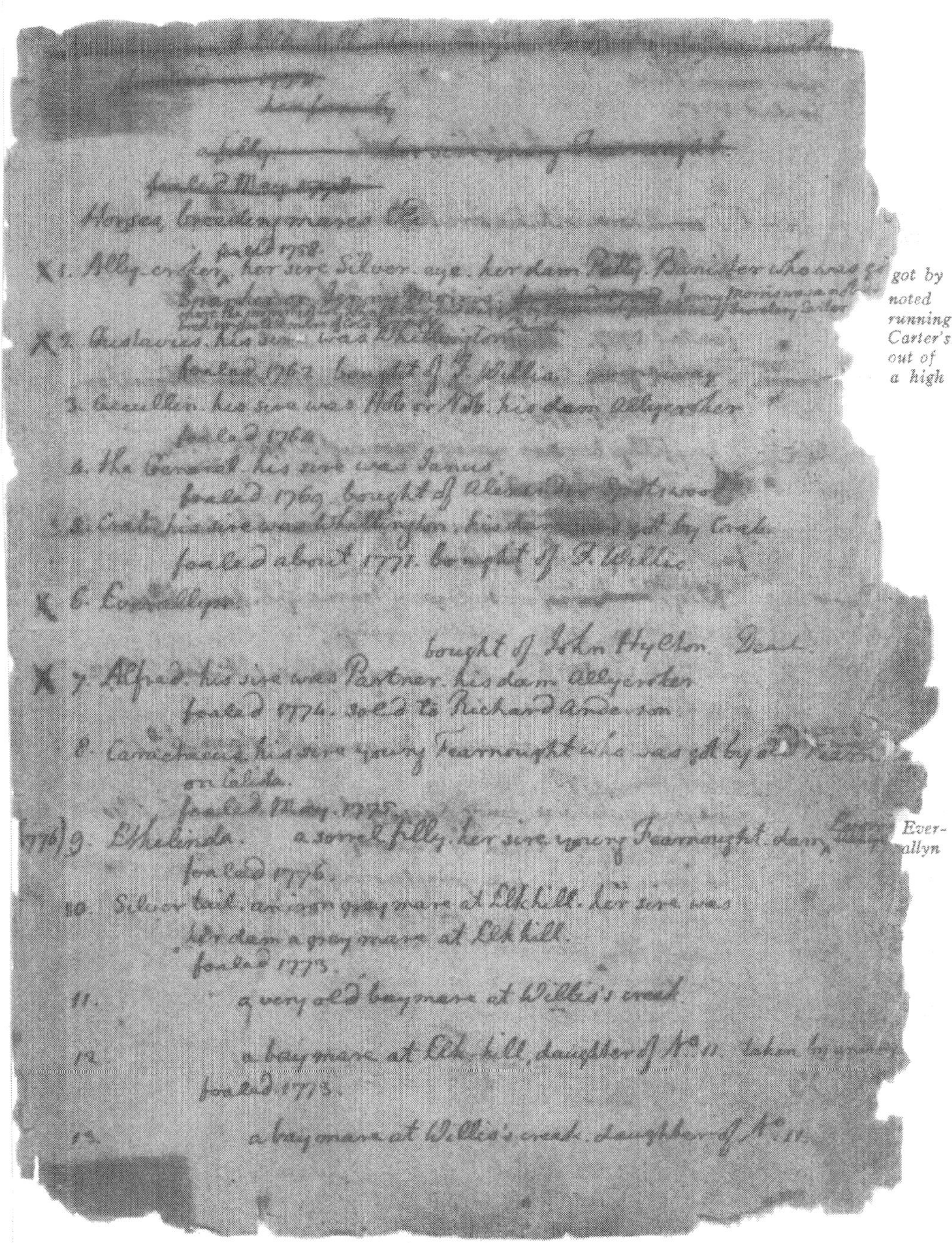

NOTES to Page 1: This page has more information about his horse, Caractacus

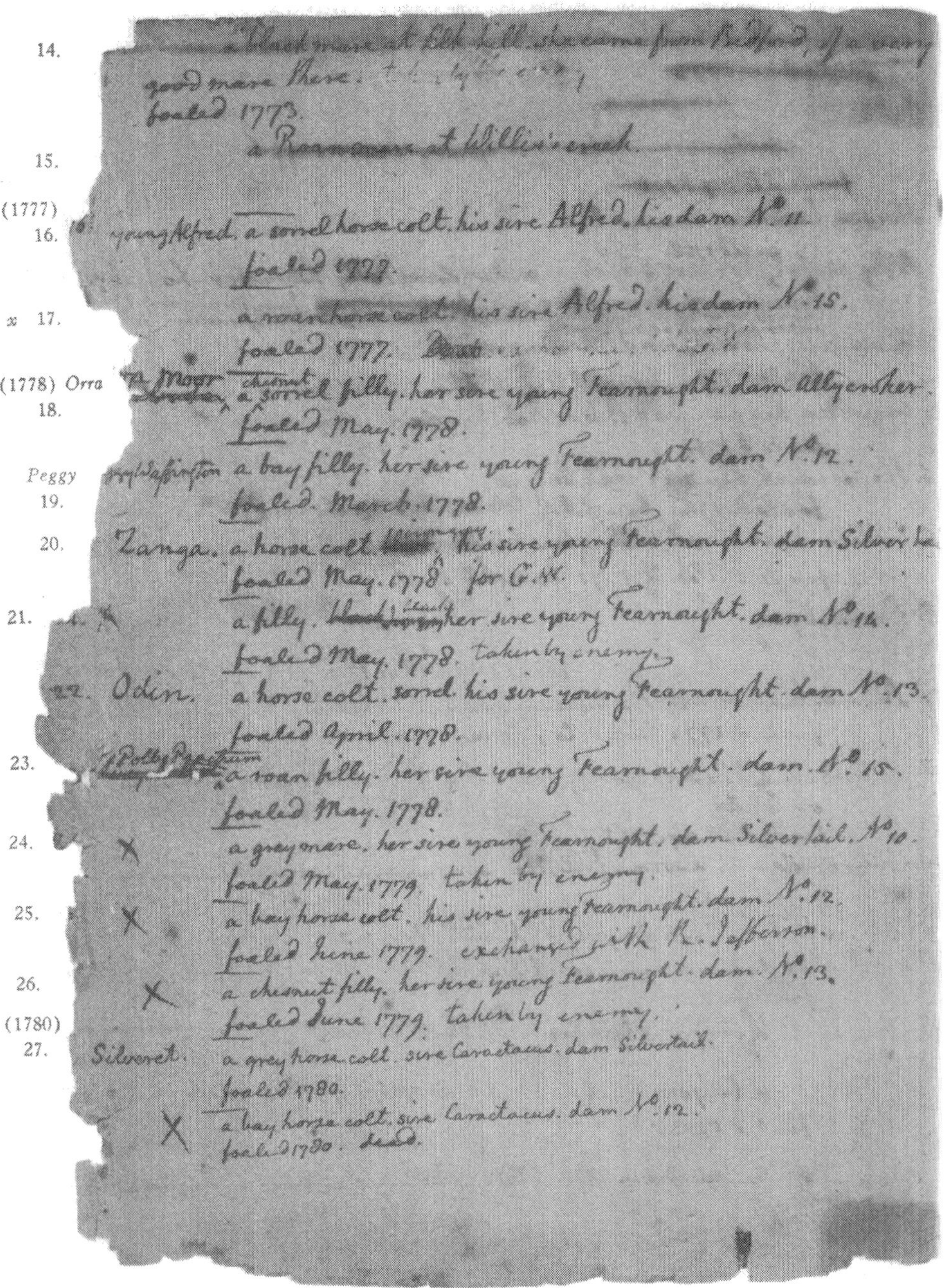

14. a black mare at Elk hill. she came from Bedford, & a very good mare there.
foaled 1773.

15. a Roan mare at Willis's creek.

(1777)
16. young Alfred. a sorrel horse colt. his sire Alfred. his dam No. 11.
foaled 1777.

x 17. a roan horse colt. his sire Alfred. his dam No. 15.
foaled 1777. Dead

(1778) Orra
18. Moor. a chesnut sorrel filly. her sire young Fearnought. dam Allycroker.
foaled May. 1778.

Peggy
19. Peggy Washington a bay filly. her sire young Fearnought. dam No. 12.
foaled March. 1778.

20. Zanga. a horse colt. his sire young Fearnought. dam Silvertail.
foaled May. 1778. for G.W.

21. a filly. black her sire young Fearnought. dam No. 14.
foaled May. 1778. taken by enemy.

22. Odin. a horse colt. sorrel. his sire young Fearnought. dam No. 13.
foaled April. 1778.

23. Polly Peachum a roan filly. her sire young Fearnought. dam No. 15.
foaled May. 1778.

24. X a grey mare. her sire young Fearnought. dam Silvertail. No. 10.
foaled May. 1779. taken by enemy.

25. X a bay horse colt. his sire young Fearnought. dam No. 12.
foaled June 1779. exchanged with R. Jefferson.

26. X a chesnut filly. her sire young Fearnought. dam No. 13.
foaled June 1779. taken by enemy.

(1780)
27. Silveret. a grey horse colt. sire Caractacus. dam Silvertail.
foaled 1780.

X a bay horse colt. sire Caractacus. dam No. 12.
foaled 1780. dead.

NOTES to Page 2: More about horses of Thomas Jefferson

A Roll of the proper slaves of Thomas Jefferson. Jan. 14. 1774.

Monticello.

* Goliah.
* Hercules.
\+ Jupiter. 1743.

* Gill.
* Fanny
\+ Ned. 1760.
Suckey 1765.
Frankey. 1767.
Gill. 1769.

* Quash
* Nell.
* Bella. 1757.
* Charles. 1760.
Jenny. 1768.

* Betty

— Juno
* Toby junr. 1753.
— Luna. 1758.

* Cate. about 1747.
Hannah. 1770.
Rachael. 1773.

Monticello.

\+ George
\+ Ursula.
George.
Bagwell
Archy. 1773

\+ Frank 1757.
\+ Bett. 1759
\+ Scilla. 1762.

* denotes a labourer in the ground.
\+ denotes a titheable person following some other occupation
— denotes a person discharged from labor on acct of age or infirmity.

NOTES to Page 5: First inventory of the Slaves of Thomas Jefferson: "A Roll of the proper slaves of Thomas Jefferson, Jan. 14. 1774." There are 29 slaves listed here.

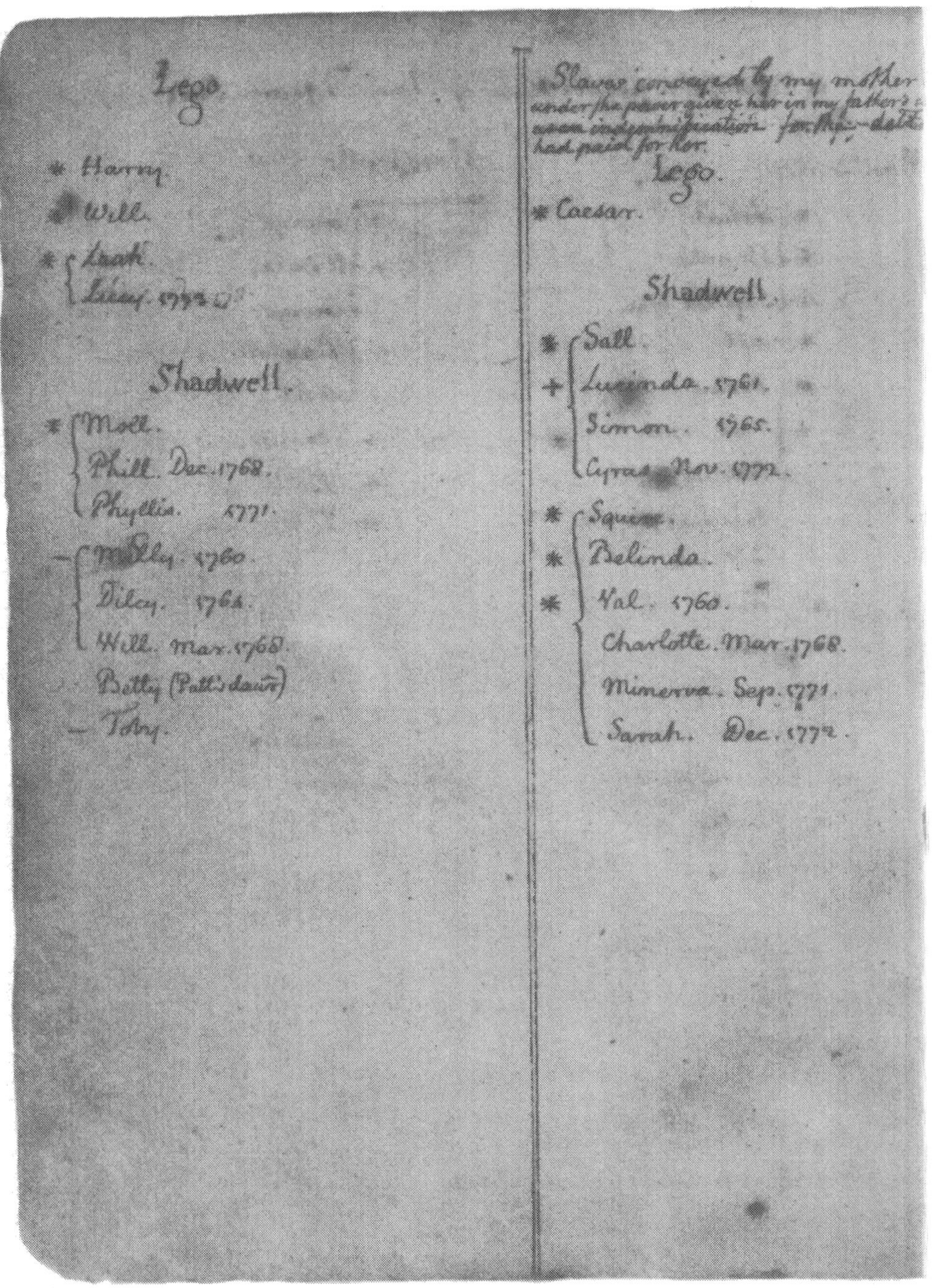

NOTES to Page 6: `Slaves conveyed by my mother to me under the power given her in my father's will upon indemnification for the debts I had paid for her'.

A Roll of the slaves of John Wayles which were allotted to T. J. in right of his wife on a division of the estate Jan. 14. 1774.

Tradesmen

+ Sanco. Elkhill } Carpenters
+ Abram. Guinea }
+ Billy boy. Poplar Forest } Smiths
+ Barnaby. 1760. Guinea }
+ Phill. Guinea. Shoemaker.
+ King. Judith's creek } Watermen.
+ Jim Hubbard. Elk-hill }
+ Peter. Crank's }

Poplar Forest.

* Guinea Will.
* Betty
Hall. Sep. 1767.
Diley. Mar. 1769.
Suckey. May. 1771.

Wingo's.

* John. 1753.
* Davy. 1755.
+ Mary. 1753.
* Doll. 1757.
* Charles.

Judith's creek, or Dunlora.

— Peg
* Judy
Hanah. Octob. 1771.
Tamar. June. 1773.

* Jupiter
— Phyllis
Shandy. Aug. 1768.
Sam. July. 1770.
Phyllis. Nov. 1772.

Crank's.

* Emanuel.
* Patt.
Prince. 1769.
Isabel. 1770.
Peter } 1772.
Sam. }
— Lucy.
— Jack.

NOTES to Page 7: A Roll of the slaves of John Wayles which were allotted to T.J. in right of his wife on a division of the estate Jan. 14 1774

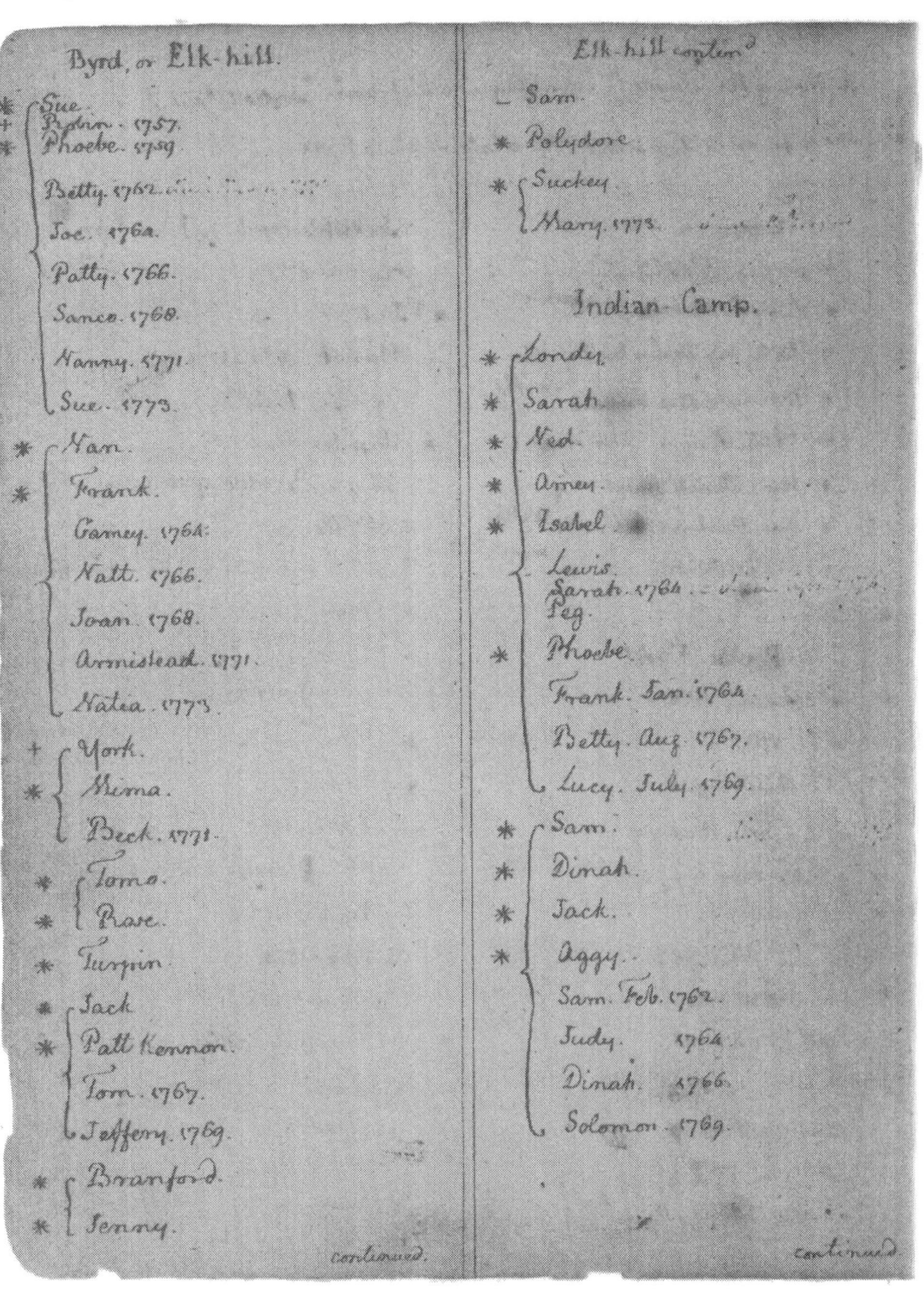

Byrd, or Elk-hill.

* Sue.
+ Robin. 1757.
* Phoebe. 1759.
Betty. 1762.
Joe. 1764.
Patty. 1766.
Sance. 1768.
Nanny. 1771.
Sue. 1773.

* Nan.
* Frank.
Gamey. 1764.
Natt. 1766.
Joan. 1768.
Armistead. 1771.
Natea. 1773.

+ York.
* Mima.
Beck. 1771.

* Tomo.
* Rose.

* Turpin.

* Jack.
* Patt Kennon.
Tom. 1767.
Jeffery. 1769.

* Branford.
* Jenny.

continued.

Elk-hill contin'd.

Sam.

* Polydore.

* Suckey.
Mary. 1773.

Indian Camp.

* Londy.
* Sarah.
* Ned.
* Amey.
* Isabel.
Lewis.
Sarah. 1764.
Peg.
* Phoebe.
Frank. Jan. 1764.
Betty. Aug. 1767.
Lucy. July. 1769.

* Sam.
* Dinah.
* Jack.
* Aggy.
Sam. Feb. 1762.
Judy. 1764.
Dinah. 1766.
Solomon. 1769.

continued.

NOTES to Page 8: Continuation of the Roll of the slaves of John Wayles

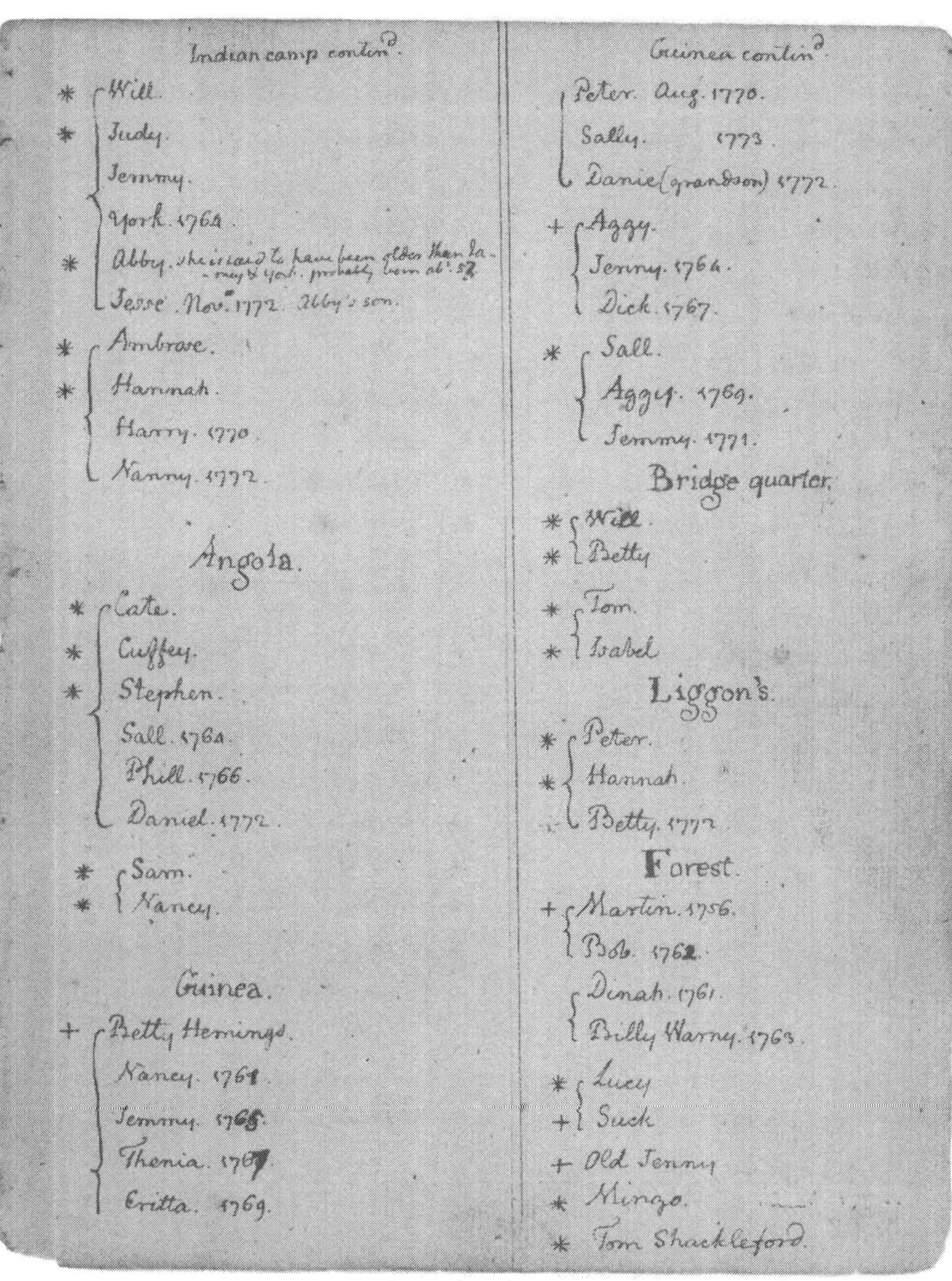

Indian camp contin^d.

* Will.
* Judy.
Jemmy.
York. 1764.
* Abby. she is said to have been older than Ja-
- mmy & York. probably born ab^t. 57
Jesse. Novr. 1772. Abby's son.

* Ambrose.
* Hannah.
Harry. 1770.
Nanny. 1772.

Angola.

* Cate.
* Cuffey.
* Stephen.
Sall. 1764.
Phill. 1766.
Daniel. 1772.

* Sam.
* Nancy.

Guinea.

+ Betty Hemings.
Nancy. 1761
Jemmy. 1765
Thenia. 1767
Critta. 1769.

Guinea contin^d.

Peter. Aug. 1770.
Sally. 1773.
Danie (grandson) 1772.

+ Aggy.
Jenny. 1764.
Dick. 1767.

* Sall.
Aggy. 1769.
Jemmy. 1771.

Bridge quarter.

* Will.
* Betty

* Tom.
* Isabel

Liggon's.

* Peter.
* Hannah.
+ Betty. 1772

Forest.

+ Martin. 1756.
Bob. 1762.
Dinah. 1761.
Billy Warny. 1763.
* Lucy
+ Suck
+ Old Jenny
* Mingo.
* Tom Shackleford.

NOTES to Page 9: Continuation of the Roll of the slaves of John Wayles

NOTES to Page 10: Blank page retained in order to keep the left-right relationship of the book.

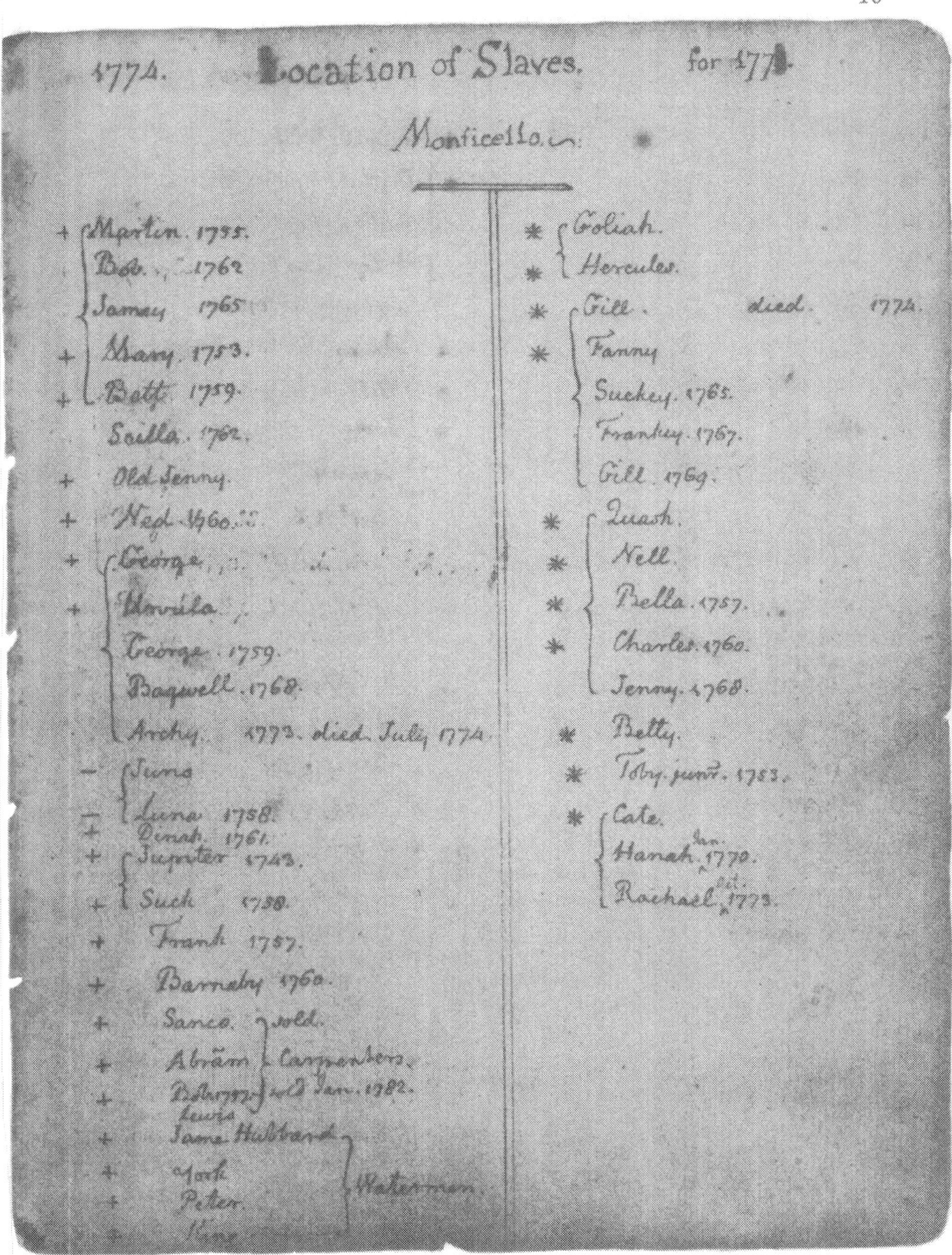

1774. Location of Slaves. for 1774.

Monticello.

+ Martin. 1755.
Bob. 1762
James 1765
+ Mary. 1753.
+ Betty 1759.
Scilla. 1762.
+ Old Jenny.
+ Ned. 1760.
+ George.
+ Ursula.
George. 1759.
Bagwell. 1768.
Archy. 1773. died. July 1774.
— Juno
— Luna 1758.
+ Dinah. 1761.
+ Jupiter 1743.
+ Such 1738.
+ Frank 1757.
+ Barnaby 1760.
+ Sanco. sold.
+ Abram Carpenters.
+ [illegible] sold Jan. 1782.
Lewis
+ James Hubbard
+ York
+ Peter Watermen.
+ King

* Goliah.
* Hercules.
* Gill. died. 1774.
* Fanny
Suckey. 1765.
Frankey. 1767.
Gill. 1769.
* Quash.
* Nell.
* Bella. 1757.
* Charles. 1760.
Jenny. 1768.
* Betty.
* Toby. junr. 1753.
* Cate.
Hanah. Jan. 1770.
Rachael. Oct. 1773.

NOTES to Page 15: Location of Slaves in 1774, Monticello

1774. Lego.

* Harry.
* Will.
* Caesar.
* Leah
Lucy. 1773.

Shadwell.

* Moll.
Phill. Dec. 1768.
Phyllis. 1771.
— Milly. 1760.
Dilcy. 1764.
Will. Mar. 1768
— Toby.
* Sall.
+ Lucinda. 1761.
Simon. 1765.
Cyrus. Nov. 1772.
* Squire.
* Belinda.
* Val. 1760.
Charlotte. Mar. 1768.
Minerva. Sep. 1771.
Sarah. Dec. 1772.

Betty (Patt's daur.) lent to H. Mullins.

Poplar Forest. 1774.

* Guinea Will.
* Betty.
Hall. Sep. 1767.
Dilcy. Mar. 1769.
Sukey. May. 1771.
* Amey.
* Will.
* Judy.
Jemmy.
York. 1764.
* Tom Shackleford.
+ Billy boy. Smith.

Wingo's.

* John. 1753.
* Davy. 1755.
* Doll. 1757.
* Charles.
* Londy.
* Sarah died July 1781.
Sarah. 1764.
Peg.
* Phoebe.
Frank Jan. 1764.
Betty. Aug. 1767.
Lucy July. 1769.
* Abby.
Jame. Nov. 1772.
* Lucy. 1747.

NOTES to Page 16: Location of Slaves in 1774, Lego, Shadwell, Poplar Forest and Wingo's

1774. Dun-lora	Elk-Hill 1774.
* Judy (Hix)	+ Phill. shoemaker.
Hanah. Octob. 1771.	* Emanuel
Thamar. June. 1773.	* Patt.
— Peg.	Prince. 1769.
* Jupiter.	Isabel 1770. given to A. S. Jeff. Feb. 1782.
— Phyllis.	Peter. } 1772.
Shandy. Aug. 1768.	Sam. } 1772.
Sam. July. 1770.	— Lucy.
Phyllis. Nov. 1772.	— Jack.
* Ned.	* Sue.
* Isabel	* Phoebe. 1759.
* Sam. died 1774.	Betty. 1762. died Nov. 15. 1774.
* Dinah.	Joe. 1764. died. 1781.
* Aggy. died 1774.	Patty. 1766. given to mrs Harris. 1777
Sam. Feb. 1762.	Sanco. 1768.
Judy. 1764.	Nanny. 1771.
Dinah. 1766.	Sue. 1773.
Solomon. 1769.	* Nan dead.
	* Frank. died 1775.
	Garney. 1764. dead.
	Natt. 1766.
	Joan. 1768.
	Armistead. 1771.
	Natia. 1773.
	* Mima.
	Beck. 1771.

NOTES to Page 17: Location of Slaves in 1774, Dunlora and Elk Hill

1774. Elk hill cont.d

* Tomo
* Aave.
* Turpin.
* Jack.
* Patt Kennon
Tom 1767.
Jeffery. 1769.
* Branford.
* Jenny
— Sam.
* Polydore
* Suckey.
Mary. 1773. died Feb. 1774
* Jack
* Ambrose.
* Hanah.
Harry. 1770.
Nanny. 1772.
* Cate.
* Cuffey
* Stephen.
Sall. 1764.
Phill. 1766.
Daniel. 1772.
* Sam.
* Nancy

Elk hill cont.d 1774

\+ Betty Hemings.
Nancy. 1761.
Thenia. 1767.
Critta. 1769.
Peter. Aug. 1770.
Sally. 1773.
Daniel. 1772.
\+ Aggy.
Jenny. 1764.
Dick. 1767.
* Sall
Billy Warny. 1763.
Aggy. 1769.
Jenmy. 1771.
* Will.
* Betty
* Tom.
* Isabel.
* Peter.
* Hanah.
Betty. 1772.
* Mingo.

187. in all.

NOTES to Page 18: Location of Slaves in 1774, Elk Hill

Blankets Beds &c. given to slaves in 1774.

Monticello.

Blankets to the following.

Martin, Bob, Mary, Bett.
Old Jenny, Ned.
George, Ursula, Little George.
Doll, Nance, Dinah, Scilla, Luna.
Barnaby, Abram, Lewis,
Jame Hubbard, York, Peter, Phill
Goliah, Hercules, Jupiter, Suck.
Fanny, Fanny's children, blankets
Quash Nell, Charles.
Betty. Toby junr. Cate.

Beds given to the following.

Mary. Ursula. Fanny. Nell. Cate.

Lego & Shadwell

Blankets to

Harry. Will. Caesar. Leah.
King. Judy. Moll. Sall.
Squire. Belinda. Charlotte &c.
Frank. Betty (Pat's daur)
Juno.

Beds to

Leah. Judy. Moll. Sall. Belinda.

Poplar Forest & Dun-lora.

Blankets to

Guinea Will. Betty. Hall &c.
Amey. Will. Judy. Jemmy.
Tom Shackleford. John. Davy. Lucy.
Londy. Sarah. Phoebe. Peg &c. Betty &c.
Abby. Peg. Jupiter. Phyllis. Shandy &c.
Ned. Isabel. Dinah. Aggy. Sam &c. Dinah &c.
Bella. Billy boy.

Beds to

Betty. Amey. Judy. Sarah. Abby. Phyllis.
Dinah.

Elk-hill.

Beds to

Sue. Nan. Hanah. Cate.

Blankets to

waterman Charles. Billy. Warny.

NOTES to Page 19: Blankets Bed given to slaves in 1774

Births and Deaths in 1774.

Births	Deaths.
Betty. ~~(Phill & Mill. Shadwell)~~	Archy. Ursula's child. July.
Patty (Guinea Will & Betty's Pop. Forest) Sep.	* Gill. (Monticello)
Judy. (Abby's child. Wingo's) Aug.	* Aggey. (Sam & Dinah's, Jud's cn)
Ambrose. (Hanah's child. Elk-hill) Jan.	~~[illegible] April.~~
Anonymus. (Black Sall's. Elk-hill) Jan.	* old Sam (Dun-lora.) May.
Nancey (Mima's child) Elk hill)	Betty (Sue's. Elkhill) Nov. 15.
Betty (Pat Kennon's Elk-hill)	Mary (Suckey's Elk-hill) Feb.
Solomon. (Bagby Peter & Hanah's) Elk-hill)	Anonymus (black Sall's Elk-hill) Feb.
~~Iris (Squire & Melinda.) Shadwell. Sep.~~	Peg. (Poplar Forest) March.

NOTES to Page 21: Births and Deaths in 1774

Births and deaths in 1775.

Births.	Deaths.
Isaac. (Ursula's. Monticello) Dec.	Frank, Mingo's wife at Elk-hill
Iris (Belinda's Monticello) July.	
John Jupiter (Jupiter & Phyllis. Ned's cr.) Feb.	
Anakey (Ned & Phoebe. Ned's cr.) July	

NOTES to Page 22: Births and Deaths in 1775

NOTES to Page 23: Blankets Beds etc. given to slaves in 1775.

Deaths among the prec
from 1783. to 1794. in

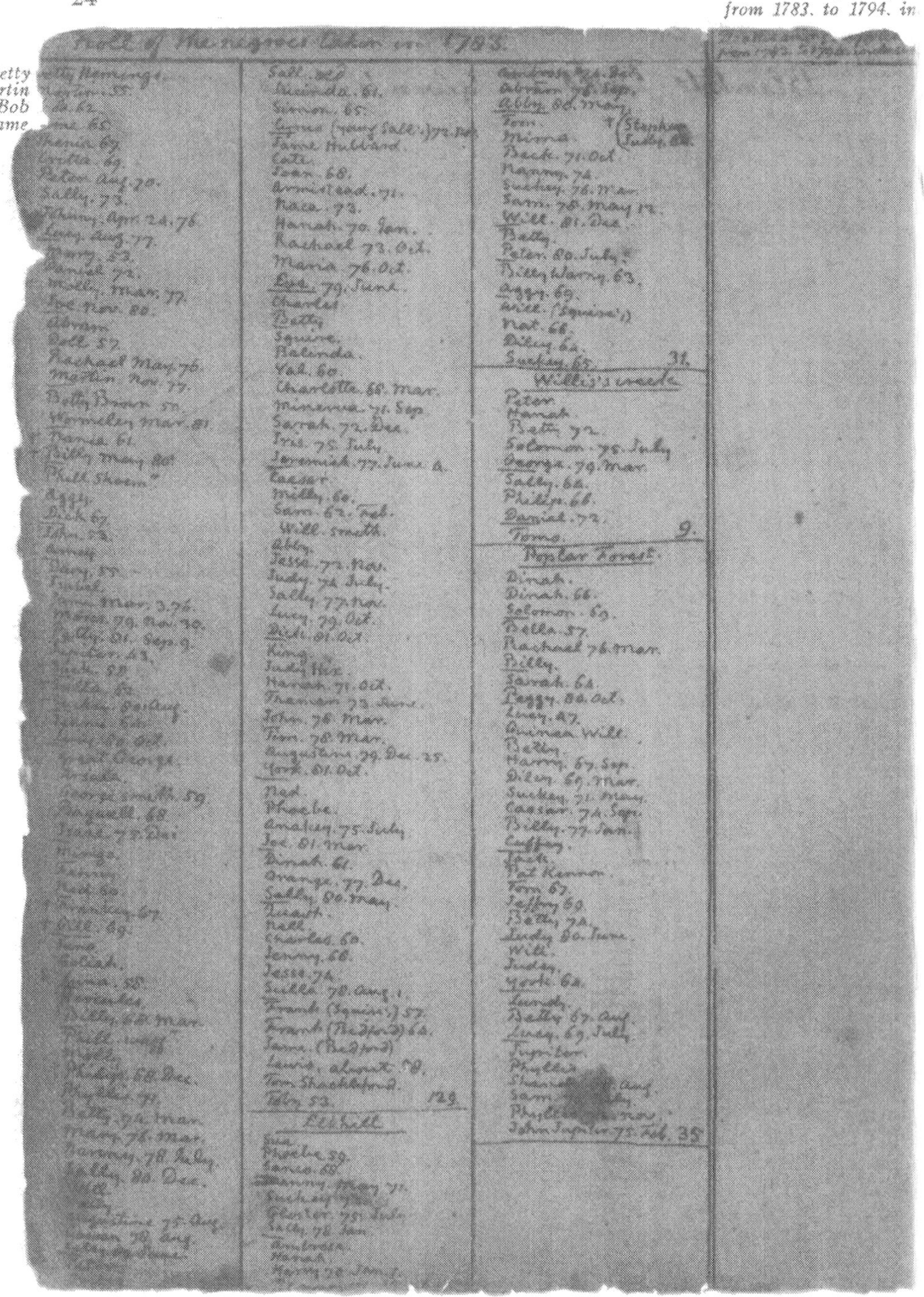

Roll of the negroes taken in 1783.

Betty
artin
Bob
Jame

Sall. 80.
Lucinda. 61.
Simon. 65.
Cyrus (young Sall's) 72.
Jame Hubbard.
Cate.
Joan. 68.
Armistead. 71.
Nace. 73.
Hanah. 70. Jan.
Rachael 73. Oct.
Maria 76. Oct.
Eve. 79. June.
Charles
Betty
Squire.
Belinda.
Val. 60.
Charlotte. 68. Mar.
Minerva. 71. Sep.
Sarah. 72. Dec.
Iris. 75. July
Jeremiah. 77. June 6.
Caesar.
Milly. 60.
Sam. 62. Feb.
Will. smith.
Abby.
Jesse. 72. Nov.
Judy. 74. July.
Sally. 77. Nov.
Lucy. 79. Oct.
Dick. 81. Oct.
King.
Judy Hix.
Hanah. 71. Oct.
Thenia 73. June.
John. 76. Mar.
Tom. 78. Mar.
Augustine. 79. Dec. 25.
York. 81. Oct.
Ned.
Phoebe.
Amey. 75. July
Joe. 81. Mar.
Dinah. 61.
Orange. 77. Dec.
Sally 80. May
[illegible]
Nell.
Charles. 60.
Jenny. 68.
Jesse. 74.
Silla 78. Aug. 1.
Frank (Squire's) 57.
Frank (Bedford) 64.
Jame. (Bedford)
Lewis, about 78.
Tom Shackleford.
Toby 52. 129.

Elkhill.
[illegible]
Phoebe 59.
Lucia. 68.
Nanny. May 71.
[illegible]
Gloster 75. July
Sally 78. Jan.
Ambrose.
Hanah.
Nanny 78. Jan.

Ambrose 71. Dec.
Abram 75. Sep.
Abby 80. May.
Tom.
Mima. (Stephen, Sally 80.)
Beck. 71. Oct.
Nanny. 74.
Suckey. 76. Mar.
Sam. 78. May 12.
Will. 81. Dec.
Betty.
Peter. 80. July.
Billy Warny. 63.
Aggy. 69.
Will. (Squire's)
Nat. 68.
Dilcy. 64.
Suckey. 65. 31.

Willis's creek.
Peter.
Hanah.
Betty 72.
Solomon. 75. July
George. 79. Mar.
Sally. 62.
Philips. 68.
Daniel. 72.
Toms. 9.

Poplar Forest.
Dinah.
Dinah. 66.
Solomon. 69.
Bella. 57.
Rachael 76. Mar.
Billy.
Sarah. 64.
Peggy. 80. Oct.
Lucy. 47.
Guinea Will.
Betty
Harry. 67. Sep.
Dilcy. 69. Mar.
Suckey. 71. May.
Caesar. 74. Sep.
Billy. 77. Jan.
Cuffey.
Jack.
Pat Kennon.
Tom 67.
Jaffry 69.
Betty 72.
Judy 80. June
Will.
Judy.
York 62.
[illegible]
Betty 67. Aug.
Lucy. 69. July
Jupiter.
Phyllis
[illegible] Aug.
Sam [illegible]
Phyllis [illegible] Nov.
John Jupiter 75. Feb. 35.

Nanny. 77. Dec.

NOTES to Page 24: Roll of the Negroes taken in 1783

Blankets, beds &c. given to slaves in 1776.

Shoemaker Phill a blanket.
Betty Hemings. a blanket.
Lucinda. Ned. Gamey. blankets
2. blankets sent to Bedford to
and to John's wife
Black Sall. Sam. blankets.
Black Sall, Doll. beds.

Number of souls in my family in Albemarle as given in this year.

	Free	Slaves
Males of 16 years old & upwds.	17	22
Females of 16 years old & upwds.	5	17
Males below 16	4	22
Females below 16	8	22
~~Number~~ of Free & slaves	34	83
Number in the whole	117	

NOTES to Page 27: Blankets Beds etc. given to slaves in 1776.

8.

Births & Deaths in 1777.

Births	Deaths.
Jeremiah (Squire & Belinda. Shadwell) July	Anon. (Ned & Phoebe. Ind's. cr.) Octob.
Sally (Will & Abby. Shadwell) Octob.	Aggey (Jup. & Suck. Monticello) Sep.
Martin (Abram & Doll. Monticello) Nov.	
Billy (Betty Brown's. Monticello)	
Orange (Dinah's. Monticello)	
Anon. (Ned & Phoebe. Ind's. cr.) Aug.	
Billy (Guinea Will & Bess. Pop. For.) January.	
Aggey (Jupiter & Suck. Monticello) July	

Births and Deaths in 1778.

Births	Deaths.
Sally (Sue's. Elk-hill)	Billy. (Betty Brown's) May.
Samson (Mima's. Elk-hill) May. 12.	
(Patt Kennon's.) July. 10.	

NOTES to Page 28: Births and Deaths in 1777

Births, Deaths &c. from 1779 to 1781. inclusive.

Other losses by the British in 1781.	Deaths &c.
[illegible] blooded mares, colts & plough horses	1781. Cumberland: Hannibal, Patty, Sam, Sally, Nanny, Fanny, Prince, Nancy } fled to the enemy & died.
59. cattle	Elkhill: Flora (Black Sall's), Quomina (Black Sall's) } joined enemy & died.
30. sheep	Black Sall, Jame (Bl. Sall's), Joe (Sue's), Cumbld. Lucy } joined enemy, returned & died.
60. hogs	[illegible], Sam, Elkhill Jenny, Shadwell [illegible], Harry } joined enemy.
200. barr. corn in the house	Monticello. Barnaby. ran away, returned & died.
500. do. growing & destroyed	Elkhill. York, Isabel, Jack, Hanah's child, Phoebe's child } caught small pox from enemy & died.
80 do. growing & lost for want of labourers	[note Judy & Nat of Elkhill & Robin of Shadwell joined the enemy, but came back again & lived. so did Will. Isabel Hannibal's daughter afterwards [illegible]
350. bush. wheat growing	Elkhill Branford } caught the camp fever from negroes who returned & died.
10. hhds tobo. in the house	Sue, Sue's daur.
12. do. growing & destroyed	Monticello Old Jenny
7. do. growing & lost for want of labourers	Elkhill Phoebe (Sue's)
250. lb hemp in the house	Nanny (Tom's) 1782
250. lb do. growing	
250. lb flax growing	
100. lb cotton growing & destroyed	
130. lb do. growing & lost for want of labourers	
75. bushels of barley growing & destroyed	
1000. pannels of fence destroyed	
houses burnt — £15-0-0	
plantation utensils — 15-0-0	
pd. Doctors attending sick 65-0-0	
expences seeks & bring back some 20-0-0	

Births. 1782.	Deaths.
Lucy. Peter & Suckey's. Monticello. Mar. 2. 1782.	
Ambrose's & Hanah. Elkhill. Mar. 3.	
Doll's. Monticello Oct. 5.	

Overseers & Stewards employed

	Monticello	Shadwell	Stewards		Monticello			Monticello	Tufton	Lego
1783		Chisolm	Key	1798.		1810				
4		Chisolm		9.						
5		[illegible]	Ballow	1800.	Lilly					
6	Clarke			1.						
7	Clarke			2.						
8	Franklin			3.						
9	Franklin			4.						
1790	Franklin			5.						
1	Rogers			6.	Freeman					
2	Clarkson	Rogers		7.	Bacon					
3	Clarkson	Rogers		8						
4	Biddle	Alexander		9						
5	Petit	Alexander								
6	Petit	Page								
7	George	Page								

George Page

NOTES to Page 29: Births and Deaths from 1779 to 1781 inclusive.

Roll of the negroes Nov. 1794. and where to be settled for the year 1795.

Monticello.

Jupiter. 43. & Jan. 1800
Martin. 55.
James. 65.
Peter. 70.
Lucy. (Jenny's) 80.
Critta. 69.
Jamey. 87. Apr. 23
Sally 73.
Joe. 80.
Betsy 83.
Betty Brown. 59.
Wormeley. 81.
Burwell. 85. Dec. 20.
Brown 85. Dec. 25.
Melinda. 87. Nov. 6.
Edwin. 93. Nov. 2.
Betty Hemings. ab^t. 35.
George.
Ursula. ab^t. 37.
George 59. } smiths
Isaac. 75. Dec. } smiths
Moses 79.
Shepherd. 82. Oct.
Barnaby 83. May 2.
Davy 85. Sep.
Ben 84.
Jamey. 82 or 83.
Kit 86.
John 53.
Davy 55.
Lewis ab^t. 60.
Abram. } Carpenters
Phill. shoem^r.
Johnny 75.
Phill. wagg^r ab^t 42. } carters
Tom Shackleford
Goliah. ab^t. 31.
Mingo.
Fanny ab^t. 36.
Betty. 81. } Spinners
Lilly. 83.
Aggy. died 98. July

Isabel
James. 76.
Edy. 87. Apr. 10.
Aggey. 89. Mar.
Lilly. 91. Feb.
Amey. 93. Mar. 1.
Doll 57.
Martin 77.
Thenia. 93. Jan.
Polly [illegible] 96. Dec. 26
Jenny (Nall's) 68.
Lewis. 88. Mar.
Jesse. 90. July.
Sally. 92. Sep. 1.
Molly. ab^t. 49.
Mary. 76.
Bartlet. 86. Jan.
Clarinda. 88. July
Goliah. 91. May.
Frank. 57.
Toby. 53.
Juno.

Tufton.

Ned. 60.
Jenny (Aggey's) 64.
Ned. 86. Feb. 15.
Fanny. 88. Mar. 31.
Dick. 90. Mar. 19.
Gill. 92. Mar. 18.
[illegible]
Rachael. 76.
Nancy. 91. Sep.
[illegible] 94 May
Black Betty.
Val. 60.
York. 81.
Nanny. 78.
Sally. 60.

Shadwell.

Squire. ab^t. 37.
Belinda. ab^t. 39.
Jerry. 77.
Iris. 75.
Squire 93. Dec. 1.
~~Rodney~~
Phillis, 68.
Phyllis 71.
Scilla. 78. Aug. 1
Nelly. 94. Feb.
Caesar. [illegible] 69.

Lego.

Bagwell. 68.
Minerva. 71.
Ursula. 87. Jan. 5.
Mary. 88. Oct. 29
Virginia. 92. May 8.
Judy Hix.
Austin 79.
Thamar. 73.
Rachael. 90. Nov.
Tim. 78.
Lucinda. 61.
Sarah. 86. Dec. 18.
Sandy. 89. Dec. 1.
Sousy. 93. Oct. 19.
~~Sall. ab^t 20~~ d. 97.

Bedford.

James Hubbard.
Cate. ab^t. 50.
Armistead 71.
Rachael. 73. Oct.
Burrel. 94
Nace. 73.
Maria. 76. Oct.
Eve 79. June.
Philip. 86. Mar.
Sarah. 88. Aug.
[illegible] 91. Sep.
Will. smith.
Abbey.
Jesse. 72. Nov.
Sal. 77. Nov.
~~Lucy 79. Oct.~~ d. 97.
Dick. 81. Oct.
Flora 83.
Davy. 85. Feb.
Fanny. 88. Aug.
~~Edy. 92. Apr.~~
~~Armstead. 94~~ [illegible]
Bess. Guinea Will's.
Hal. 67. Sep. smith
Caesar. 74. Sep.
~~Cuffy. ab^t 79~~ d. 96
Suck. (Bess's) 71. May
Cate. 88. Mar.
Daniel. 90. Sep.
Stephen. 94.
Hercules. ab^t. 33.
Bet.
Austin. 75. Aug.
Gawen. 80. Aug.
Cate. 88. Mar.
Mary 92. Jan.
Hercules. 92. [illegible]
Hanah. Cate's. 70. Jan.
Lucinda. 91. [illegible]
Reuben. 93. [illegible]
Solomon. 94
Dick. 67. [illegible]
Dinah 66.
John. 88. Nov.
Aggey. 89. Mar.
Moses. 92. Jan.
[illegible] 94 [illegible]
Will. old.
Judy. old

NOTES to Page 30: 'Roll of the Negroes Nov. 1794 and where to be settled for the year 1795. Monticello Sally 73.'

Register of births. B. denotes Bedford

Males	Females
79. Moses. Isabel's	Eve. Cate's. B.
Austin. Judy Hix's.	Lucy. Abby's. B.
Cuffy. Betty's. d. 96 B.	
80. Joe. Mary's.	Lucy. Jenny's
Gawen. Bet's B.	Sally. Molly's
	Cate. Bett's. B.
81. Wormeley. Bett Br's.	Patty. Isabel's.
York. Judy's.	
Dick. Abby's. B.	
82. Shepherd. Doll's	
James. Cate's. qu. 83.	
83. Barnaby. Jenny's.	Lucy. Molly's
Burwell. Bet Br's.	Flora. Abby's. B.
84. Davy. Isabel's. Sep.	
Ben. Judy Hix's.	
85. Brown. Bet Br's	
Davy. Abby's. B.	
John. Dinah's. B.	
86. Bartlet. Molly's.	Sarah. Lucinda's.
Ned. Jenny's	
Kit. Judy Hix's.	
Philip. Cate's. B.	
87. Jamey. Critta's	Malinda. Bet Br's. I.E.
	Edy. Isabel's
	Ursula. Minerva's.
88. Lewis. Jenny's	Clarinda. Molly's. I.E.
	Fanny. Jenny's.
	Mary. Minerva's.
	Sarah. Cate's. B.
	Fanny. Abby's. B.
	Cate. Suck's. B.
89. Sandy. Lucinda's. I.E.	Aggey. Isabel's
	Aggy. Dinah's. B.
90. Jesse. Lewis's.	Rachael. Thamar's. I.B.
Dick. Jenny's.	
Daniel. Suck's. B.	
91. Goliah. Molly's. I.E.	Lilly. Isabel's
	Nancy. Rachael's
	Nancy. Cate's. B.
	Lucinda. Hanah's. B.
92. Gill. Jenny's. Ned's	Sally. Jenny's. Lewis's
Moses. Dinah's. B.	Edy. Abby's. B.
	Mary. Bett's. B.
93. Edwin. Bet Br's.	Amy. Isabel's.
Squire. Iris's. I.E.	Thenia. Doll's.
Scotty. Lucinda's. I.E.	Virginia. Minerva's.
Reuben. Hanah's. B.	
94. Abram. Rachael's	Molly. Scilla's. I.E.
Burwell. Rachael's. B.	Scilla. Jenny's.
Stephen. Suck's. B.	Dolly. Doll's.
Armstead. Abby's. B.	
Hercules. Betty's. B.	
Evans. Dinah's. B.	
Solomon. Hanah's. B.	
95. Jamey (Jenny Lewis's) [illegible]	[illegible] Minerva's. Mary
[illegible] (Sally) [illegible]	[illegible] Phyllis. Apr. 20. I.E.
[illegible] Lucinda's. Sep. I.E.	[illegible] Sally. Oct. 5.
	[illegible] Critta's [illegible] B.

males	Females
96. May. 6. Joyce. Iris's. I.E.	96. Lucy. Thamar's. I.E.
June 1. Zachary. Lucy's	Aug. 18. Letty. Scilla's. I.E.
14. James. Ned & Jenny	Aug. Hanah. Dinah's. B.
Aug. Nace. Maria's. B.	Suck's. B.
	Abby's. B.
	May 5. Sucky. Mary's
97.	Mar. 22. Maria. Rachael's
	30. [illegible] Isabel's
	Oct. 22. Evelina. Lewis & Jenny
	Bec. Minerva's
98. Apr. Beverly. Sally's	Mar. 98. Maria. Nanny's
Oct. 29. [illegible]	July 13. Emily. Phyllis's
	June. 8. Dinah. Mary's
	Oct. 25. Aggy. Ned's Jenny
99. June 22. Thruston. Isabel's	Apr. 10. Nanny. Minerva's

NOTES to Page 31: Register of births Bdemotis Bedford. Squeezed in at the bottom of the page there is an illegible entry under births which says, `H-, Sally's, October 5, 1795'.

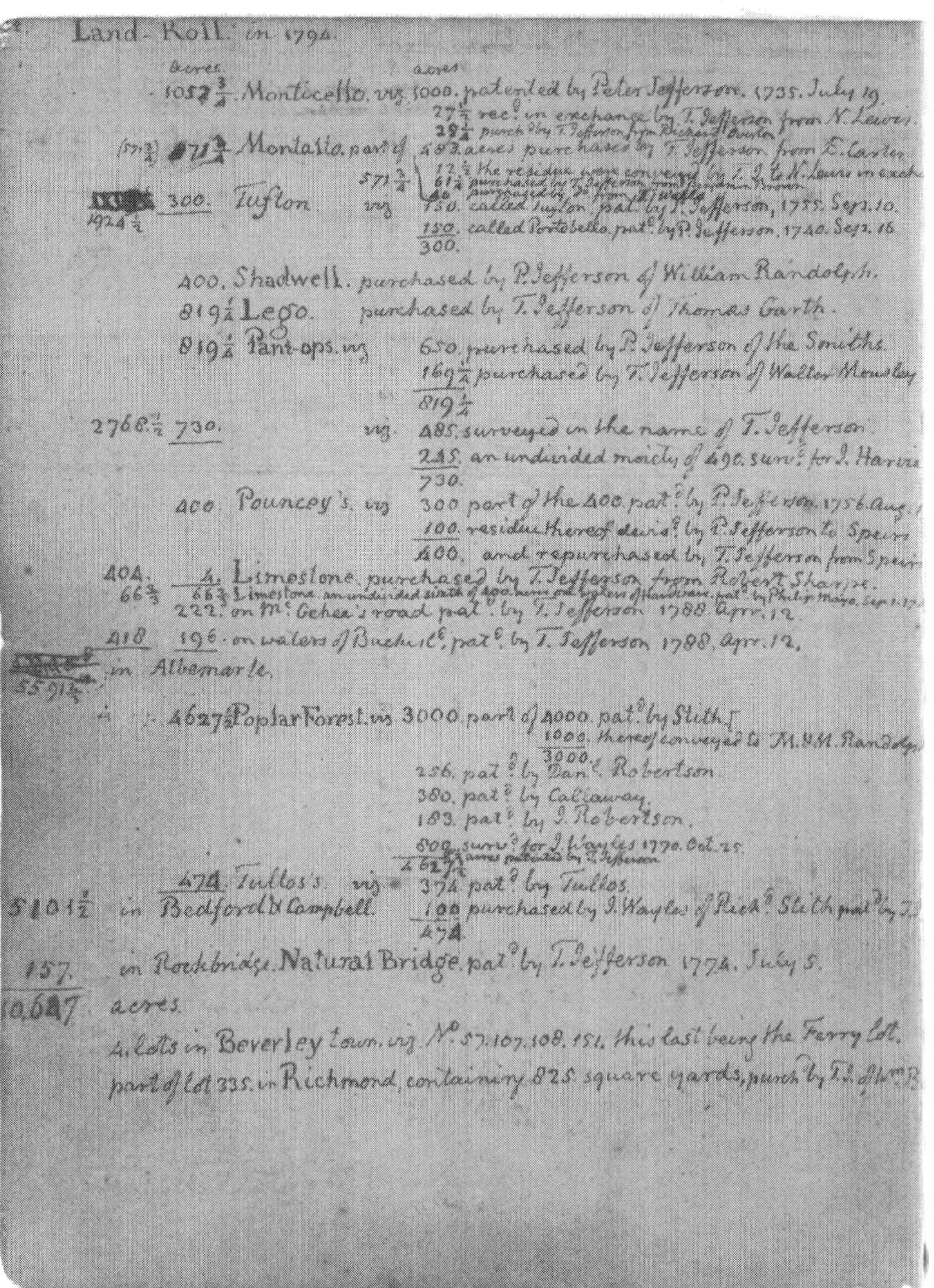

Land-Roll. in 1794.

acres. acres

1052¾. Monticello. viz. 1000. patented by Peter Jefferson. 1735. July 19.
27½ rec^d. in exchange by T. Jefferson from N. Lewis.
29¼ purch^d by T. Jefferson from Richard Overton

(571¾) 571¾ Montalto. part of 483. acres purchased by T. Jefferson from E. Carter
571¾ 12½ the residue were conveyed by T. J. to N. Lewis in exch.
61½ purchased by T. Jefferson from Benjamin Brown
40 purchased by do. from [illegible] Wells

1924½ 300. Tufton viz 150. called Tufton, pat. by P. Jefferson, 1755. Sep. 10.
150. called Portobello, pat^d. by P. Jefferson. 1740. Sep. 16
300.

400. Shadwell. purchased by P. Jefferson of William Randolph.
819¼ Lego. purchased by T. Jefferson of Thomas Garth.
819¼ Pant-ops. viz 650. purchased by P. Jefferson of the Smiths.
169¼ purchased by T. Jefferson of Walter Mousley
819¼

2768½ 730. viz. 485. surveyed in the name of T. Jefferson
245. an undivided moiety of 490. surv^d. for J. Harvie
730.

400. Pouncey's. viz 300 part of the 400. pat^d. by P. Jefferson. 1756. Aug.
100. residue thereof devis^d. by P. Jefferson to Speirs
400. and repurchased by T. Jefferson from Speirs

404. 4. Limestone. purchased by T. Jefferson from Robert Sharpe.
66⅔ 66⅔. Limestone. an undivided sixth of 400. acres on Tufton of Hardware. pat^d. by Philip Mayo. Sep.
222. on M^c. Gehee's road. pat^d. by T. Jefferson 1788. Apr. 12.
418 196. on waters of Buck isl^d. pat^d. by T. Jefferson 1788. Apr. 12.

5591⅔ in Albemarle.

4627½ Poplar Forest. viz 3000. part of 4000. pat^d. by Stith.
1000. thereof conveyed to M. & M. Randolph
3000.
256. pat^d. by Danl. Robertson
380. pat^d. by Callaway.
183. pat^d. by J. Robertson.
800. surv^d. for J. Wayles 1770. Oct. 25.
8 acres patented by T. Jefferson
4627½

474. Tullos's. viz 374. pat^d. by Tullos.
5101½ in Bedford & Campbell. 100 purchased by J. Wayles of Rich^d. Stith pat^d by T.
474.

157. in Rockbridge. Natural Bridge. pat^d. by T. Jefferson 1774. July 5.
10,647 acres.

4. lots in Beverley town. viz. N°. 57. 107. 108. 151. this last being the Ferry lot.
part of lot 335. in Richmond, containing 825. square yards, purch^d by T. J. of W^m. R.

NOTES to Page 32: Land Roll in 1794.

		1792	1793 april	94 mar.	Xmas	95.	Dec.	96. spring	fall	97. spring	fall
Monticello. Tufton.	workhorses	2		6	6		5		7		9
	mules			5	7		1				
	broodmares	16		3.	[illegible]		1		3		
	colts			1							
	Steers & bulls	5		8	3+2		15				6
	cows	11.		23.	15		14				
	3. y. old males			3	2		2				1
	females	6		3	5						4
	2. y. old males	8		8	1		4				2
	females			8	7		5				2
	yearlings	6		9	10		10				
	calves	1.		5							6
	Ewes above 6 & Wethers	39			8+2						
	Ewes 1 to 6. y. old				17						
	lambs				17						
	Sows & boars	12		19	9+1		5		5		12
	shoats	18		27	26		15		7		10
	pigs.	43		23	30		13				
	bacon hogs	40		21	30		22		9		8
	beeves.	1		2							
Shadwell. Lego.	Work-horses	5		5	6		8				3
	mules						2				2
	broodmares			2	4		2				3
	colts				3+4 2.3.3 1.3.4		4				
	Steers & bulls	5		8	10		10		5		9
	cows	24		11	10		9		9		11
	3. y. old males			5	1		1				1
	females	4		3	4		2				3
	2. y. old males	5		3	3		3		10		2
	females			4	2		1				1
	yearlings	10			5		4				
	calves	9		6	5		7		5		10
	Ewes above 6 & Wethers			3			11				23
	Ewes from 1. to 6. y. old										
	lambs				32						
	Sows & boars	21.		7	8		8				9
	shoats	51		42	20		21				2
	pigs.	55		7	35		11				42
	bacon hogs	84		60	32		20				18
	beeves	1		1.							
Poplar Forest	Workhorses	5	9			[illegible]					
	mules										
	broodmares		3.								
	colts.		5								
	Steers & bulls		23	17.		7+2	8	11		14	
	cows	19	31.	40		40	35	40.		44	
	3. y. old males	3		5		8	8	6		8	
	females	6		7		8	7	8		11	
	2. y. old males	6		10		11	11	14		11	
	females		13	11		15	10.	12		10	
	yearlings.	11	11	24		10+15	24	21		23.	
	calves.	5	19.	25		29	41	21		23	
	Ewes above 6. y. old & Wethers	24									
	ewes from 1. to 6. y. old										
	lambs										
	Sows & boars.	10	114	121		20		19		17	
	shoats	42				75		120 +30		85 +12	
	pigs	25	26	73		70				62	
	bacon hogs	44				110					
	Beeves	7				[illegible]					

NOTES to Page 33: Inventory of livestock on Monticello, Tufton, Shadwell, Lego, Poplar Forest

NOTES to Page 34: Blank page retained in order to keep the left-right relationship of the book.

Rates of estimating builder's work.

	£ s d
Framing is from 7/6 to 15/ the square of 100. sq. f. according to the quality from the slightest to the strongest, & if found provisions &c. 1/5 is to be deducted. call 1. square then	0 - 15 - 0
sawing the stuff (about 50. f.)	0 - 3 - 0
133. f. of feather edge plank (it laps 2. I. & shews 6. I.)	0 - 8 - 0
planing & putting up	0 - 7 - 6
100. 20d. nails	0 - 1 - 9
100. square feet of lathing @ 3d ½ the square yard	0 - 3 - 3
450. 4d. nails	0 - 3 - 9
painting 3. coats of white lead, paint & oil included	

The same work done in brick of 1½ bricks thick would take 1800. bricks, worth, making, laying, finding &c. @ 40/	3 - 12 - 0

The same done in stone would take 6 perch (18 I. thick) the laying of which is worth	0 - 15 - 0

NOTES to Page 37: Rates of estimating builders work.

Peach trees planted Dec. 1794.

		trees
Monticello.	in the North orchard, between the apple trees	263
	dividing lines between the feilds - - - - - - - -	537
	do. between the Quarry feild & Long feild - - -	70.
Lego.	dividing lines between the feilds - - - - - -	287.

NOTES to Page 38: Peach trees planted Dec. 1794

Distribution of blankets.

1792.5.8.1801.

~~Jupiter~~
Betty Brown
Critta.
Sally.
Nance
Abram.
Doll.
Martin
Phill. shoem^r.
Amey.
Isabel (4.ch.)
Edy
Jenny. (4.ch.)
Jenny.
Molly's 3. chdr.
Phyllis
Mary.
Davy. Bedford
John (Bedford)
Goliah.
Mingo.
Bagwell.
Bartlet.
Belinda
Val
Jerry
I..s.
Tom
Austin
York
Thamar.
Sall
31.

Suck

1793.6.0.1802.

Betty Brown's 2 chd.
Wormeley.
Burwell.
Jamy
Joe
Johnny. joiner
Shepherd.
Ben Snowden
Cary.
~~Great George~~
Ursula.
Ursula
~~George smith~~
Isaac.
~~Aggey~~.
John gardener
Davy.
Isabel's childr^n
Moses.
Ned
Ned
Jenny's 4. chdr.
Dick.
Lewis
Lewis
Jenny's 3 chdr.
Scilla.
Molly
Tom Shacklef^d.
Fanny.
Minerva.
black Betty
Frank
Juno.
Phill Hubbard
28

Scilla.

1794.7.0.1803.

Betty Hemings.
~~James~~.
Peter.
Brown
Betsy.
Doll's chdr
Rachael.
her 3. chdr.
Isabel's chdr.
James.
Patty
Davy.
Jenny's 4. chdr.
Lilly.
Barnaby.
Jenny's chdn.
Phill wag^r.
Phillis.
Nanny.
Sally
Lucy
Jame Hubbard.
Minerva's 3. chdr.
Caesar
Toby.
Squire
Sally Hix.
~~Brown~~
~~Hix~~
Lucinda.
Lucinda's 3. chdr.
28

Distribution of Crocus beds.

1794.7.0

Betty Brown.
Amey.
Jenny (Lewis's)
Molly.
Fanny.
Jenny. Ned's
~~Thamar~~
~~Sally~~
Peter

1795.8.

Betty Hemings.
~~Nance~~
Rachael
Ursula.
Aggey.
Scilla.
Minerva.
Juno.
Lucinda.
Mary

1796.9.

Critta.
Sally.
Doll.
Isabel.
~~[illegible]~~
Betty. black.
Belinda.
Sally Hix
house boys.
Patty
9.

NOTES to Page 39: Distribution of blankets: Sally along with her sisters, Critta and Nancy, are mentioned as having received a blanket in various years.

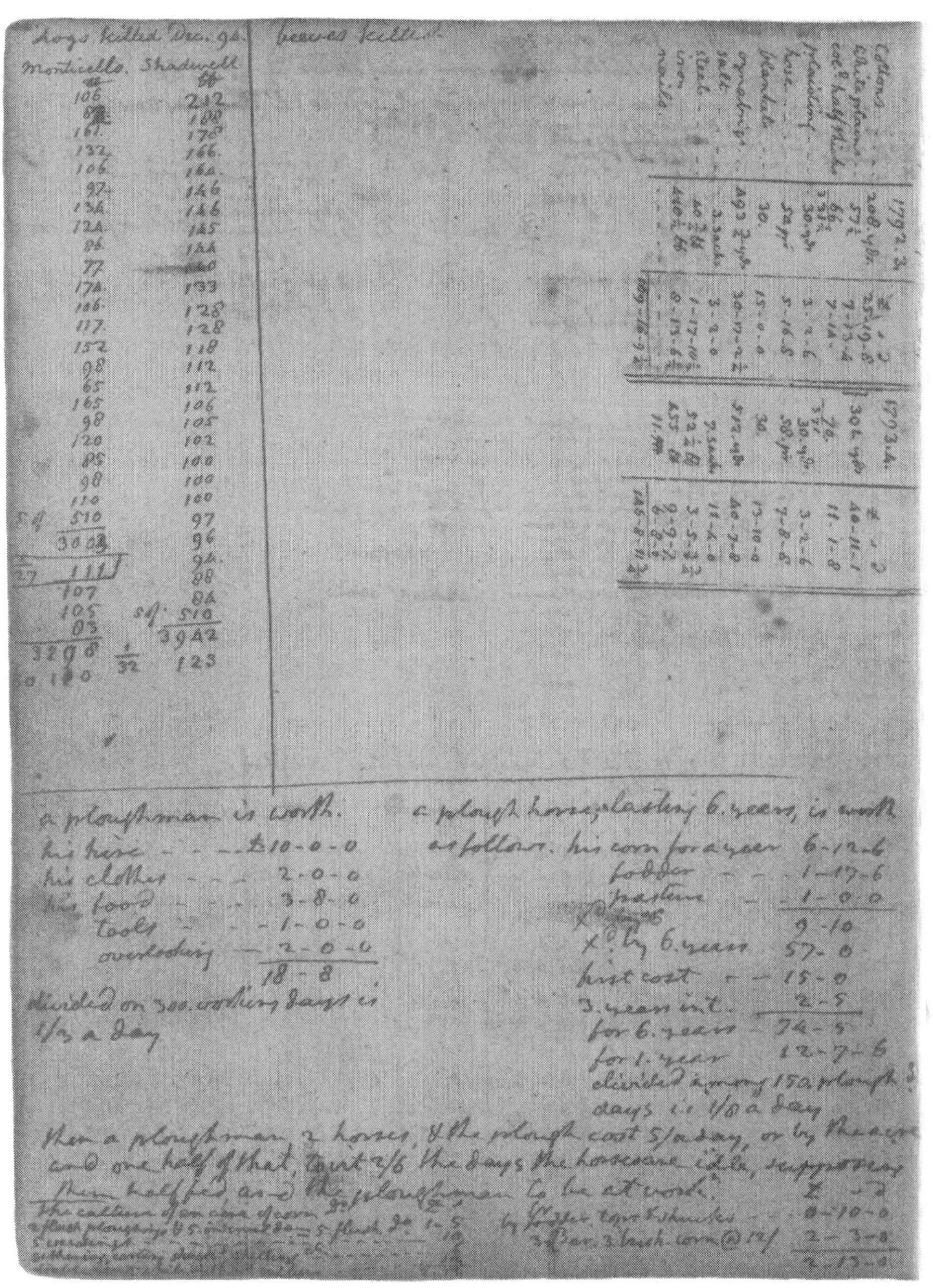

NOTES to Page 40: Logs killed Dec. 94, Monticello, Shadwell

Distribution of clothes for Dec. 1794.

Rule for the oznabrigs & woollen, supposing the latter 3/2 yd. wide

the blanket & linen given a newborn infant serves till next cloathing time.

to find the age, subtract the year of birth from the present year without regarding the month.

call those of		yards of linen	yards of 3/4 cloth
1 year old	1st size	1/2 2	1 2/3 2
2.3.4.	2d size		
5.6.7.	3d size	3	3
8.9.10.	4th	4	4
11.12.13.	5th	5	5
14.15.16.	6th	6	6
common sized men or women	7th	7	7
very large do.	8th	8	8

3. skaines of thread to each shirt make give 3 more to mend it.
3. do. to a suit of cloth + 3 to mend.
9 skaines weigh 2. oz.
1. lb of thread contains from 100. to 130. skaines.
8. yds of rolls to a bed.
6. lb. oznabr. thread hav yielded 926 skains which is 154. to the lb.

Jupiter	10½ yds Irish linen	coat, waistcoat, breeches of cloth	2 pr worsted stockings. 1. pr cotton.
James	10½ yds Irish linen	coat, waistc. & overalls of cloth	2 pr worsted stockgs. 1 pr cotton
Peter	10½ yds Irish linen	coat, waistc. & overalls of cloth	2. pr worsted stockgs. 1. pr cotton.
Critta	10½ yds Irish linen	11. yds callimanco 3½ yds flannel	3 pr cotton stockgs.
Sally	10½ yds Irish linen	11. yds callimanco 3½ yds flannel	3 pr cotton stockgs.
Betty	9 yds Irish linen	8. yds callimanco 3½ yds flannel	3 pr cotton stockgs.
Joe	6. yds ozn.	3 yds bearskin	
Wormley	5. yds ozn.	3 yds bearskin	
Burwel	5. yds ozn.	3 yds bearskin	
Brown	4. yds ozn.	3 yds bearskin	

	yds. of linen	half ells of cloth		skains of thread	pr stockings.	blanket	bed	shoes
George	8	9		6 + 3	1			1
Ursula	8	9 3/4		6 + 3	1			1
sm. George	7	8		6 + 3	overalls			1
Isaac	7	8		6 + 3	overalls			1
James (Critta's)	2		3	6 + 3				
Lucy (Jenny's)	7	8		6 + 3	1			1
Betty Brown	7	8		6 + 3			1	1
Melinda	3		4	6 + 3				
Edwin	2		3	6 + 3				
Betty Hemings	7	8		6 + 3	1	1.		
Moses	6		8	6 + 3				1
Shepherd	5		7	6 + 3				1
Barnaby	5		7	6 + 3		1		1
Davy	4		6	6 + 3		1		1
James Hubbard	4 ½		6	6 +		1		1
Ben	4		6	6 + 3		1		1
Kit	2		6	6 + 3		1		1
	90 ½	58 3/4	56		4	4	1	

continued

NOTES to Page 41: Sally, Critta and others were given clothing in December 1794.

[illegible]	Yds of linen	[illegible]	[illegible]	Skeins of thread	prs of stockgs	[illegible]	[illegible]	[illegible]
John Carpent.	7	8		6 + 3	1			1
John gardn.	7	8		6 + 3	1			1
Davy	7	8		6 + 3	1			1
Lewis	7	8		6 + 3	1			[illegible]
Abram	7	8		6 + 3	[illegible]			1
Phill shoem.	7	9		6 + 3	1			1
Phill wagg.	7	8		6 + 3	1	1		1
Tom	7	8		6 + 3	1			1
Goliah	7	8		6 + 3	1			1
Minga	7	8		6 + 3	1			1
Fanny	7		8	6 + 3	1		1	1
Patty	5	6	6	9	1			1
Lucy	5		6	6 + 3	1	1		1
old Aggey	7	8		6 + 3	1			1
Isabel	7	8		6 + 3	1			1
James	7	8		6 + 3	[illegible]	1		1
Edy	3		4 c	9				
Lilly	2		3 c	9		1		
Amey	2		3 c	9				
Doll	7	5		6 + 3	1			1
Martin	7	8		6 + 3	1			1
Thenia	2		3 c	6				
Jenny Lew's	7		8	6 + 3	1		1	1
Lewis	3		4 c	9				
Jesse	2		3 c	9				
Sally	2		3 c	9				
Amey	7	8	8	6 + 3	1		1	1
Aggey (Isabel's)	3		2 c	9				
Molly	7	8		6 + 3	1		1	1
Bartlet	4		5 c	9				
Clarinda	3		4 c	9				
Goliah	2		3 c	9				
Frank	7	8		6 + 3	1			1
Toby	7	8		6 + 3	1	1		1
Juno	7		8	6 + 3	1			1
Ned	7	8		6 + 3	1			1
Jenny	7	8		6 + 3	1		1	1
Ned	4		5 c	9			1	
Fanny	3		4 c	9				
Dick	3		4 c	9		1		
Gill	2		3 c	9				
Billy	2		3 c	9				
Rachael	7		8	6 + 3	1	1		1
Nancy	2		3 c	9				
[illegible]	2		3 c	9				
Ol. Betty	7		8	6 + 3	1			1
Tim	7	8		6 + 3	1			1
York	6	7		6 + 3	1			1
Nanny	7		8	6 + 3	1	1		1
Sally	6		7	6 + 3	1	1		1
[illegible]	[illegible]	[illegible]	[illegible]		[illegible]		[illegible]	

NOTES to Page 42: Sally was given 2 yards of linen and other items in 1794.

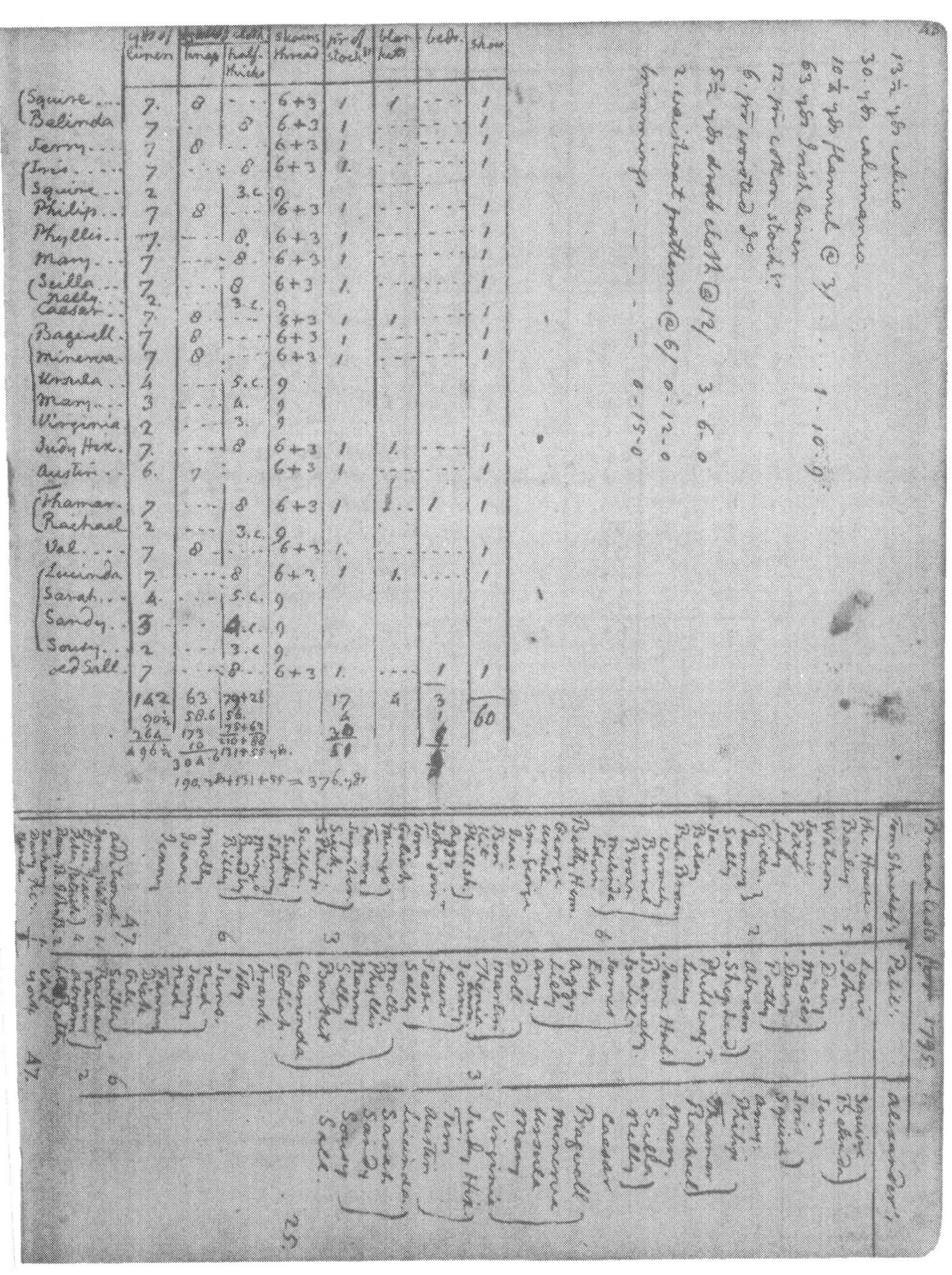

	yds of Linen	[illegible]	half thicks	skeins thread	pr. of stockings	blankets	beds	shoes
Squire	7.	8	--	6+3	1	1	--	1
Balinda	7		8	6+3	1			1
Jerry	7	8		6+3	1			1
Iris	7		8	6+3	1			1
Squire	2		3.c.	9				
Philip	7	8		6+3	1			1
Phyllis	7		8.	6+3	1			1
Mary	7		8	6+3	1			1
Scilla	7		8	6+3	1.			1
nelly	2.		3.c.	9				
Caesar	7	8		6+3	1	1		1
Bagwell	7	8		6+3	1			1
Minerva	7	8		6+3	1			1
Ursula	4		5.c.	9				
Mary	3		4.	9				
Virginia	2		3.	9				
Judy Hix	7.		8	6+3	1	1.		1
Austin	6.	7		6+3	1			1
Thamar	7		8	6+3	1	1	1	1
Rachael	2		3.c.	9				
Val	7	8		6+3	1.			1
Lucinda	7		8	6+3	1	1.		1
Sarah	4.		5.c.	9				
Sandy	3		4.c.	9				
Sowsy	2		3.c	9				
old Sall	7		8	6+3	1.		1	1
	142	63	79+26		17	4	3	60
	90½	58.6	56.		4		1	
	264	173	75+63		30			
	496½	10	210+88		51			
		304.6	131+55 yds.					

190 yds + 131 + 55 = 376 yds

13½ yds white
30 yds calimanco
10½ yds flannel @ 3/ ... 1-10-9
63 yds Irish linen
12 pr cotton stockings
6 pr worsted do
5½ yds drab cloth @ 12/ 3-6-0
2 waistcoat patterns @ 6/ 0-12-0
[illegible] — — — 0-15-0

Bread list for 1795

Tom Shackelford's	Patt's	Alexander's
[illegible] 47	[illegible] 47	[illegible] 25

NOTES to Page 43: Both 'Betty Hem' and several Sallys are on the bread fist for 1795.

"Estimate for the issues of the corn on hand Dec. 15. 1794.

	Barrels	shrinkage	Barrels
towit. Monticello. on hand	241½	12.	229½
Shadwell do.	270.	13½	256½
			486.
Oats at do.			20
			506

	from Dec. 15 to Apr. 1. 106. Days.	from Apr. 1. to July 15 106. Days.	from July 15 to Nov. 15. 123. Days	Total 335. Days	
	Barrels				
120. persons	90.	90	105	285	@ 1. peck a week each
8. riding horses	32	21		53	@ 1½ gall. a day in winter & 1. gall. in summer
5. broodmares	13.			13	@ 1. gallon a day
3. colts	2			2	
7. mules	14			14	@ 3. qts. a day each
16. work horses	56	36		92	@ 2. gal. on ploughg. days & 1. in do. of rest. winter and half that in summer
12. oxen	18			18	@ 1½ gal. on workg. days, supposed 60.
cattle	10			10	@ 1½ B. pr. month on each side the river
3. beeves	4			4	@ 1. gal. a day for 135. days in all.
hogs	21			21	@ ½ bush. a day on each side the river
Total	260	147	105	512	

Repartition of do. between Monticello & Shadwell.

Monticello

Polit.	Dec. 15. to Apr. 1. 106. Days	Apr. 1. to July 15. 106. D.	July 15 to Nov. 15. 123 Days	Total 335. D
67. persons	35.	35	41½	111½
8. work horses	28	18		46
4. oxen	6			6
cattle	5			5
3. beeves	4			4
hogs	10½			10½
	88½	53	41½	183
Jupiter for 8. horses	32	1		35 (a)
1 mule	2			
Will & mule	12			12 (b)
George's man	2½			2½
Total	137 + 54 + 41½ = 232½			

Shadwell.

Alexander	Dec. 15 to Apr. 1. 106. D.	Apr. 1. to July 15 106. D.	July 15. to Nov. 15. 123. Days	Total 335 D.
26. persons	19½	19½	23	62
4. broodmares	10½			10½
3 colts	2			2
8 work horses	28	18		[illegible]
8. oxen	12			12
cattle	5			5
hogs	10½			10½
	87½	37½	23	148
Tom. 67 persons	35	35	41½	111½ (c)
Jupiter, for horses & mule			oats	20
Total.	122½ + 72½ + 64½ = 279½			

(a) at 11. bush. a week till Apr. 1. & 5½ till July 15.
(b) @ 4. bush. a week till Apr. 1.
(c) at 11. bush. 2. pecks a week.

NOTES to Page 44: Estimate of the issues of the corn on hand Dec. 15, 1794.

Diary for 1795.

The fall of 1794. had been fine, yet little ploughing was done, partly from the want of horses, partly neglect in the overseers, & a three months confinement by sickness in myself, viz from Sep. 1. to the latter end of Nov.

Petit came to Monticello about the middle of Nov. & soon after they began to plough on both sides, first with one plough, then 2, then 3. they did not get the 4th. plough each till the 2d. week in Mar. in the mean time 8. horses for each had been made up by purchasing 5.

Before Christmas, at Tufton the Highfield of about 35. acres, & at Monticello a part of the River field, to wit about 20. acres, & about 15. acres for an Oatfield were ploughed, say about 70. a.

On the other side about 25. or 30. a. of the Square field were ploughed.

1795. Jan. } Not a single ploughing day in either of these months. a degree
Feb. } of cold of extraordinary severity, with many little snows, prevailed through the whole of them.

Petit cut down & grubbed about 8. acres between Franklin & Poggio fields, grubbed the S. Orchard cleaned part of the Hollow & Knob. f.

Alexander grubbed the patches in Square field
employed his men in Mauling & cart in hauling rails to inclose Lastf.
& repair the fences in general.

Mar. 9. at night. John & his 4. companions have turned over the brick-earth.
have cut for firewood 23. cords, & for coal 50. cords.
the mule carts have brought in 403½ hampers of coal.
12. loads of dung from Shadwell to the Lucerne.

19. P.M. John &c. have cut 86. cords of ~~wood~~ pine & 2 of hiccory, & 28½ of firewood.
Alexander has about 90. a. ploughed.
Petit about 113. viz Highfield 30. & 8 a. of Hollow f. for corn, 15 a. of the Riverf. 30. of Slatef. for wheat, 20 for oats & about 10. a. of S. orch. for pease.

Apr. 4. began to plant corn at Lego.
finished bringing dung to the Lucerne with the Mule carts.
peaches & cherries in blossom.
Martins came to Charlottesville about the 24th. of March.

Apr. 1. began to sow clover. on trial with the box it took 11. gills to the acre. Col. N. Lewis sowed an acre with 12. gills, but not so well done. the sowings are Anthony f. and an Oatfield at the head of Slatef. about 15. a. also about 4. or 5. acres to complete Poggio.
at Shadwell began to sow the Upper field about 30. a.

6. the Oatfield has taken 135 gills of clover seed, so, at 11. gills to the acre, there must be about 12¼ acres

20. finish sowing clover this day. 15. gallons have sowed Outfield & Infield at Tufton

May 6. the fallowing is finished here to about 10. a.

9. the clover at Poggio in general blossom. begin now only to cut it for green food. it has not been high enough till now

10. the first lettuce comes to table.

14. strawberries come to table.

NOTES to Page 45: Dairy for 1795.

46.

June 18. cut barley at Shadwell.
22. do. at Tufton.
27. began to cut wheat at Shadwell. the force employed as follows.
17. cradlers. { Ned. Toby. James. Val. Bagwell. Caesar. Jerry. Philip. Davy. John. Lewis. Johnny. George (smith) Isaac. Isaac. Peter Patrick.
5. reapers. Frank. Martin. Tim. Austin. Phill shoemaker.
7. stackers. Gr. George. Abram. Essex. Squire. Goliah. Tom. waggoner Phill.
36. gatherers. Isabel. Ned's Jenny. Lewis's Jenny. Doll. Rachael. Mary. Nanny. O. Betty. Molly. Sally. Amy. Minerva. Lucinda. Judy Hix. Thamar. Iris. Scilla. Belinda. Phyllis. Moses. Shepherd. Joe. Wormly. Burwell. Bram. Jamy. Barnaby. Davy. Ben. Davy. John. Kit. Patty. Lucy. Lucy.

65.

July 3. began to cut wheat on this side the river.

3d. & 4th. these 2. days they cradled 73 a. there were but 12. cradlers at work on an average, & they stopped cutting by an hour by sun the 4th. (Saturday) that all that was cut might be secured. they cut therefore fully 3. a. a day each, & may be counted on for that.

the ox carts carry the sheaves of about 7. bushels of wheat at a load. one of them with 3. loaders besides the driver, loads in 15'. and to go 1/4 of a mile & return took 22'. they would load, go & return 1/8 mile in 30'.

6th. finished cutting wheat.

7th. finished cutting rye.

8. began to tread at Monticello with 7. horses.

Were the harvest to go over again with the same force, the following arrangement should take place.

the treading floors should be laid down before harvest.

1/2 a doz. spare sythes should be mounted, & fingers for 1/2 a dozen more ready formed, bent & mortised, & some posts should be provided.

1. great George, with tools & a grindstone mounted in the single mule cart, should be constantly employed in mending cradles & grinding sythes. the same cart would carry about the liquor, moving from tree to tree as the work advanced.

18. cradlers should work constantly. Smith George. John, Davy, Lewis, Johnny, Isaac, Peter Patrick, Isaac; Ned, Toby, James, Val, Bagwell, Caesar, Jerry, Tim, Phill, Philip.

18. binders of the women & abler boys. Isabel, Jenny, Jenny, Doll, Molly, Amy, Minerva, Lucinda, Judy, Belinda, York, Burwell, Jamy, Barnaby, Davy, Patty, Lucy, Lucy.

6. gatherers, to wit 5 smallest boys & 1. larger for a foreman. Wormly, Bram, Day, John, Ben, Kit.

3. loaders. Moses, Shepherd & Joe, loading the carts successively with the drivers.

6. stackers. Squire. Abram. Shoemr. Phill. Essex, Goliah. Austin.

2. cooks. O. Betty & Fanny.

4. carters. Tom. Phill. Frank. Martin.

58.

8. would remain to keep half the ploughs a going. Rachael. Mary. Nanny. Sally. Thamar. Iris. Scilla. Phyllis.

66.

in this way the whole machine would move in exact equilibrio, no part of the force could be lessened without retarding the whole, nor increased without a waste of force.

this force would cut, bring in, & shock 54. a. a day, and complete my harvest of 320. a. in 6. days.

the proper allowance 4. gallons of whiskey, 2 quarts molasses, 1 midling besides fresh meat per day, with peas.

July 29. began to buy fallow Slatefield.

NOTES to Page 46: One Sally is mentioned as a gatherer at Shadwell. Another Sally is on the list of eight women who 'would remain to keep half the ploughs a going'.

Aug. 9. the Knobfield was sown the last fall with wheat on the North side of the road, and 47.
rye on the South side. before harvest I laid off an acre on each side of the road where the ground appeared nearly equal. that of the wheat however was somewhat the best, but the wheat & the rye having been sown at the same time which was very late for the wheat & in good time for the rye this circumstance was thought to make up for the difference in the quality of the ground. the wheat & rye being stacked separately, each stack measured exactly 4.8 cubic yards; & the wheat yielded 3. bushels 3. pecks, & the rye 3½ bushels of clean grain.

the bulk of wheat in the stack then was to the bulk of grain as 129.6 : 4.6875 :: 27.64 : 1
that of rye - - - - - - - - - - - - - - as 129.6 : 4.375 :: 29.62 : 1

31. one fallow field is sowed on each side the river.

Sep. 1. begin to gather fodder. Colo. N. Lewis began a week ago.
begin to gather peaches for mobby.

11. the rains have been so constant that it has been impossible to tread out the wheat at Shadwell. 5. stacks of about 30. bushels each are still untrodden.

22. finish treading wheat at Shadwell. no weavil yet to do injury.
fodder got & stacked at Shadwell. at Monticello it took but 7. or 8. days.

Oct. 21. began to gather corn, & to dig potatoes.

Wheat sowed on each side of the river & the dates of sowing.

Monticello		acres	Shadwell			acres
Aug. 20. — 31.	Riverfield about	36.	Aug. 20 — 31.	Eastfield - - -		35
Sep.	Highfield	36	Sep.	Triangle	10.	
	Newground	8		Pantops - - -		10
	Longfield	20		Road - - -		60
Oct. 10 — 26.	Slatefield	35	Oct. 18 — 26.	Triangle - -	20	30
[illegible]	[illegible]	5	27. — Nov. 21.	Middlefield - -		35
		135				170 = 305

Ploughing days this year have been as follow, 1795.

Jan. } not one.
Feb. }

Mar.	23.	during the Summer months of this year there were probably twice as many wet days as in common years, for nothing like it has ever been seen within the memory of man. yet these 10. months, being 43. weeks & 3. days have given 220. ploughing days, which average more than 5. a week. the account stands thus
Apr.	24½	
May.	20½	
June	20.	
July	24.	
Aug.	19.	
Sep.	22	
Oct.	24.	
Nov.	23	
Dec.	20	
	220.	

		days
In these 10. months are - - - - - - - -		306.
of these there were Sundays & holidays - - -	49	
ploughing days - -	220	
wet, frozen, &c do. - -	37	306.

List of tools given in by Alexander Nov 1795. for Shadwell & Lego.

6. large ploughs & tackle.
7. single ploughs.
8. pr chain traces.
1. harrow.
2. dung forks
2. corn rakes.
2. ox chains.

Bagwell, Phill, Caesar, Jerry, Judy, Lucinda, Phyllis, Scilla, [illegible]

Hogs killed Dec. 1795.

Monticello. Shadwell. Bedford.

10. for B. Clarke
2. for [illegible]
10. for negroes.
1. for carryg &c.
60. for Monticello.
83

NOTES to Page 48: Hogs killed Dec. 1795

Clothes. 1795.

	yds linen	3/4 yd	3/4 yd cotton	stockings	shoes	blanket	bed
George	8	8		1	1		
Ursula	8	8		1	1		1
Lucy cook	12	7		1	1		
Betty Brown	7	7		1	1	1	
melinda 87	4	4					
Edwin. 93	2	2					
Betty Hemings	7	7		1	1		1
Nance	7	7		1	1	1	1
smith George	7	7		1	1		
Isaac	7	7		1	1		
Moses. 79	6	6			1		
Shepherd. 82	5	5			1		
Jamey Hubbard 83	5	5			1		
Barnaby 83	5	5			1		
Davy (Isabel's) 84	5	5			1		
Ben. 84 100	5	5			1		
Brown 85	4	4			1		
Bedford John 85	4	4			1	1	
Bedford Davy 85	4	4			1	1	
Kit. 86	4	4			1		
John joiner	7	7		1	1		
John gardener	7	7		1	1		
Davy carpenter	7	7		1	1		
Lewis	7	7		1	1		
Abram	7	7		1	1		
Phill shoemaker	7	7		1	1	1	
Phill waggoner	7	7		1	1	1	
Tom	7	7		1	1		
Goliah.	7	167	7	1	1	1	
Mingo	7		7	1	1	1	
Fanny	7		7	1	1		
Patty 91. 99	6		6	1	1		
Lucy (Molly's) 83	5		5	1	1		
Aggy	7		7	1	1		1
Isabel	7		7	1	1	1	
Edy. 87	4		4			1	
Aggy 89	3		3				
Lilly 91.	2		2				
Amy. 93	2		2				
Johnston 96	1						
Doll.	7		7	1	1	1	
Martin 77.	7		7	1	1	1	
Thenia. 93.	2		2				
Dolly 94	1		1 2/3				
Jenny (Lewis's)	7		7	1	1	1	
Lewis 88	3		3				
Jesse. 90	3		3				
Sally 92	2		2				
James 9[illegible]							
Molly	7		7	1	1		
Bartlet 86	4		4			} 1	
Clarinda 88	3		3				
Goliah. 91	2		2				
Nad	7		7	1	1		
Jenny	7		7	1	1	1	
Ned. 86	4		4				
Fanny 88 100	3		3				
Dick 90	3		3				
Gill. 92	2		2				
Scilla. 94	1		1 2/3				
Rachael	7		7	1	1		1
Nanny 91.	2		2				
Abram 94	1		1 2/3	30			

	yds linen	3/4 yd	3/4 yd cotton	stockings	shoes	blanket	bed
black Betty	7		7	1	1		
Toby	7		7	1	1		
Juno	7		7	1			
Frank	7		7	1			1
Val	7		7	1	1		
James	7		7	1	1	1	
York 81	6		6	1	1	1	
Mary	7		7	1	1	3	1
Nanny	7		7	1	1		
Sally	6		6	1	1		
Squire	7		7	1	1		
Belinda 98	7		7	1	1	1	
Jerry	7		7	1	1	1	
Iris	7		7	1	1	1	
Squire 92	2		2				
Bagwell	7		7	1	1	1	
Minerva	7		7	1	1		1
Ursula. 87	4		4				
Mary. 88	3		3				
Virginia. 93	2		2				
Esther. 96	1						
Scilla	7		7	1	1		1
Nelly 94	1		1 2/3				
Judy Hix	7		7	1	1		
Tim	7		7	1	1	1	
Austin	6		6	1	1	1	
Philip	7		7	1	1		
Thamar	7		7	1	1	1	
Rachael 90	3		3				
Amy	7		7	1	1	1	
Lucinda 99	7		7	1	1		1
Sarah 86	4		4				
Sandy 89	3		3				
Sousy 93	2		2				
Barnet. 95	1						
Phyllis	7		7	1	1	1	
Sophia. 96	1						
Old Sal	7		7	1		1	
Caesar	7		7	1	1		
Joe. 80	6	6			1		
Wormeley 81	6	6			1		
Burwell 82	5	5			1		
Jamy. 87 53	4	4			1		

Critta 9 yds lin. 6½ yds calico, 10 yds ribbon, 9 yds flan. 2 pr cotton blank.
Sally do. do. do. do. do.
Betsy. do. do. do. do. do.
Jupiter. 9 yds linen cloth. 2 pr worsted, 1 pr cotton. blanket, shoes
Peter. do. do. do. do.

Hired people

	yds linen	3/4 yd	3/4 yd cotton	stockings	shoes	blanket	bed
Essex	7	7		1	1		
Isaac	7	7		1	1		
Peter	7	7		1	1		
Patrick	7	7		1	1		
James. Lucy Wood	7		7	1			
Dick. Jane Wood	7			1	1		
Reuben. Jm Wood	7			1		1	
Bob. do	7		7	1		1	
Patrick do	7		7	1	1	1	
Billy. mrs Carter							
Cain. do					74		

NOTES to Page 49. Clothes 1795: Sally is on the list as receiving various items of clothing in 1795.

Bread-Lists for 1796. per week

Monticello (pecks)

	pecks
the House	3
Mr. Bailey	3
Mr. Buck	5
Mr. Watson	2
James	1
Peter	1
Lucy, cook	1
Betty Brown, Wormely, Burwell, Brown, Melinda, Edwin	6
Joe	1
Betsy	1
Nance	1
Critta, Jamey	2
Sally, Edy	2
Betty Hemings	1
George, Ursula	2
Smith George	1
Smith Isaac	1
Ben, Kit	2
Philip	1
John, joiner	1
Phill shoemaker, Aggy	2
Tom	1
Goliah	1
Mingo, Fanny	2
Jupiter, Suck, Philip	3
Suckey	1
Johnny	1
~~[illegible]~~	1
Molly	1
Peter, Isaac, Patrick, Jamey, Dick, Reuben, Bob, Patrick, Billy, Cain, Isaac, Tom — 1¼ each, 15; Moses, Shepherd, Jame Hub, Barnaby, Dan, Ben, Kit, John, Davy	9
	75

Mr. Petit. (pecks)

	pecks
~~John gardener~~, Amy	2
Davy, Isabel, ~~Moses~~, ~~Davy~~, Patty, Aggy, Lilly, Amy	8
Lewis, Jenny, Lewis, Jesse, Sally, m. ~~Davy Bedf.~~	6
Abram, Doll, m ~~Shepherd~~, Thenia, Dolly	5
Martin	1
Rachael, Nanny, Abram	3
Ned, Jenny, m ~~Barnaby~~, Ned, Fanny, Dick, Gill, Scilla	8
Phill waggoner, Molly, Lucy, Bartlet, Clarinda, Goliah, m ~~John Bedf.~~, m ~~James Hub~~	8
Jerry, Mary	2
m ~~Smith Isaac~~, Iris	2
Old Betty	1
Val	1
Frank	1
Toby	1
Juno	1
York	1
	42

Mr. Page. (pecks)

	pecks
Squire, Belinda	2
Bagwell, Minerva, Ursula, Mary, Virginia	5
Philip, Thamar, Rachael	3
Judy Hix, Tim, Austin	3
Lucinda, Sarah, Sandy, Sousy, old Sall	5
Phyllis, Nanny, Sally	3
Scilla, Nelly	2
Jerry	1
Caesar	1
	25

Laboring hands on each side.

Monticello & Tufton	Shadwell & Lego
Frank born 1757	Squire born 27
Toby 53	Caesar 49
Ned 60	Bagwell 68
Val 60	Philip 68
Jerry 77	James 76
Martin 77	Tim 78
York 81	Austin 79
old Betty	Belinda 39
Molly 49	Judy Hix
Isabel	Lucinda 61
Amy	Minerva 71
Doll 57	Phyllis 71
Jenny, Ned's 64	Thamar 73
Jenny, Lewis's 68	Scilla 78
Iris 75	Nanny 78
Rachael 76	Sally 80
Mary 76	

NOTES to Page 50: Bread Lists for 1796 per week

Ration lists for 1796.

57.

ration	Monticello	fish
3.	George & Ursula	12
	Smith George	8
	Bet. Melinda. Edwin	8
	Nance. Critta	8
2	Critta. Jamey	8
	Sally. Edy	8
	Suck. Philip	8
	Molly	8
	Betsy	4
	Zachary	4
	John joiner	4
1	Phill shoemaker	4
	Aggy	4
	Tom	4
	Goliah	4
	Mingo	4
	Fanny	4
	Isaac	4
	Moses	4
1	Joe	4
	Wormely	4
	Shepherd	4
	Jame Hub^d	3
3/4	Barnaby	3
	Burwell	3
	Davy	3
	Brown	2
	Ben	2
1/2	John	2
	Davy	2
	Kit	2
	Bartlet	2
	Ned	2
	Phill	2
1 1/2	12 hiredmen	72
		228

ration	Mountain	fish
3 1/2	Davy. Isabel. Betty. Aggy. Lilly. Amy	18
3	Lewis. Jenny. Lewis. Jesse. Sally	12
2 1/2	Abram. Doll. Thenia. Dolly	10
1 1/2	Rachael. Nanny. Abram	6
3 1/2	Ned. Jenny. Fanny. Dick. Gill. Scilla	14
3	Phill. Molly. Lucy. Clarinda. Goliah	12
	Mary	4
	Sally	4
	Nanny	4
	Old Betty	4
	Jamey	4
1	Martin	4
	Val	4
	Frank	4
	Toby	4
	Iris	4
	Betty Hemings	4
	York	4
		116

ration	Shadwell	fish
2	John. Amy	8
2	Squire. Belinda	8
3 1/2	Bagwell. Minerva. Archy. Mary. Virginia	14
2	Philip. Thenia. Rach^l.	8
3	Lucinda. Sarah. Sandy. Sary. Old Sall	12
	Scilla. Nelly	4
	Judy	4
	Tim	4
1	Austin	4
	Phyllis	4
	Iris	4
	Jerry	4
	Caesar	4
		82

228
116
82
42[illegible]

NOTES to Page 51: Ration lists for 1796

52 Clothes 1796

Name	Cam	wool	stockings	hats	blankets	shoes
George	8	8	1	1		1
Ursula	8	9	1	1		1
Betty Hemings	7	7	1			1
Betty Brown	7	7	1	2		1
melinda 87	4	4				
Edwin 93	2	2		1		
nance	7	7	1			1
Lucy 00	12	7	1			1
Zachary 96	1	1.6				
Smith George	7	7	1	1		1
Isaac	7	7	1	1		1
Moses	7	7	ov.	1		1
Joe	7	7	ov.	1		1
Wormely 81	6	6	ov.	1		1
Shepherd 82	6	6	ov	1		1
Jamey Hub. 83	6	6	ov			1
Barnaby 83	6	6	ov			1
Burwell 83	6	6	ov	1		1
Davy Isabel's 84	5	5	ov			1
Brown 85	5	5	ov			1
Ben Judy's 84	5	5	ov			1
John Bedford 85	5	5	ov			1
Davy Bedford 85	5	5	ov			1
Phill Bedford 86	5		ov	1		1
Cary	5	5	ov	1		
Ben Snowden	5	5	ov	1		1
John Hemings	7	7	1	1		1
John gardener	7	7	1	1		1
Davy Carpenter	7	7	1	1		1
Lewis	7	7	1	1		1
Abram	7	7	1			1
Phill shoemaker	7	7	1			1
Phill waggoner	7	7	1			1
Tom	7	7	1	1		1
Goliah	7	7	1			1
Mingo	7	7	1			1
Fanny	7	7	1	1		1
Isabel	7	7	1		1	1
Edy 87	4	4				
Aggy 89	4	4				
Lilly 91	3	3		1		
Amy 93	2	2				
Thruston 96	1	1 2/3				
Doll	7	7	1		1	1
Thenia 93	2	2				
Dolly 94	2	2				
Jenny Lewis's	7	7	1			1
Lewis 88	4	4				
Jesse 90	3	3		1		
Sally 92	3	3				
Jamey 95	1	1 2/3				
Molly	7	7	1	1		1
Bartlet 86	5	5				
Clarinda 88	4	4				
Goliah 91	3	3				
Ned	7	7	1	1		1
Jenny	7	7	1			
Ned 86	5	5				
Fanny 88	4	4				
Dick 90	3	3				
Gill 92	3	3		1.		
Scilla 94	2	2				
James 96	1	1 2/3				
Rachael	7	7	1			1
Nanny 91	3	3				
Abram 94	2	2				
Hark Betty	2	2	1	1	1	1
[illegible]	7	7				

Name	Cam	wool	stockings	hats	blankets	shoes
Val	7	7	1			1
Frank	7	7	1	1		1
~~James~~	7	7	1			1
Martin	7	7	1			1
York 81	6	6	1			1
Mary	7	7	1			1
Suckey	1	1 2/3				
Nanny	7	7	1			1
Sally	7	7	1			1
Lucy 83	6	6	1			1
Patty 81	6	6	1			1
Aggey	7	7	1	1		
Juno	7	7	1	1		
Squire	7	7	1			1
Belinda	7	7	1		1	1
Jerry	7	7	1			1
Iris	7	7	1		1	1
Squire	2	2				
Joyce 96	1	1 2/3				
Bagwell	7	7	1			1
Minerva	7	7	1	1		1
Ursula 87	4	4		1		
Mary 88	4	4				
Virginia 93	2	2				
Esther 96	1	1 2/3				
Scilla	7	7	1	1		1
Nelly 94	2	2				
Judy Hix	7	7	1		1	1
Kit 86	5	5				1
Tim	7	7	1			1
Austin	7	7	1			1
Philip	7	7	1			1
Thamar	7	7	1			
Rachael 90	3	3				
Lucy	1	1 2/3				
Amy	7	7	1			1
Lucinda	7	7	1			1
Sarah 86	5	5				
Sandy 89	4	4				
Sousy 93	2	2				
Barret 95	2	2				
Phyllis	7	7	1			1
Sophia 96	1	1 2/3				
Caesar	7	7	1			1
Sal	7	7	1			
Critta				1	1	
Jamey 87				1		
Sally					1	
Harriet						
Betsy						
Jupiter						
Peter						
Hired people						
Peter	7	7	1	1		1
Isaac T.	7	7	1	1		1
Patrick T.	7	7	1	1		1
James W.	7	7	1	1		1
Dick	7	7	7			1
Patrick	7	7	7			1
Bob						1
Reuben		7				1
Cain	7	7	1			1
Isaac H.	7	7	1			1
Tom	7	7	1			
Wapping						
Joe						
James B.						
Moses	7	7	1	1		

Bread list May 1797

Monticello		Mountain		Sha[dwell]
Peter	1	George, Ursula	2	Squi[re]
Lucy, Zachary	2	Davy, Isabel, Patty, ~~Edy~~, Lilly, Amy, Thruston	7	Bel[inda]
Betty B., Melinda, Edwin	3	Ned, Jenny, Ned, Fanny, Dick, Gill, Scilla, James	8	Bag[well]
nance, Critta	2	Phill W., Molly, Lucy, Bartlet, Clarinda, Goliah	6	Min[erva]
Critta, Jamey	2	Lewis, Jenny, Lewis, Jesse, Sally, Jamy	6	Ursu[la]
Sally, Harriet, ~~Aggy~~	3	Abram, Doll, Thenia, Dolly	4	Mar[y]
Betty H.	1	Rachael, Nanny, Abram	3	Virg[inia]
George S.	1	Isaac, Iris, Joyce	3	Esth[er]
John H.	1	Jerry, Mary, Suckey	3	Phil[ip]
Phill S., Aggy	2	John, Amy	2	Tha[mar]
Tom	1	~~Phill~~, ~~Aggy~~		Rac[hael]
Goliah	1	~~[illegible]~~	1	Lu[cy]
Mingo, Fanny	2	~~[illegible]~~	1	Sa[...]
Moses, Joe, Wormly, Shepherd, Jame H., Barnaby, Burwell, Davy I., ~~Brown~~, Ben I., John B., Davy B., Phill B., Cary, Ben S.	15	Betty	1	Sa[...]
Jupiter, Suck, Philip, Johnny	4	Val	1	Sou[sy]
Peter H., Jamy, Dick, Patric, Moses	6	Frank	1	Bar[ret]
Betsy	1	Martin	1	Sci[lla]
Molly, child	2	York	1	Ne[lly]
Betsy	1			[illegible]
Mason	1			Ju[dy]
House	6			Tim
	58		51	Au[stin]
				Ph[yllis]
				So[phia]
				Na[nny]
				Sa[l]
				Ja[...]
				Ca[esar]

NOTES to Page 52: Clothes 1796, Bread List May 1797

53.

Name	fish
George Smith	8
Betty Brown, Malinda, Edwin	8
Nance, Critta	8
Critta, Jamey	8
Sally, Harriet	8
[Suck, Philip]	8
Molly, child	8
Peter Hawkins	6
Jamey	6
Dick	6
Patrick	6
Moses	6
Betty Hemings	4
John Hemings	4
Tom	4
Goliah	4
Mingo	4
Fanny	4
Betty	4
[Betty]	4
Moses	4
Joe	4
Wormely	4
Shepherd	4
Jame Hubbard	4
Barnaby	3
Burwell	3
Davy, Isabel's	3
Brown	3
Ben Isabel's	3
John Bedford	2
Davy Bedford	2
Phill Bedford	2
Cary	2
Ben Snowden	2
Patty	3
Lucy	3
	169

Name	fish
George, Ursula	20
Davy, Isabel, Edy, Aggey, Lilly, Amy, Thruston	14
Ned, Jenny, Ned, Fanny, Dick, Gill, Scilla, James	14
Phill waggoner, Molly, Lucy, Bartlet, Clarinda, Goliah	14
Lewis, Janey, Lewis, Jesse, Sally, Jamy	12
Abram, Doll, Thenia, Dolly	10
Isaac, Ivis, Joyce	8
Jerry, Mary, Suckey	8
John, Amy	8
Phill, Aggey	8
Rachael, Nanny, Abram	6
Juno	4
Toby	4
Betty	4
Val	4
Frank	4
Marke	4
York	4
	150

Name	
Bagwell, Minerva, Ursula, Mary, Virginia, Esther	14
Squire, Belinda	8
Phill, Thamar, Rachael	8
Lucinda, Sarah, Sandy, Sooey, Barnett	8
Scilla, Nelly, child	6
Judy	4
Tim	4
Austin	4
Phyllis, Sophia	4
Nanny	4
Sally	4
Jamey	4
Caesar	4
	76

169
150
76
395

NOTES to Page 53: Ration list of fish for each slave

54.

Diary 1796.

Jan. 1. Petit has ploughed the Knobfield abt 30. as. Franklin's, 26. as.
Page has ploughed the Chapel ridge 40. as. Mountn field 40. as.
Mar. ~~[illegible]~~ for cattle is out at Monticello this day.
Apr. 26. there has been a most extraordinary drought through the whole spring to this tim
the seeds sown for a long time past have not sprouted. copious rains now fall
for 38. hours, gentle at first, heavy at last.
30. the weather is become very cold. a great frost in the neighborhood.
May. 1. the first blossom I see of red clover.
5. began to cut clover to feed.
6. Doll's lays in with a boy Joyce.
10. began to sow peas.
June 1. Lucy lies in with a boy. Zachary.
6. began to cut clover for hay.
14. finished cutting clover.
Ned's Jenny lies in with a boy. James.
23. the White pea beginning to blossom.

Diary of harvest.

		acres	stacks	
June 23.	Eastfield	35	100.	3.6.
25.	Riverfield,	40	65	
28	Poggio nuygd.	8		40.6.
29.	Triangle	30	63.	
	Pantops	9		95.
30.	Culpeper	7	27.	4.6.
July 1.	Springfield	16	48	
2.	Smith's	48	74.	
4.	Highfield	32	72	
5.	Slatefield	55.	70	
.	Longfield			
7.	Middlefield	abt 20	27	
		300	546	4.135.6

one oxcart of 4. or 6. oxen which did little.
2. carts of 3. mules each.
1. cart with 4. horses.
a waggon aided 4. days.
July. 2. we stopped our ploughs; the pickers up[illegible] not keeping up with the cutters.
tho' 18. mowers had been fixed on & furnished wi[illegible] 27. scythes, yet the wheat was so heavy for the mo[illegible] part that we had not more than 13. or 14. mowers [illegible] cutting on an average.
13. cutters × 12 days = 156. which gives nearly 2. as. a[illegible] for each cutter, supposing 300. acres.

9. sowed Buckwheat at Monticello.
Aug. 18. Scilla has a child born.
22. our Threshing machine begins to work at the Riverfield.
Nov. 23. on this day a very severe spell of weather set in. on the 23d. it was at fre[illegible]
freezing point. 24th. at 23°. 25th. at 21°. 26th. at 12°. other indispensable
work had prevented the digging our potatoes, & tho' the earth was remarkab[illegible]
dry (for it had not rained since the middle of Octob.) the whole were lost by free[illegible]
27. we finished sowing our 3d. field of wheat over the river (Dogfield). May the[illegible]
the 4th. which should have been in wheat, we thought better to put into ry[illegible]
Dec. 10. we finish sowing our 3d. field of wheat on this side the river (Ridgefield). May [illegible]
our 4th. (Brokenfield) which should have been in wheat, is to be in ry[illegible]
concluded with George that we will keep 12. breeding sows here.
children born at Bedford this year. Hanah (Dinah's) Aug. – a girl (Suck[illegible]
a girl (Abby's) Nace (Maria's) Aug.
ploughing days have been, this year, as follows. Jan. 6. Feb. 15. Mar[illegible]
Apr. 25. May 17. June 19. July 23. Aug. 24. Sep. 20. Oct. 29. Nov. 24. Dec. 1[illegible]
List of tools at Monticello & Tufton. given in by Hugh Petit Nov. 96.
18. hoes. 5. axes. 10. reaphooks. 6. large ploughs. 8. small ploughs.
8. pr. chain traces. 3. oxchains. 1. toothed harrow.

NOTES to Page 54: Dairy 1796

1799. Oct.	yds linen	yds wool	stock	blankt	beds	shoes
Bagwell	7	5 bl.		98		1
Minerva.	7	5		1	98	1
		3				
Mary. 88	4 1/3	3 1/2				
Virginia. 93.	2 2/3	2		97		
Esther 95	2	1 3/4				
Dec. 97.	1 1/3	1 1/2				
Nanny. 99.						
Ned	7	5		1		1
Jenny	7	5		98	97	1
Ned. 86.	5	4		1		1
Fanny 88.	4 1/3	3 1/2				
Dick. 90.	3 2/3	3		1		1
Gill. 92.	3	2 1/2				
Scilla. 94.	2 1/3	2		97		
James 96.	1 2/3	1 1/2				
Aggy. 98.						
Davy	7	1 1/2		1		1
Isabel	7	5		98		1
		1 1/2				
Peggy 89.	4	3 1/2		1		
Lilly 91.	3 1/3	2 3/4				
Amy 93.	2 2/3	2 1/4				
Thruston 95.	2	1 3/4		97		
Eldridge 97.	1 1/3	1 1/2				
Sally	7	5		97		1
Lewis	7			97		1
Jenny	7	5		98	97	1
Jesse 90.	3 2/3	3				
Sally 92.	3	2 1/2		1		
Jamy 95.	2	1 3/4				
Evelina 97.	1 1/3	1 1/4				
Abram	7			98		1
Doll	7	5		98	1	1
Thenia. 93.	2 2/3	2 1/4		98		
Dolly 94.	2 1/3	2				
Rachael	7	5		97	98	1
Nanny 91.	3 1/3	2 3/4				
Abram. 94.	2 1/3	2		97		
Lazarus. 97.	1 1/3	1 1/4				
Squire	7	5		97		1
Belinda	7	5		98	1	1
Jerry	7	5. bl.		98		1
Mary	7	5		98	98	1
Suckey 96	1 2/3	1 1/2				
Phill	7	5 bl.		97		1
Molly	7	5		1	97	1
John	7	5. bl.		1		1
Amy	7	5		98	97	1
Betty, black	7	5		1	1	1
Caesar	7	5		97		1
Toby	7	5		97		1
Frank	7	5		1		1
Ursula	7	7 bl.		1	98	1
Goliah	7	5		98		1
Mingo	7	5		98		1
Fanny	7	5		1	97	1
Tom	7	5. bl.		1		1
Phill shoem.	7	5		98		1

1799. Oct.	yds linen	yds wool	stock	blankt	beds	shoes
Betty Hemings	7	5 bl.		97	98	1
Peter Hemings				97		1
Betty Brown	7	5		98	97	1
Edwin. 93.	2 2/3	2 1/2				
Nance	7	5 bl.		98	98	1
Critta				98	1	1
Jamy 87	9	4		1		1
Sally				98	1	1
Beverly 98		1 1/2				
John Hemings	7	5 bl.		1		1
Moses 79	7	5		1		1
Joe 80	7	5		1		1
Wormly 81.	7	5		1		1
Jame Hubbd. 83	6	4 3/4		97		1
Barnaby 83	6	4 3/4		97		1
Shepherd 82.	6 1/3	5		1		1
Isb's Davy 84	5 2/3	4 1/2		97		1
Brown 85.	5 1/3	4 1/2		97		1
John Bedfd. 85	5 1/3	4 1/2		98		1
Bedfd. Davy 85.	5 1/3	4 1/2		98		1
Smootd. Ben 85	5 1/3	4 1/2		1		1
Cary. 85.	5 1/3	4 1/2		1		1
Louis 88	4 2/3	3 1/2		1		1
Phill Hub. 86.	5	4		1		1
Hattel 86	5	4		98		1
Burwell 83.	9	4 3/4		1		1
Ursula 87	12	4		1		1
Edy 87	4 2/3	4		98		1
Jupiter				98		1
Simon	7	5				1
Stepney	7	5				1
Moses	7	5				1
Frank	7	5				1
	481 1/3	165 1/2				65

rule. for linen 1 yard the 1st year + 1/3 every year after to 7. yds.
woollen 1 yard the 1st year + 1/4 every year after to 5. yds.

	yards
cotton.	181 1/4
cold. plains	165 1/2
oznabrigs	481 1/3
bedlinen	56
blankets	29.
shoes.	65. pr.

NOTES to Page 55: Beds, Shoes Oct. 1799

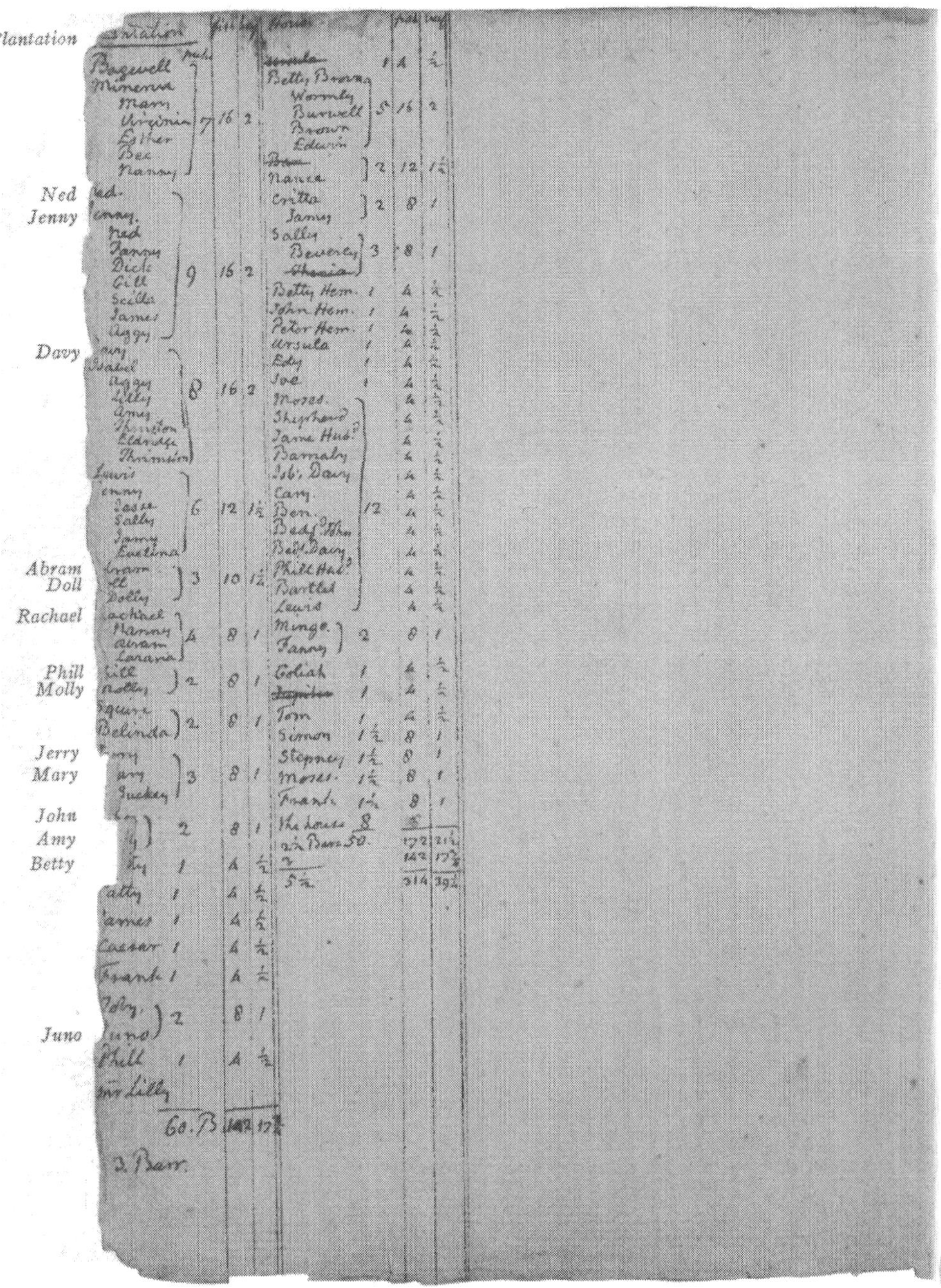

NOTES to Page 56: Plantation. Sally has a line through Thenia.

Roll of the negroes in the winter of 1798.9

Monticello.

Bagwell. 68.
Minerva. 71.
Ursula. 87. Jan. 5.
Mary. 90. Oct. 29.
Virginia. 93. May 8.
Esther. 95. Mar. 19.
Bec. 97.
Ned. 60.
Jenny. 64.
Barnaby. 83. May 2.
Ned. 86. Feb. 15.
Fanny. 88. Mar. 31.
Dick. 90. Mar. 19.
Gill. 92. Mar. 18.
Scilla. 94. Apr. 14.
James. 96. June 14.
Davy. 1759. 98. Oct. 25.
Isabel
James. 76.
Moses. 79.
Patty. 81.
Davy. 84. Sep.
Edy. 87. Apr. 10.
Aggey. 89. Mar.
Lilly. 91. Feb.
Amy. 93. Mar. 1.
Thruston. 95. July 1.
Eldridge. 97. Mar. 30.
Lewis. ab^t. 60.
Jenny. 68.
Lewis. 88. Mar.
Jesse. 90. Jul.
Sally. 92. Sep. 1.
Jamy. 95. Apr.
Evelina. 97. Oct. 24.
Abram.
Doll. 57.
Shepherd. 82. Oct.
Thenia. 93. Jan.
Dolly. 96. Dec. 26.
Rachael. 76.
Nanny. 91. Sep.
Abram. 94. May.
Lavania. 97. Mar. 22.
Squire. ab^t. 27.
Belinda. ab^t. 29.
Jerry. 77.
Mary. 76.
Suckey. 96. May 5.
Dingo. 98. June. d. July 99
Phill. ab^t. 44.
Molly. ab^t. 49.
Bartlet. 86. Jan.
John. 53.
Amy.
Betty. black.
Caesar. ab^t. 49.
Toby. 53.
Frank. 57.
George. 30. d. Nov. 2. 99
Ursula. 38. d. 1800.
Goliah. ab^t. 31.
Mingo.
Fanny. ab^t. 36.
Tom Shackleford.
Phill shoemaker.
Jupiter.

Betty Hemings. ab^t. 35.
Peter Hemings. 70
Betty Brown. 59.
Wormely. 81.
Burwell. 83. Dec. 24.
Brown. 85. Dec. 25.
Edwin. 93. Nov. 2.
Robert. 99. Dec. 22.
Nance. 61.
Critta. 69.
Jamy. 87. Apr. 22.
Sally. 73.
Beverly. 98. Apr. 1.
John Hemings. 75.
Joe. 80.
George. smith. 59. d. 99. June
Jame Hubbard. 83.
Phill Hubbard. 86. Mar.
Ben Hix. 84. d. Nov. 2. 99.
Ben Snowden. 85.
Cary. 85.
John Bedford. 85. Nov.
Davy. Bedford. 85. Feb.
Jupiter. 43. d. 99. 90

Bedford.

Jame Hubbard.
Cate. ab^t. 50.
Armstead. 71.
Rachael. 72. Oct.
Burrel. 94. Cate 98
Nace. 73.
Maria. 76. Oct. epileptic
Nace. 95. Aug. Nicy 9.9
Eve. 79. June. Sancho Apr. 97
Sarah. 88. Aug.
Nancy. 91. Sept. an idiot
Will smith.
Abby.
Jesse. 72. Nov.
Sal. 77. Nov. (Bowman's wife)
Isabel. 95. June. Milly 97.
Dick. 81. Oct.
Flora. 83.
Fanny. 88. Aug.
Edy. 92. Apr.
Manuel 94.
Amy. 96.
Bess. Guinea. Will's
Hal. smith. 67. Sep. husb^d. of Hanah
Caesar. 74. Sep.
Suck. Bess's. 71. May.
Cate. 88. Mar.
Daniel. 90. Sep.
Stephen. 94.
Philip. 96. Ambrose June 99.
Hercules. ab^t. 33.
Bet.
Austin. 75. Aug.
Gawen. 78. Aug. Sal's husb^d.
Cate. 88. Mar. 8.
Mary. 92. Jan.
Hercules. 94. Nov. 20. Feb. 1800 Jupiter
Hanah. Cate's. 70. Jan.
Luanda. 91. June.
Reuben. 93.
Solomon. 94. Sally Sep. 97
Dick. 67. Betty July 99
Dinah. 66.
Aggey. 89. Mar.
Moses. 92. Jan.
Bryan. 94.
Hanah. 96. Aug. Lucy July 1800
Kit. 86.
Will. old.
Judy. old.
Nanny. 78.
Maria. 98. Mar.
Lucy. 85

Rations	fish	flour
George, Ursula	16	2
Betty Brown, Wormley, Burwell, Brown, Edwin, Melinda	16	2
×Ban, Nance, ×Critta	14	$1\frac{3}{4}$
Bagwell, Minerva, Mary, Virginia, Esther, Bec	14	$1\frac{3}{4}$
Ned, Jenny, Ned, Fanny, Dick, Gill, Scilla, James	14	$1\frac{3}{4}$
Davy, Isabel, Aggey, Lilly, Amy, Thruston, Eldridge	14	$1\frac{3}{4}$
Lewis, Jenny, Lewis, Jesse, Sally, Jamy, Evelina	12	$1\frac{1}{2}$
Abram, Doll, Thenia, Dolly	10	$1\frac{1}{4}$
Jerry, Mary, Suckey	10	$1\frac{1}{4}$
Phill, Molly	8	1
Squire, Belinda	8	1
John, Amy	8	1
Mingo, Fanny	8	1

1799	fish	flour
Rachael, Nanny, Abram, Lavaria	8	1
Critta, Jamy	8	1
Sally, Beverly	8	1
Smith George	8	1
×Frank	8	1
×Moses	8	1
×Simon	8	1
×Stepney	8	1
Moses	4	$\frac{1}{2}$
Joe	4	$\frac{1}{2}$
Shepherd	4	$\frac{1}{2}$
Jame Hubbard	4	$\frac{1}{2}$
Barnaby	4	$\frac{1}{2}$
Davy Isabel's	4	$\frac{1}{2}$
Ben Hix	4	$\frac{1}{2}$
Cary	4	$\frac{1}{2}$
Ben Snowden	4	$\frac{1}{2}$
John Bedford	4	$\frac{1}{2}$
Davy Bedford	4	$\frac{1}{2}$
Phill Hubbard	4	$\frac{1}{2}$
Bartlet	4	$\frac{1}{2}$
Caesar	4	$\frac{1}{2}$
Toby	4	$\frac{1}{2}$
James	4	$\frac{1}{2}$
Frank	4	$\frac{1}{2}$
Betty	4	$\frac{1}{2}$
Patty	4	$\frac{1}{2}$
Phill shoemaker	4	$\frac{1}{2}$
Goliah	4	$\frac{1}{2}$
Tom	4	$\frac{1}{2}$
Betty Hemings	4	$\frac{1}{2}$
John Hemings	4	$\frac{1}{2}$
Peter Hemings	4	$\frac{1}{2}$
James	4	$\frac{1}{2}$
Jupiter	4	$\frac{1}{2}$
Ursula	3	$\frac{1}{2}$
Edy	3	$\frac{1}{2}$
×Priscilla	4	$\frac{1}{2}$
	336	42

NOTES to Page 57: Roll of the Negroes in the Winter of 1798.9

58.

1799. June 27. arrangement of the harvest.

Cradlers	Binders.	Loaders	Drivers	Stackers	Cooks	water tenders	liquor & grindstone in a cart	Ploughmen	sick
John Hem	Ned's Jenny	Abram	Joe	Bagwell	Betty	Lewis	Squire	Sh. Phill	Lewis
James.	Doll	Jame Hub.	Caesar	Wormly	Fanny	Ned		Mary	Shepherd
Davy	Lewis Jenny	Brown	Toby	Belinda				Patty	Isabel
John	~~Minerva~~	Cary	Phill					Sn. Ben	Frank burn-
Ned	~~Rachael~~	Bedfd John						Phill Hub.	-ing coal
Jerry	Amy	Bedfd Davy							
~~Moses~~	Molly	Bartlet							
Ben	Ursula								
Simon	Edy								
Stepney	Barnaby								
Moses	Isab. Davy								
Frank	Ben Hix.								

		Diary of harvest	as.	stacks
June	27.	Southfield. rye.	35	
July.	1. 2.	Chapelridge. wheat	40	41
	3.	Middlefield. do.	20	19
	4.	Poggio. mayswheat	23½	37
	5.	do. common do.	9	
	6	Franklin's.. do.	24	
			16	

The actual crop of 1799.

	Monticello	Tufton	Shadwell	
Wheat	....	Poggio Franklin's	Chapel ridge Middlefield	132½
rye.			Southfield	35
oats	l.g. of Riverf.	Oatfield		35
corn	[illegible]	[illegible]	....	94
tobo.	[illegible]	[illegible]		

June. Lewis's Jenny lies in with a daughter

July. Patty lies in with a son.

1809. Aug. Fanny lies in with a daughter

July 26. began to cut tobo.

Sep. 10. began to gather fodder.

Oct. 17. 18. first white frost.

Dec. 8. corn already used 68. barrels

still on hand 145

made in all 213

maize at Shadwell 16

bot. of Perrone 12

of Jorril 5

of Page 40½

of James Key 50

of D. Minor

of C. L. Lewis

1800. July 15. ripe figs. a considerable gathering both red & white

cradlers	binders	loaders	drivers	stackers	cooks	ploughm.
Bagwell	Ned Jenny	Abram	Jerry	Frank	Betty	Sh. Phill
John Hem.	Doll	Jame Hub	Toby	hired Joe	Belinda	Mary.
James	Isabel	Brown	Caesar	Bedf. Davy	Fanny	Phill Hub.
Davy	Minerva	Cary		Wormly		Bartlet
Lewis	Rachael	Shepherd				
John	Amy	hired Moses			water tenders	
Ned	Molly				Lewis	sick
Moses	Ursula				Ned	Lewis's Jenny
Joe.	Edy					Patty
8. hired	Barnaby					
	Isab. Davy					
	Ben					
	Bedf. John					

Crop of 1800.

		as.
Wheat.	Highf.	40
	Oatf.	15
	Inf.	8
	Riverf. Ragendf.	31
	Park	18
		112
Oats	Oatf.	25
Corn.	Poggio	32
	Franklin's	40
	Riverf.	15
		87
Peas.	Slatef.	20
clover sown	Highf.	40
	Park	18
	Ragendf.	[illegible]

NOTES to Page 58: 1799 June 27 arrangement of the harvest.

1800. Po. F.	yds lin.	y. wool	stock.	blank.	beds	shoes
Bagwell	7	5	1	98		
Minerva.	7	5	1	99		
Mary 88	5	4				
Virginia 93	3 2/3	2 3/4				
Esther 95	2 2/3	2 1/4				
Bec. 97	2	1 3/4		1		
Nancy 99	1 1/3	1 1/2				
Ned	7	5	1	99		
Jenny	7	5	1	98	1	
Ned 86	5 2/3	4 1/2		99		
Fanny 88	5	4				
Dick 90	4 2/3	3 1/4		99		
Gill 92	3 2/3	3				
Scilla 94	3	2 1/2				
James 96	2 1/3	2		1		
Aggey 98	1 2/3	1 1/2				
Isabel	7	5	1	98		
Aggey 89	4 2/3	3 3/4				
Lilly 91	4	3 1/2		99		
Amy 93	3 1/3	2 3/4				
Thruston 95	2 2/3	2 1/4				
Eldridge 97	2	1 3/4		1		
Thomasine 99	1 1/3	1 1/2				
Jenny (Lewis)	7	5	1	98	1	
Jesse 90	4 1/3	3 1/4				
Sally 92	3 2/3	3		99		
Jamy 95	2 2/3	2 1/4				
Evelina 97	2	1 3/4		1		
Molly 1800	1	1				
Doll	7	5	1	98		
Thenia 93	3 1/3	2 3/4				
Dolly 94	3	2 1/2		1		
Rachael	7	5	1	1		
Nanny 91	4	3 1/4				
Abram 94	3	2 1/2		1		
Lavinia 97	2	1 3/4				
Patty	7	5	1	1		
Beverly 1800	1	1				
Mary	7	5	1	98		
Suckey 96	2 1/3	2				
James	7	5	1	1		
Caesar	7	5	1	1		
Toby	7	5	1	1		
Frank	7	5	1	99		
Amy	7	5	1	98	1	
Molly	7	5	1	99	1	
Betty	7	5	1	99		
Belinda	7	5	1	98		
Squire	7	5	1	1		
Juno	7	5	1	99		
	230 1/3	168 1/2				

	yds lin.	y. wool	stock.	blank.	beds	shoes
Davy	7	5	1	99		
Lewis	7	5	1	99		
Abram	7	5	1	98		
Jerry	7	5	1	98		
John	7	5	1	99		
Phill way	7	5	1	1		
Phill Shoem.	7	5	1	98		
Goliah	7	5	1	98		
Mongo	7	5	1	98		
Fanny	7	5	1	99	1	
Tom	7	5	1	99		
Betty Hemings	7	5		1		
Peter Hemings			1	1		
Betty Brown	7	5	1	98	1	
Edwin 93	3 1/3	2 3/4				
Robert / Nance	7	5	1	98		
Critta				98		
Jamy 87	[illegible]	4 1/4		99		
Sally			1	98		
Beverley 98	1 2/3	1 1/2				
John Hemings	7	5	1	99		
Moses	7	5	1	99		
Joe	7	5	1	99		
Wormley	7	5		99		
Jame Hub. 83	6 2/3	5		1		
Barnaby 83	6 2/3	5		1		
Shepherd 82	7	5		99		
Isb's Davy 86	6 1/3	5		1		
Brown 85	6	4 3/4		1		
John Bedf. 85	6	4 3/4		98		
Davy Bedf. 85	6	4 3/4		98		
Ben 85	6	4 3/4		99		
Cary 85	6	4 3/4		99		
Lewis 88	5	4		99		
Phill Hub. 86	5 2/3	4 1/2		99		
Bartlet 86	5 2/3	4 1/2		98		
Burwell 83	7	5		99		
Ursula 87	[illegible]	4 1/2	1	99		
Edy 87	5 1/3	4 1/2	1	98		
				19	6	
Simon	7	5	1	1		
Stepney	7	5	1	1		
Moses	7	5	1	1		
Joe	7	5	1	1		
John	7	5	1	1		
Nat	7	5	1	1		
~~Harry~~ Isaac	7	5	1	1		
	275 3/4 230 1/3 506	203 3/4				

note the * denotes the delivery of blue thread.

NOTES to Page 58a: 1800 beds and shoes

NOTES to Page 58b: Blank page retained in order to keep the left-right relationship of the book.

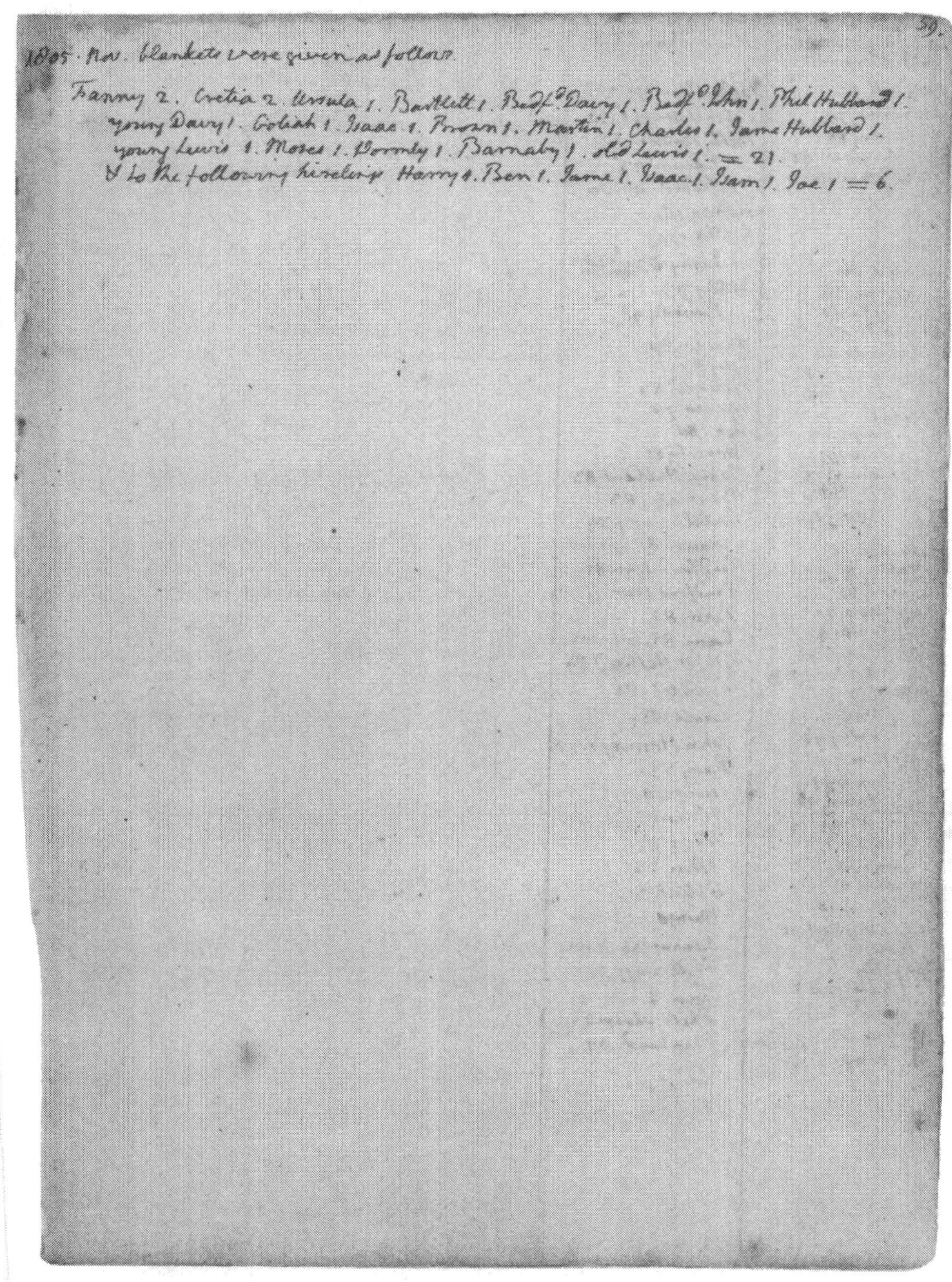

59.

1805. Nov. blankets were given as follows.

Fanny 2. Cretia 2. Ursula 1. Bartlett 1. Bedfd. Davy 1. Bedfd. John 1. Phil Hubbard 1.
young Davy 1. Goliah 1. Isaac 1. Brown 1. Martin 1. Charles 1. Jame Hubbard 1.
young Lewis 1. Moses 1. Dolly 1. Barnaby 1. old Lewis 1. = 21.
& to the following hirelings Harry 1. Ben 1. Jame 1. Isaac 1. Sam 1. Joe 1 = 6.

NOTES to Page 59: 1805 Nov. blankets were given as follows.

60.

1801. negroes leased to J. H. Craven.

Bagwell 68.
Minerva. 71.
  Mary. 88
  Virginia. 93.
  Esther. 95.
  Bec. 97.
Ned. 60.
Jenny. 64.
  Ned. 86.
  Fanny 88.
  Dick 90.
  Gill 92.
  Scilla 94.
  James 96.
  Aggy. 98.
Isabel
  Aggy 89.
  Lilly 91.
  Amy 93.
  Thruston 95.
  Eldridge 97.
James. 76
~~Sally~~ 81 d. Sep. 06.
Jenny 68
  Jesse 90.
  Sally 92.
  Jamy 95.
  Evelina. 97.
Doll 57.
  Thenia. 93.
  Dolly 94.
Rachael 76.
  Nancy 91.
  Abram 94.
  Lazaria 97.
Squire 27.
~~[illegible]~~da. 39. d. 08
Molly 49.
Mary 76.
  Suckey 96.
Amy
d. Betty
  Caesar. 49.
  ~~[illegible]~~ 53. d. July. 05
  ~~Frank~~. 57. d. Jul. 09
  ~~[illegible]~~. d. 1801.

Negroes retained.

~~Betty~~ Hemings. 35. d. 07
Peter Hemings. 70.
Betty Brown. 59.
  Edwin 93.
  Robert. 99. Dec.
Nance. 61.
Critta. 69.
  Jamy 87 runaway Apr. 04.
Sally 73.
  Beverly 98.
Ursula. 87.
Edy 87
Fanny 88
Burwell 85.
Moses 79.
Joe. 80.
Wormly 81.
Jame Hubbard 83.
Barnaby 83.
Isabel's Davy 84.
Brown 85. sold 1806
Bedford John 85.
Bedford Davy 85.
Ben. 85.
~~Cary~~ 85. sold 1803.
Phill Hubbard 86.
Bartlet 86.
Lewis 88.
John Hemings 75.
Davy 55.
Lewis 60.
Abram. about 1740.
Jerry 77.
John 53.
Goliah 31.
~~Hanga~~ d. 1802.
~~Fanny~~ 36. d. 1802.
Phill wagg. 40.
~~Tom~~ d. 1801.
~~Phill shoem.~~ d. July 2. 1809
Shepherd. 82.
Isaac 70.
Charles. 81.
~~Martin~~ d. 07.

Negroes in Bedford
July 1805.
Jame Hubbard
Cate. ab. 1747.
Armistead. 71.
Nace. 73.
Sarah. 88. Aug.
~~Cancey~~ 91. Sep. d. Oct. 08.
Rachael. Oct. 73.
  ~~Burrel~~. 94. d. 1808
  Cate. 97. Aug.
  Joe. 1801.
  Lania. 1805
Maria. 76.
  Nace 96. Aug.
  Nisy. 99.
  Johnny 1804. Sep.
Eve. 79
  Sanco. 97. Mar.
Will. smith.
Abbey.
  Jesse. 72. Nov.
  Dick. 81. Oct.
  Fanny 88. Aug.
  Edy. 92. Apr.
  Armistead. 94. (Mason)
  Amy. 97. Jan.
Sal. 77. Nov.
  ~~Isbel~~ June 95 d. 07
  Milley 97. Mar.
  Betty 1801. Jan.
  Abbey. 1804. Nov.
Flora. 83.
  Gawen. 1804. July
Hanah. (Cate's) 70. Jan.
  Lucinda. 91. June
  Reuben. 93.
  Solomon. 94.
  Sally 98.
  Billy 99.
  Jamey 1805. Aug.
Bess. (Guinea Will's)
  Hal. (smith) 67. Sep.
  Caesar. 74. Sep.
Suck (Bess's) 71. May
  Cate 88. Mar.
  Daniel 90. Sep.
  Stephen. 94.
  Philip. 96.
  Ambrose 99.
  Prince. 1804.

~~Hercules~~. ab. 1733. d. 180
Bet.
  Austin. 75. Aug.
  Gawen. 78. Aug.
  Cate. 83. Mar. 8.
  Mary. 92. Jan.
  Hercules. 94. Nov. 20.
  ~~Jupiter~~. 1800. Mar. d. 1809.
Dick. 67.
Dinah. 66.
  John 85. Nov.
  Aggy. 89. Mar.
  Moses. 92. Jan.
  Evans. 94.
  Hanah. 96. Aug.
  Lucy 99.
  Jamey. 1802.
Juby (old)
Nanny (Phill's) 78. July
  Maria. 98. Feb. 24.
  Phill. 1801. Aug.
  ~~Sally~~. 1804. July. d. 1807.
Lucy. (Phill's) 82. July
  Robin. 1805.

NOTES to Page 60: 1801 Negroes leased to J.H. Craven, Negroes retained, Negroes in Bedford

Aphonoms, Observations, Facts in husbandry.

I. Implements of husbandry & operations with them.
the plough. pa. 62. harrow. 63. roller. 63. hoes. 64. axes. 64.
waggons. 65. carts 65. slides 66. wheelbarrows. 66.
II. Farm buildings & conveniencies.
Threshing machine. 67. Treading floor 68. Granary. 68.
Roads. 69. fences 70. fuel 71. timber 71.
III Animals. viz. Horses. 72. mules 72. oxen 73. cattle 73.
sheep. 74. goats 75. hogs. 75.
IV. Overseers. 76. Labourers. 77.
V. Provisions 78.
VI. Preparation of ground. to wit fallow. 79.
green-dressings. vetch. 80. buckwheat 81. Turneps. 80.
Manure. 82.
VII. Plants. to wit Wheat 84. Rye. 85. Oats 85. Barley. 86. Corn 86.
Potatoes. 87. Peas. 88. Clover 89. fodder 91. straw. 91.
Lucerne 92. Succory 92. other grasses. 93. Artichokes 94.
Cotton. 95. hemp & flax 95. Pasture. 96. Orchards. 96.
VIII. Rotation of crops. 97.
IX. Calendar of work. 100.
X. Building. Brick 102. Stone 103. Wood. 104. Lime. &c. 105.
XI. Mill 106.
XII. Still. 108. Brewing
XIII. Smith's shop. 109. nailery 110. Coal 113.
XIV. Carpenters. 114. XV. Spinning. Weaving, 116
XVI. Potash. 117.
XVII. Tenants. 119.

NOTES to Page 61: Aphonoms, Observations, facts in husbandry

Implements of husbandry.

The Plough see pa. 36.

after the 15th or 20th of March the use of the great plough in grounds not before broken up with it, becomes injurious.

NOTES to Page 62: Implements in husbandry, the plough

NOTES to Page 63: Harrow. Roller.

Hoes.

clean the locks of fences of every thing but the good grasses.

a laborer will weed 500 cornhills a day flush.

2 laborers will follow one plough & weed the intervals between the hills.

a laborer will grub from half an acre to an acre a week of common brushy land in win

2 hands grubbed the grave yard 80. f. sq. = $\frac{1}{7}$ acre in $3\frac{1}{2}$ hours.

1. do. will grub $1\frac{1}{2}$ acre a week in summer, of the worst woodlands. inclosed lands in thicket are worse

the price of grubbing is 24/ pr. acre in Augusta, & cutting down & cutting up the large timber ready for burning is 18/

Axes.

NOTES to Page 64: Hoes, Axes

Waggons.

1772. Aug. 20. the waggon brings 5. cord of wood at 10. loads, 300 yards, in a day.

It brings 28. rails at a load up a steep part of the mountain.

a good general size to be established for the boxes of wheels is $2\frac{3}{4}$ I. & $4\frac{3}{4}$ I. which is rather stout for waggon wheels & rather small for ox cart wheels. but the advantage will be that when a wheel breaks down, you may borrow another from any cart or waggon happening to be idle, till the broken wheel can be replaced. diam. of the wheel 5 f.

Carts.

NOTES to Page 65: Waggons, Carts

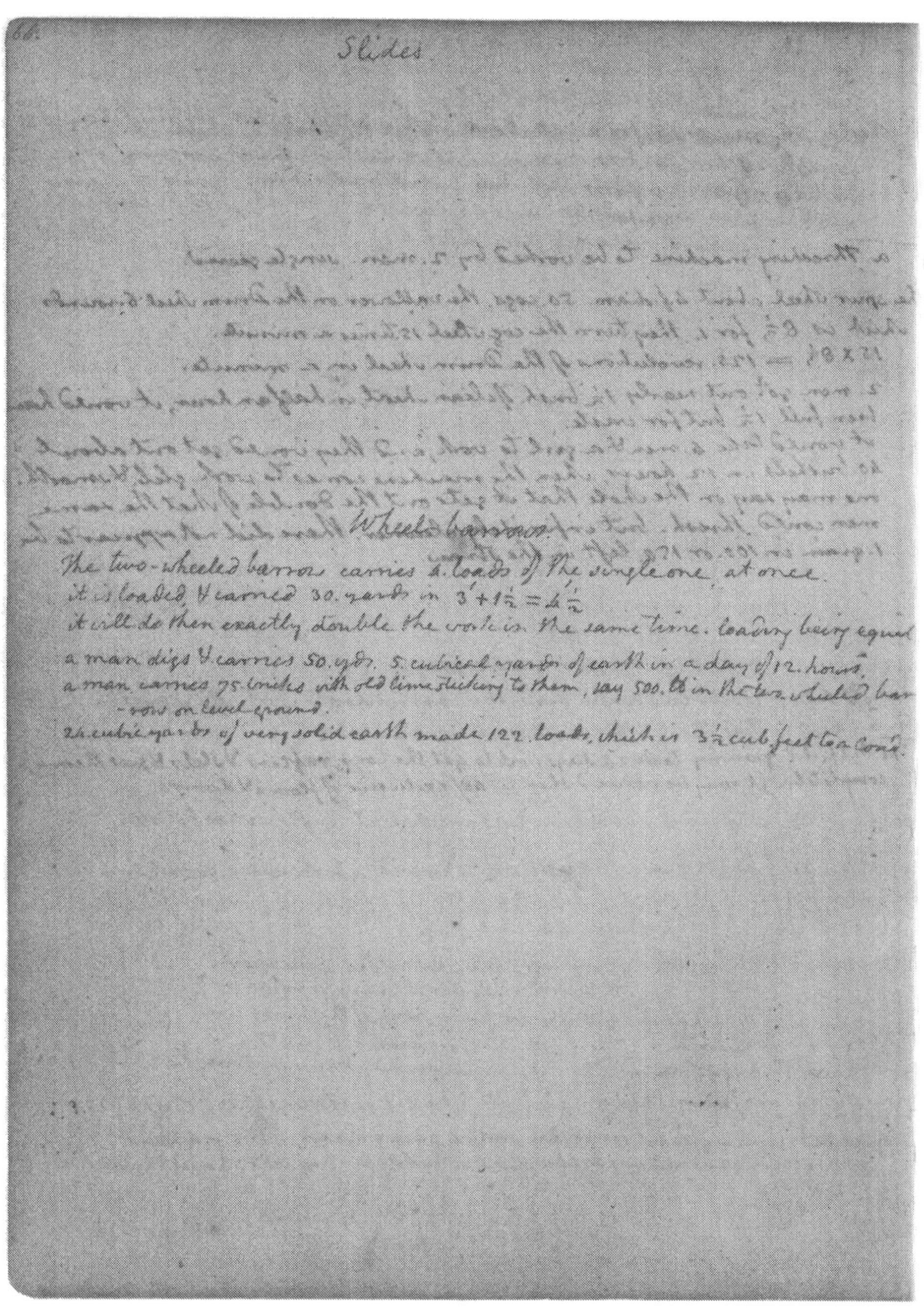

66.

Slides

Wheel barrows.

The two-wheeled barrow carries 4. loads of the single one, at once.
it is loaded & carried 30. yards in $3' + 1\frac{1}{2} = 4\frac{1}{2}'$
it will do then exactly double the work in the same time. loading being equal
a man digs & carries 50. yds. 5. cubical yards of earth in a day of 12. hours.
a man carries 75. bricks with old lime sticking to them, say 500. ℔ in the two wheeled barrow on level ground.
24. cubic yards of very solid earth made 122. loads, which is $3\frac{1}{2}$ cub. feet to a load.

NOTES to Page 66: Slides, Wheel barrows

67

II. Farm buildings & Conveniences.

Threshing machine.

	cogs	rounds			
1st wheels.	56.	11	is 5. for 1.	at about 4½ I. making 254.5 circumference	diam = 81.9
2d.	36	9	4. for 1.	- - - - - - 122.5 circumference	= 39.9
3d.	30	6	5. for 1.		
			100. for 1.		

a threshing machine to be worked by 2. men. single geared.

the spur wheel about 4f. diam. 50. cogs. the wallower on the Drum wheel 6. rounds which is 8⅓ for 1. they turn the cog wheel 15. times a minute.
15 X 8⅓ = 125. revolutions of the Drum wheel in a minute.
2. men got out nearly 1½ bush. of clean wheat in half an hour, it would have been full 1½ but for waste.
it would take 4. men & a girl to work, and they would get out about 40. bushels in 12 hours, when the machine comes to work glib. & smooth. one may say on the whole that it gets out the double of what the same men could thresh. but infinitely cleaner. there did not appear to be 1. grain in 100. or 150. left in the straw.

Houses for Laborers.

Davy & Lewis & Abram have done the carpenter's work of Bagwell's house in 6 days, getting the stuff & putting it together.
the Outfield granary took 24. days work to get the logs, rafters & slabs & put them up completely. it may be valued then @ 48/ exclusive of floors & doors.

1810. Aug. the threshing machine I am now erecting at Tufton is as follows.

the horsewheel has	128. cogs.	it's wallower 23. rounds. which gives	5.5652. turns for 1.
~~Spur wheel~~	60.	16	3.75
band wheel	92. Inches diameter. whirl 22.2		4.1818

5.5652 X 3.75 X 4.1818 = 87.272 turns of Drum for 1. of the horse wheel.
~~[illegible]~~ 3. beaters, or strokes at every revolution
261.816 strokes for every turn of the horse wheel
the diameter of the drum is 5. feet, it's circumference 15.708
the diam. of the horse circle is 28.f. it's circumference 88f. he performs it in 29" @ 3 f. pr second
the velocity then of ~~every~~ a beater is to that of the horse as 15.708 X 87.272 : 88 or as 15.57 : 1
to wit 46 f. in a second.
1814. Sep. this machine gets out 170. b. a day, working as in ordinary, with 5. or 6. horses.
Oct. 6. the treble geared machine at Lego got out 66. bushels in a day, with 3. horses & 2 mules.

NOTES to Page 67: Farm Buildings and conveniences, threshing machines, houses for laborers

68.

Granaries.

NOTES to Page 68: Treading floor, granaries

Roads & fords. 69.

Moore's ford over the Rivanna, cost £28. on an accurate estimate

1772. Nov. in making the Upper Roundabout, 3 hands ~~grubbed~~ 80. yds a day in the old field, = 26. yds a day, but in the woods where they had stumps to take away, not more than 40 & sometimes 25 yds = 13, or 8 this walk is 926. yds = .5261 mile in circumference

1790. Oct. in making the road from where it begins to rise 1. f. in 10. a little above the Antient field to the upper Roundabout, 5. hands did 127. yds the first day, & 165. yds the second, = 25 to 33 yds a day. it was 12. f. wide & they crossed 3. or 4. considerable gullies which they filled with stone.

1794. Apr. Path of the Orchard Roundabout, 2 hands did 90. yards of it, 4. f. wide in 2. hours. it was set with briars & some grubbing. they grubbed 76. yds 6. f. wide in 2. hours, in the thicket West of S. orchard after it was grubbed 1. hand did 20. yds in an hour.

1792. Sep. 18. the Orchard Roundabout, passing above the garden along the Mulberry row, measured by the Odometer of the Phaeton 1473 1/3 yds = .837 mile

1795. Jan. 8. the road which leads from the Grave yard gate, descending 1. foot in 10. into that leading to the Secretary's ford, being 250. yards took 21. days work, which is 12 yds each. there was some stone and gravel to dig, but ne'er a tree to take up. it may be estimated @ 1 1/4 d a yard or 30. Dol. a mile It was 10. f. wide.

1799. Dec. Diary of work on the road from the Park branch to Milton. 8. feet wide.

	days work	yards in ~~[illegible]~~	yds per day for each hand
Nov. 30 (6 hands) Dec. 1. (7 hands)	9.5	120.	12.6
Dec. 2. 3. (7 hands each	14.	125	9.
4. (7. do.)	7.	60	8.5
5. 8. (7 do.)	14.	155	11.
9. 10. (5. do.)	10	40	4.
11. 12. 14. (5. do.)	15	184	12.26
15. 16. 17. (5. do.)	15	203	13.5
21. (20. do.)	20	549	27.5
22. (20 do.)	20	283	14.15
23. (20. do.	20	821	41.
24. half a day. (20. do.)	20.	261	26.
Total	154 1/2	2801	= 18 average

reckoning the days work @ 2/ the 2801. yds done in 154 1/2 days comes £15-9 the whole or £9. 14 the mile, or 1 1/3 d the yard.

Estimate of Ascent, Level & Descent, in yards	ascent	Level	Descent	total
Upper hill	225	225	206	656
Indian branch bottom	....	28	....	28
middle hill	77 } 187 }	126 } 246 }	116	752
Portobello hill	30	413	....	443
from Po. Bo. branch undg.	70	155	....	225
begg. of digging to Milton	....	697	....	697
Total	589	1890	322	2801

Estimate of height of Milton above the river — feet
~~from beginning of road at the Park branch~~
rise of upper hill at 1 foot in 10. — 67.8 [illegible]
deduct Descent of same hill to the Indian branch — [illegible]
Ascent of Middle hill or Morgan's hill — [illegible]
whole height of that hill — [illegible]
Descent of Morgan's hill to Morgan's branch — [illegible]
Ascent of Porto Bello hill — 9.
Do. of just beyond Porto Bello branch about — 14.
Do. at entrance of town — [illegible]
whole height of Milton above beginning of road — [illegible]
Descent from beginnt. of road to river at plank Park head — 6.
fall of river from Park bra. to mas mill about — 14.
Do. at Mountain falls — about — 12.
height of Milton above river opposite the town abt. [illegible]

In making a path 4 f. wide down the South side of the River field, with to the commencement of lowgrounds (to be joined to the Milton road)

in going thro the woods
5. men did 280. yds in 7 H 15' which is 7 3/4 yds per hour each

in going thro the old field
5. men did 77. yds in 45' which is 20 1/2 yds per hour each

see next page. roads continued

NOTES to Page 69: Roads & Fords

70.

Fences.

1773. Rep. Randolph's fencing chain weighs ½ lb per foot, & is 3 f 3 I. from the groun[d]

1772. Park-paling, every other pale high, the tall pales to have 5. nails, the low ones 4. nails is worth but 30/ the 100. yds, out & ont. calculated by Skip Harris.

a man will cut & maul 300. chesnut rails a day thro' the year. &

1815. July 1. of the chain inclosing the semi-oval level in front of the house 182. f. weighs 90 [...]

Roads continued from page 69.

1811. May. I think the road from the Pierhead up the river side, about 60. or 70. yards which is now finished, has cost about 100. D. it took 22. lbs of powder, about 14. days w[ork] of 2 men & 2. boys blowing, repair of augers, about 60. days work of common labour[ers] last year, & about 15. days work of common labourers now. (with them 42. days)

1812. Sep. in making the Carlton path on the high mountain, thro' the woods & exceedingly steep, Wormeley & Ned did about 50. yds a day, 4 f. wide. which is 25. yds apiece.

1822. Feb. 10. Cr. in making a horse path on the 3^d^. Roundabout & North side where it is very steep Wormly did 60. yds a day thro' the wood lands.

NOTES to Page 70: Fences, Roads continued from page 69.

71.

Fuel and light

Comparative expence of candles and lamps. a common glass lamp, with a flat wick ½ an I. wide was placed beside a mould candle of the size called sixes, & allowed both to burn 16½ hours without being moved in that time 2⅗ candles were consumed, & ⅓ pint of oil. from the experiment it appears that 1. gallon of oil will burn 402. hours, and that it requires 10⅗ ℔ of candle to burn the same time so that supposing oil to be .75 per gallon, it will be equal to mould candles at 7. cents per ℔. which shews the advantage of oil.

½ oz. of powdered brimstone will instantly extinguish a chimney on fire, if thrown on the burning coals on the hearth.

May 22. 1826. a gallon of lamp oil, costing D 1.25 has lighted my chamber nightly 25. nights, for 6. hours a night which is 5. cents a night & 150. hours

Timber.

Get bark for tanning where your next clearing is to be, felling the tree & stripping it clean.

maul up every cut of timber which will make rails, stacking those not wanting for the present. let them be large.

NOTES to Page 71: Fuel and light, timber

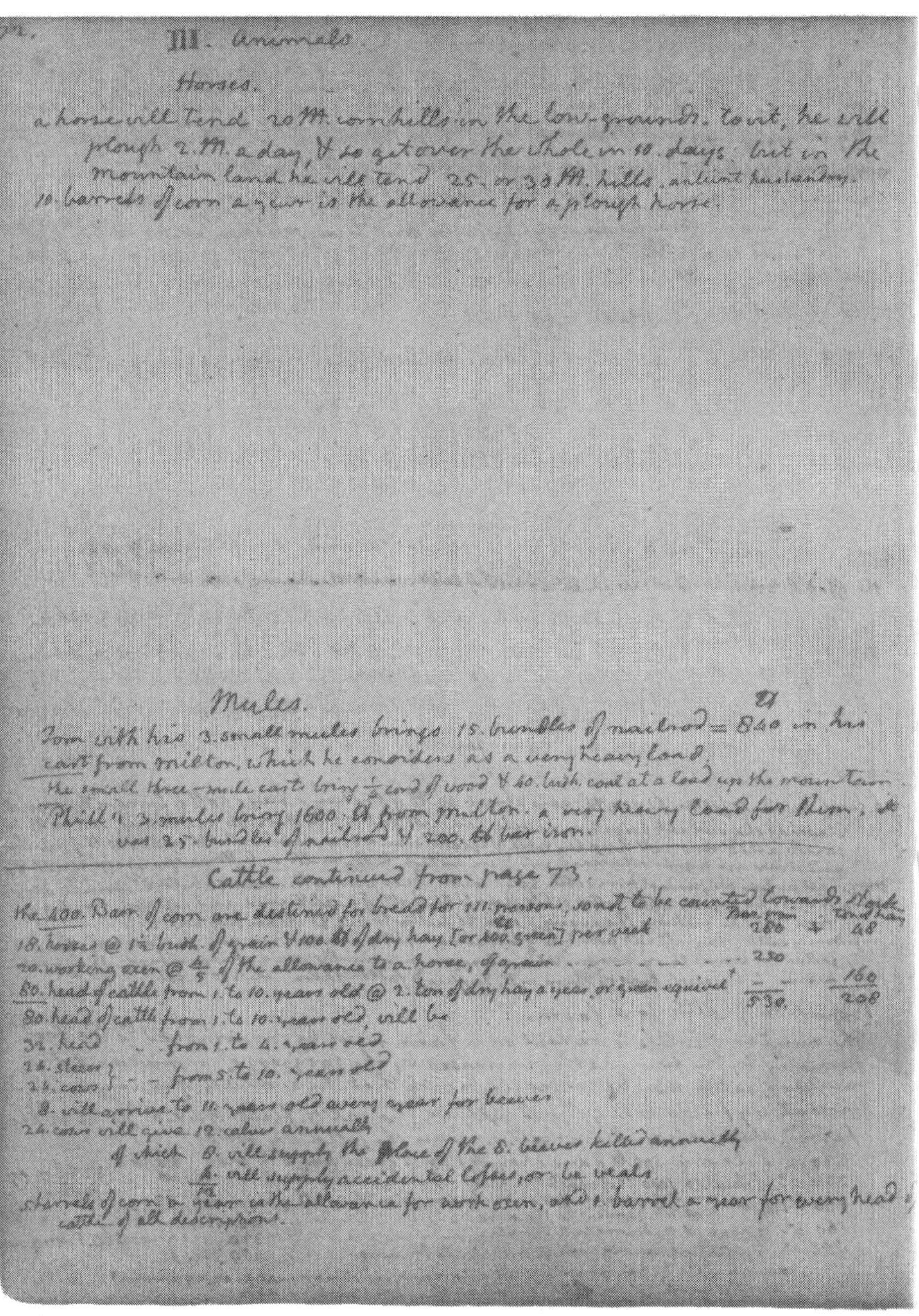

72.

III. Animals.

Horses.

a horse will tend 20 M. cornhills in the low-grounds. to wit, he will plough 2. M. a day, & so get over the whole in 10. days. but in the mountain land he will tend 25. or 30 M. hills. antient husbandry.
10. barrels of corn a year is the allowance for a plough horse.

Mules.

Tom with his 3. small mules brings 15. bundles of nailrod = 840 in his cart from Milton, which he considers as a very heavy load.
the small three-mule carts bring ½ cord of wood & 40. bush. coal at a load up the mountain.
Phill & 3. mules bring 1600. lb from Milton. a very heavy load for them. it was 25. bundles of nailrod & 200. lb bar iron.

Cattle continued from page 73.

the 400. Barr of corn are destined for bread for 111. persons, so not to be counted towards stock.

	Barr grain		tons of hay
18. horses @ 1½ bush. of grain & 100. lb of dry hay [or 400. green] per week	280	&	48
20. working oxen @ 4/5 of the allowance to a horse, of grain	250		
80. head of cattle from 1. to 10. years old @ 2. ton of dry hay a year, or green equival^t	–		160
	530.		208

80. head of cattle from 1. to 10. years old, will be
32. head — from 1. to 4. years old
24. steers } — from 5. to 10. years old
24. cows }
8. will arrive to 11. years old every year for beeves
24. cows will give 12. calves annually
of which 8. will supply the place of the 8. beeves killed annually
4. will supply accidental losses, or be veals
12

5. barrels of corn a year is the allowance for work oxen, and 1. barrel a year for every head of cattle of all descriptions.

NOTES to Page 72: Animals, Horses, Mules, Cattle

73.

Oxen.

45 break all your steers at 3. 4. old, so that when an ox is fatigued, you may have others to relieve him. this costs nothing as you feed oxen only when you work them.
with feeding & working they make better bullocks than without.
Oxen should be fatted & killed at 10. years old; not sooner. Logan.
Toby with 4. oxen & a horse brings in a cart from Milton 28. bundles of nail rod = 1568 lb

Cattle

the offal of 300. Barr. corn will winter 40. head of cattle. so will the straw of 1000 bush. wheat.
Veals are best from 6. to 8. weeks old, but may do from 5. to 9. weeks.
~~Dr.~~ Logan buys bullocks in July, & in 2. months they are fat & sell double the money
kill all calves which fall after the 1st. of June.
keep from 5. to 6. head of cattle to every hand. old husbandry.
Dr. Logan allows 2. ton of hay per head in wintering his cattle
kill cows (as well as steers) at 10. years old.
a cow (which will fatten to 700. lb) eats about 40. lb of dry hay a day. 50 lb of turneps & as much straw as she will eat keeps her as well. she will eat 83. lb of carrots and straw, but 50. lb of carrots and straw will keep her well & yield much & excellent butter & milk. 50. lb of potatoes and straw are a good allowance, and give no taste to the milk or butter. A. Young's ~~exp~~ exp. 368–371
Young in estimating the product from cattle rates milk ½d per pint or lb. cream 6d. butter 6d. cheese 2½d. ib. 372
his cows yield in a year 84 lb butter 186 lb cheese & 8/7 worth of milk & cream each. ib. 372–375. but in page 377. he reckons the average 100. lb butter & 200. lb cheese per cow.
in fattening cattle, they will eat from ⅓ to ½ of their weight of turneps per day besides hay. they will fatten in 4. month on turneps & hay alone, or in 3. months on a change of food. they prefer carrots to turneps, ~~fewer~~ of them will suffice & fatten faster. ib. 380–386.

Proportion of cattle to a farm.

The number of cattle to be kept on a farm must be proportioned to the food furnished by the farm. as this increases by the progress of improvement the number of cattle may be increased, & with that the quantity of manure. suppose all my fields once got into culture, to wit 7. fields of 40. a. each of the farms, the rotation of crops will produce the following food.

320. a. of clover @ 500. lb of dried hay, or 1. ton of green hay to the acre — 80. tons
320. a. of wheat @ 1000 lb straw to the acre — 160
160 a. of corn { yielding fodder tops & shucks equivalent to 400. lb of hay p. acre — 32. } 272 tons of fodder
at 2½ barrels to the acre — 400. Barr.
160. a. of peas at 2. Barrels to the acre — 320.
80. a. of potatoes among corn @ 6. Barr. to the acre. — 480 } = 560. Barr. grain
so much of the 320 a. as are not put into clover must be in peas as an equivalent.
see the application of this food on the ~~preceding~~ page.

NOTES to Page 73: Oxen, Cattle

74.

Sheep.

never let the ram go to ewes till Michaelmas, or 1st. of Oct. Gl. Washington

kill all lambs which fall after the 1st. of May.

at sheering time mark the age of your sheep. the 3 first years by a nick each year in the right ear, & the 4th. & 5th. ~~& 6th.~~ years by nicks in the left ear. the 6th. ~~&c.~~ crop the left ~~ear~~ & fatten them for muttons.

it is best never to house sheep. ewes which yean in a house among other sheep sometimes disown their lambs, losing knolege of them in the crowd

a sheep requires about $\frac{1}{5}$ or $\frac{1}{6}$ the food of a cow. Ronconi. voce 'Medica.'

muttons are put into the cornfeild about the 23d. July. W. Cary.

5. sheep will eat as much & dung as much as one cow. Taylor.

a sheep may be wintered on 10. cwt of turneps. but it is not an ample allowance. a ewe and lamb will eat 12. lb of hay a week having very little food besides. A. Young's exp. agr. 391.392. they will do very well & fatten on any kind of grass. ib. 390.

Young says turneps should not be depended on for sheep later than March. that the turnep cabbage is then in perfection and continues 6. weeks longer, yielding from 22. to 28. tons per acre. A. exp. agr. 394.—397.

NR. allows ½ lb hominy a head to his sheep from christmas to March. about 3 pecks each and ½ lb of fodder a day for each, varying, according to the weather from a bundle to 4. sheep, to a bundle a piece. others allow but a gill a day of <u>meal</u> to each.

also about a spoonful of salt a head once a week. i.e. ½ of a gill. or a quart a week for 32.

NOTES to Page 74: Sheep

Goats.

kids are fit for the table from 3. weeks to 3. months old.

Hogs.

keep a breeding sow to every 2. laborers. Antient husbandry.

a hog of a year old takes 1. barrel of corn to fatten him. he will weigh 100.lb he eats a bushel of corn a week while fattening.

my mark in Albemarle is a Crop & slit in the Right ear.
an Underkeel & slit in the Left ear.

2. bushels of corn keep a grown hog a year.

a hog (suppose of 100.lb) eats 1 bushel of corn a week, & in ~~between~~ 7. weeks will weigh 175. lb. consequently every bushel of corn adds 10.lb to his weight

every hog raised & fattened (including the stolen & lost) will have eaten 3. barrels of corn.

the young hogs require a bushel of corn a month for 4 months, their 1st. winter, & no more till they are put up to be fattened. then 1½ barrel. this makes him cost
B. 6
2-1½ but to this should be added 2. bushels eaten by the young hogs which are lost, and which make a part of the cost of those brought to slaughter.

NOTES to Page 75: Goats, Hogs

IV. Persons

Overseers,

Articles for contracts with them:

the employer to have his share of grain at a fixed price at the end of the year, if he chuses it.

not to share till seed-grain is taken out, & then of what is sold or eaten by measure only.

allow ½ a share for every horse, & the same for a plough boy.

a share for every 8. hands as far as 16. but never more than 2 shares.

provision 400. lb pork if single, 500. lb if married.

to be turned off at any time of year if his employer disapproves of his conduct, on paying a proportion of what shall be made accord-ing to the time he has staid.

to pay for carrying his share of the crop to market.

to pay the carriage of all refused tob°.

to pay his own taxes & levies.

to pay his share of liquor & hiring at harvest.

to exchange clear profits with his employer at the end of the year, if the employer chuses it.

not allowed to keep a horse or a goose, or to keep a woman out of the crop for waiting on them.

NOTES to Page 76: Contracts for Persons

Labourers. 77.

build the Negro houses near together that the fewer nurses may serve
& that the children may be more easily attended to by the super-
-annuated women.

children till 10. years old to serve as nurses.
from 10. to 16. the boys make nails, the girls spin.
at 16. go into the ground or learn trades.

a barrel of flour yields 17. pecks of flour, & the labourers prefer recieving 1. peck
of flour to 1½ peck of Indian meal.

a barrel of fish, costing 7.D. goes as far with the laborers as 200.lb of pork worth 14.D.

a side of upper leather & a side of soal make 6. pr shoes, & take ½ lb thread, so
that a hide & 1.lb of thread shoe 12. negroes.
worth of a pair of shoes. upper leather 3/ soal leather 1½ lb 3/
thread 6d. making 2/ } = 8/6

NOTES to Page 77: Labourers

78.

V. Provisions.

100. ℔ of green pork makes 88. ℔ pickled do. or 75 ℔ of bacon.
green pork when made into bacon loses one fourth. C. H. Harrison
herrings cost 18d. a hundred, pickled & barrelled, on Patowmack, 2 are a ration.
1. ℔ of salt is necessary for curing every 10. ℔ of pork for bacon. but another
opinion is that a bushel of salt (of the weight of wheat) will cure 1000. ℔ of bacon, which
is 1. ℔ salt to 16. ℔ pork, or 7½ ℔ to a hog of 120. ℔ nett, say 1. gallon to a hog of 125. ℔
1. quart of salt saturates 1. gallon of water. per mr D. M. Randolph.

NOTES to Page 78: Provisions

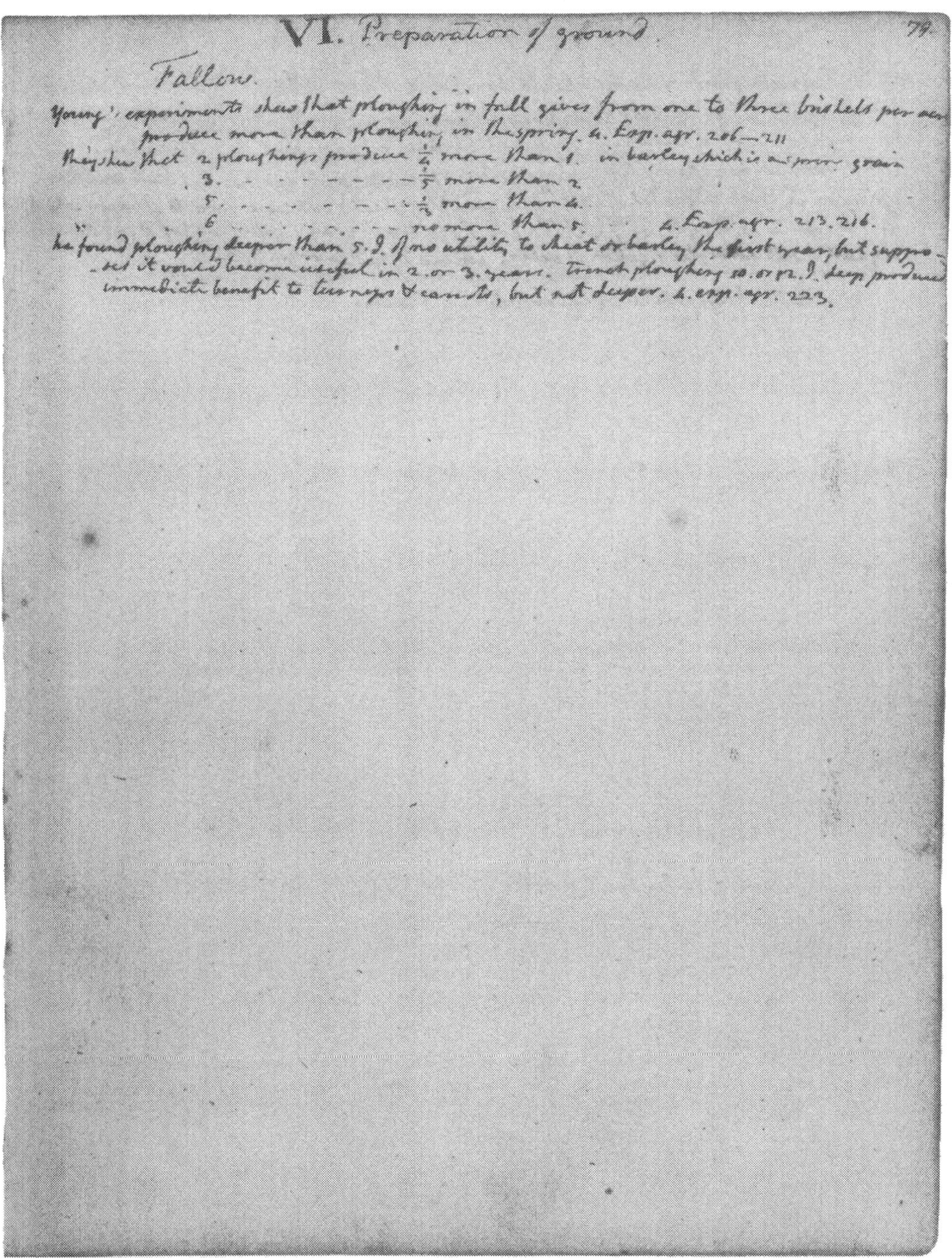

VI. Preparation of ground.

79.

Fallow.

Young's experiments shew that ploughing in fall gives from one to three bushels per acre produce more than ploughing in the spring. 4. Exp. agr. 206—211

they shew that 2 ploughings produce $\frac{1}{4}$ more than 1. in barley which is as poor grain
3. - - - - - - - - - $\frac{1}{5}$ more than 2.
5. - - - - - - - - - $\frac{1}{3}$ more than 4.
6 - - - - - - - - - - no more than 5. 4. Exp. agr. 213. 216.

he found ploughing deeper than 5. I. of no utility to wheat or barley the first year, but supposes it would become useful in 2. or 3. years. trench ploughing 10. or 12. I. deep produced immediate benefit to turneps & carrots, but not deeper. 4. exp. agr. 223.

NOTES to Page 79: Preparation of Ground Fallow

80.

Dreſsings

Turnepss.

A. Cary sowed an acre of turneps for every 10 sheeps. he turned his we-
-thers on them as soon as the graſs failed, and his ewes about
a month before they yeaned. he folded them on

a pint of seed sows an acre of ground.

Turneps do not exhaust land, if dug before Christmas. Taylor

turneps sowed on the wheat stubble succeed well without hoeing, and folded
off with sheeps are very advantageous. Parker.

Vetch.

sowed the last of September & ploughed in in May, a fine green dreſsing. Report on manures. ap. 17

NOTES to Page 80: Dressings Turnips

81.

Buckwheat.

When buckwheat is sown for seed, it should be in the last week of June.
it's produce is very precarious. Alexander reckons on about 10. bushels
to the acre on an average.
to make seed, it requires strong land.
it is 10. weeks from the seed to it's harvest.

when sowed for a green dressing, it should be thick, i.e. 3 pecks for
the acre. Alexander.
in 5. weeks it is fit for ploughing in.
it rots in the ground completely in a fortnight. G. Washington
a dressing of buckwheat is equivalent to a coat of dung of about 10. loads
to the acre; calling the load a cubic yard, or ton-weight. Logan.

NOTES to Page 81: Buckwheat

82.

Dung.

Folding. mr Taylor says he knows by accurate & constant experience that 40. head of cattle, folded of nights only, dung completely 20. yds square.
before folding the ground should be coultered & covered with straw, then folded one week, and the straw & dung immediately turned in with the great plough.
an Experiment to be tried. lay off a square acre & put 25 loads [$\frac{4}{30}$] of dung on it. lay off 8 acres separately around it. fold 4. of them with a given number of cattle, & the other 4. with 5. or 6 times as many sheep, giving 1. week to one acre, 1½ to the 2d. 2 weeks to the 3d. & 2½ to the 4th. sow the whole with wheat, and see which of the folded acres is equal to the dunged one, in order to ascertain the equivalence between folding & spreading dung.
Dung beneficially used as a top dressing in the spring. Report on Manures. pa. 15.
Dung hill should be on a level, paved, with a wall round it, shaded, channels at bottom to lead off superfluous moisture. ib. 27. plant trees round it. ib. Append. 7.
Young sais that 20. head of sheep will fold 1. acre a year in a manner to equal 20. loads of dung. then the folding of one sheep a year is equivalent to one load of dung. 3. exp. agr. 166. this makes 20 sheep only equal to 1. cow. mr Taylor's estimate in folding makes 1. cow fold $\frac{2}{10}$ of an acre in a year. this makes 1. cow equal to 18. sheep.

Long dung.

Potted dung. cattle, little & big, will make 10 loads [cubic yds] in 6. months if well littered. Logan. D. M. Randolph.

25. such loads serve to manure an acre. Logan.

it would be well worth while to confine & litter cattle in a yard thro' the summer. Logan.

each head would then manure an acre a year.

dung is carried on in Dec. Jan. Feb.

Marle. an easy method of estimating accurately the quantity of calcareous earth they con-tain by dropping spirit of nitre till saturated, on that & on unburnt limestone. Rep. Manures. pa. 78

Gypsum a calcareous earth combined with a mineral acid. when the calcareous earth is predo-minant it is a good manure, when the 2. ingredients are balanced so as to neutralize it perfectly it is neither good nor bad, when the acid abounds it is injurious. ib. pa. 85.

NOTES to Page 83: Potted dung, cattle, little & big

84. # VII. Plants

Wheat.

G. Divers supposes that every Cubic yard of a stack of wheat yields generally 2. bushels of grain. a common good barn yields 4¾ bushels of grain & 475 ℔ of straw & chaff, or perhaps ¼ of a ton.

Jo. Watkins says he knows from actual experiment that wheat loses 2 ℔ in the bushel, weight, from Oct. to January which is 1. per cent per month.

he reckons the offal of a bushel of wheat worth 1/ see below.

2½ bush. of seed wheat to the acre produces the maximum. 1. Young exp. agric. 271

drilling in equidistant rows, those 1. foot apart produce the maximum. ib. 286. 292. 290.

in this way 2 bush. of seed per acre seems better than 2½ ib. 298.

all September & the first fortnight of October in England, for sowing, produces most. 310.

too early sowing does more mischief after a clover lay than after a fallow. ib. 306

as to change of seed he establishes these points. 1. wheats from the most opposite climates are best. 2. from opposite soils also, as clay wheats on gravel soil, or gravel wheats on clay soil. 3. wheat which has for some years been of the same neighborhood is worse than any change that can be made. 1. Exp. agr. 321.

for 5½ bushels of wheat a miller should give a barrel of fine flour, he keeping the offal

for 6. bushels he should give a barrel of ~~fine~~ flour, he finding barrel & nails, & return^d the offal

6. bushels of wheat weigh – – – –	360		
a barrel contains of fine flour	196		
allowance for waste – – – –	20		d
Offal. Seconds 25 = ~~½ a bush. of corn~~ —	25 = ½ bush. of corn	– –	1-6
Shorts 2. bushels – – – –	50.	– – – –	1-6
bran 3. bushels – – – –	69 @ 1/ per bushel	– –	3
			6-0

when wheat is @ 6/ per bush. then the offal is worth 1/ per bushel

to have a barrel of flour & the offal for 6/ instead of a barrel for 5½ is getting 6/ for the odd half bushel of wheat

1800. Sep. 9. on accurate trial 3. bush. of wheat in the chaff as it came from the threshing machine yielded 1. bush. of clean wheat.

1812. May 3. the period for sowing wheat is from Oct. 10. to Nov. 10. what is sown either earlier or later is subject to the fly.

NOTES to Page 84: Plants, wheat

85.

Rye.

it is thought that any ground will yeild as much wheat as rye, & that wheat exhausts less than rye.

D. Ross has found that 1. bush. of rye furnish as much nutriment to horses as 5. bushels of corn. both supposed to be ground. also that a feed of 3. quarts of ground corn are as nutritive as 4. quarts of unground.

G. Divers thinks that 4. measures of bran are but equal to one of rye or corn.

Oats.

a common sheaf of oats, chopped, will fill a peck, & contains about a pint of the grain.

a good sheaf will weigh 2. ℔.

100. ℔ in the sheaf will yield a bushel of grain, if the straw was not very rank

NOTES to Page 85: Rye, Oats

86.
Barley

Indian corn.

1. gallon of plaister mixed in tar suffices to roll 1. bushel of corn.
1. bushel of corn plants 8. acres of ground in drills 5½ f. apart, with single plants
at from 18 I. to 30 I. or say 2. f. distance in the drill
so that 1. pint of plaister is enough for an acre.

NOTES to Page 86: Barley, Indian Corn

Potatoes. 87

planted alone in drills 5.f. apart, take 8. bushels of seed to the acre, if cut into eyes.

the unrotted dung of the last winter may be carried out in Mar. Apr. or May, & the potatoe furrow being made, & potatoes dropped in, this dung is then put over them, trodden in, & covered with a thin coat of earth. mr Taylor thinks this much the most oeconomical way of using dung. it becomes well rotted & in a proper state for the succeeding crop of grain. a

1795. Dec. Colo. N. Lewis's. this year in drills 4f. apart yielded 5. bush. to 140. yds. in the row = 130 bush. per acre he says a hand will dig $\frac{1}{3}$ of an acre per day, say 43. bushels per day

Young finds the planting at a foot apart all over the ground produce most & prepare the ground best for wheat. 2 Exp. agr. 240.

mixed with corn.

one way is to drill the corn in 8.f. rows, & 18. I. apart in the row, then to drill the potatoes between. with good ploughing this is the best method. G. Washington.

this method takes about 5. bushels of seed to the acre, if cut into eyes.

Peters has tried this method many years. & measuring the produce of several acres it has been 40. bush. of corn & 120. bush. of potatoes to the acre.

June is the best time for planting potatoes, by which time the corn may have been worked over 3 times. mr Parker.

another way is to plant the corn & potatoes in 4.f. rows both ways, every other row being potatoes. this takes 2. or $2\frac{1}{2}$ bush. of seed to the acre, & with bad ploughmen, is the best, because of crossploughing.

to feed with potatoes, they are put into a trough with some water, and stirred about with a switch broom, then put into a dry trough & chopped with an S, the blade of which is $7\frac{1}{2}$ I long, 3 I. deep, & has a socket to receive the handle which is as long as a spade handle.

a double measure of potatoes yield as much nutriment as a single one of corn. Logan.

a peck of potatoes a day serves a horse. a handful of bran, or ryemeal &c. is mixed in for them.

a bushel a day serves a fattening ox.

NOTES to Page 87: Potatoes

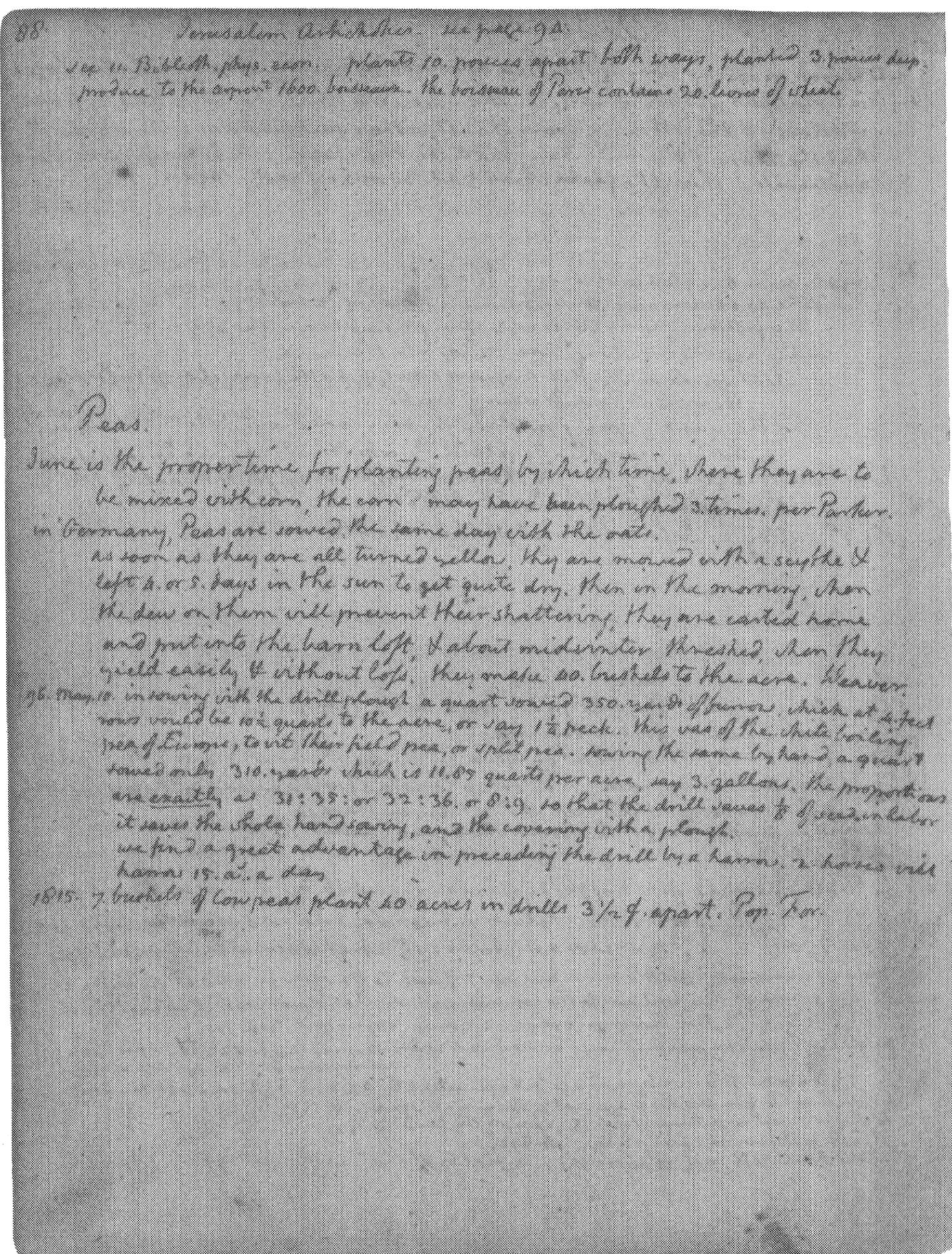

88. Jerusalem Artichokes. see page 94.
see in Biblioth. phys. econ. plants 10. pouces apart both ways, planted 3. pouces deep.
produce to the amount 1600. boisseaux. the boisseau of Paris contains 20. livres of wheat.

Peas.
June is the proper time for planting peas, by which time, where they are to
be mixed with corn, the corn may have been ploughed 3. times. per Parker.
in Germany, Peas are sowed the same day with the oats.
as soon as they are all turned yellow, they are mowed with a scythe &
left 4. or 5. days in the sun to get quite dry. then on the morning, when
the dew on them will prevent their shattering, they are carted home
and put into the barn loft, & about midwinter threshed, when they
yield easily & without loss. they make 40. bushels to the acre. Weaver.
96. May. 10. in sowing with the drill plough a quart sowed 350. yards of furrow, which at 4. feet
rows would be 10½ quarts to the acre, or say 1½ peck. this was of the white boiling
pea of Europe, to wit their field pea, or split pea. sowing the same by hand, a quart
sowed only 310. yards which is 11.85 quarts per acre, say 3. gallons. the proportions
are exactly as 31 : 35 : or 32 : 36. or 8 : 9. so that the drill saves ⅛ of seed, in labor
it saves the whole hand sowing, and the covering with a plough.
we find a great advantage in preceding the drill by a harrow. 2 horses will
harrow 15. as. a day
1815. 7. bushels of Cowpeas plant 40 acres in drills 3½ f. apart. Pop. For.

NOTES to Page 88: Jerusalem Artichokes, Peas

Clover.

89.

White clover growing among the Red does not lessen the crop of the latter. Logan
Try two Rotations, differing only in the circumstance that one has 3. years of
red clover, & the other 3. years of rest, either successive or interspersed,
& at the close of the rotation, that with the clover will be very much more
meliorated, than the field which had 3. years of rest. Logan.

Dr. Logan sows his clover alone in the fall.
the next summer is it's prime, yielding 2 cuttings.
the following year gives one cutting & pasture instead of a 2d.
his average cuttings are 2. tons to the acre.
wheat sowed on it after 2. years crops, yield the heaviest crop possible, as
the ground is still clear of weeds.
if the want of spring pasture renders expedient to let it remain still
another year, then, to get rid of weeds, it will require an extra ploughing.
the 2d. cutting is generally best for the quantity, & always for the quality of the hay.
it is also best for the seed. Peters.
the 1st. cutting is before harvest, & the 2d. after.

Clover hay, if well stacked, will spoil but a little way in. however it is
best to put it under barracks.
hay is generally stacked in Pensylva in stacks of about 3, 4, or 5 tons; but in
England they pack in 15 or 20. tons, as hard as wood. it keeps the bet-
-ter the larger the stack, & the harder packed.
clover when dried weighs ¼ of what it did when green. Kaims. 168.

the Seed-produce is very precarious in quantity. Dr. Logan thinks 2. bush-
-els a average crop: Peters 4. bushels, & he has seen vastly more
to the acre. the heads are combed off, which does not sacrifice the hay.
Young's experiments yielded on an average 2¾ bush. to the acre. he made it from the 2d crop.
he suspects that contrary to the common opinion, when clover seeds it injures the succeed-
-ing crop, whether clover or grain. 3. Young's exp. agric. 300. 360.
the quantity of seed to an acre producing the maximum is in manured lands 12½ ℔. pa. 393
unmanured 20. ℔ pa. 387
[these quantities sown by hand are but equivalent to 4½ and 7½ ℔ sown with the box.]
his experiments are decisive against autumnal sowing. ib. 367.
he thinks it best to continue clover 3. years on the land. ib. 321.
it is the best summer feed for hogs. ib. 292.
a field of 10. a. will pasture more than 2. fields of 5. a. each. ib. 299.

NOTES to Page 89: Clover

90

Vetch.

if for fodder it is sown about the Autumnal equinox. 2 Dickson 212.

Young' average crop of hay is 43 C.R. to the acre. the seed 12. bush. 3 Young, agr. pa. 21 27.

he thinks it best that the manure designed for wheat should be laid on the spring vetch, and the wheat sowed on the stubble in autumn. pa. 32. it would seem best to let clover precede wheat in the strong fields and vetches in the weak ones.

NOTES to Page 90: Vetch

91.

Fodder.

an acre of corn yields in blades, tops & shucks what is equivalent to about 400. lb of blades.

8. or 10. lb of blades serve a horse a night.

blades are generally put into cocks of about 1000. lb.

Straw.

2600. lb of effect straw to the acre is reckoned a tolerable crop. Agri-cult. of Middlesex pa. 29.

another estimate is 100. lb of straw & chaff to every bushel of grain yielded.

NOTES to Page 91: Fodder, Straw

92. Lucerne

green Lucerne, when dried, loses $\frac{3}{4}$ of it's weight. 2. Dickson. 230.
a cow eats of green Lucerne about 66.℔ per day. of St. foin 66.℔ neither gives any taste to the milk
nor will clover if the cow be not confined to it. A. Young's. exp. agr. 362–367.

Succory.

~~[illegible]~~ Pumpkins.

Nov. 1796. less than an acre of pumpkins have fed 9 horses at Shadwell 5. weeks, as well as a gallon & a half of corn a day would have done. equal then to 35. days × 9. horses, × 1½ gall^s. of corn = 12 barrels of corn. besides this a great proportion of the pumpkins had rotted. an acre of pumpkins then is equivalent to 5. acres of corn.

to feed all the work horses, oxen, milch cows from Sep. 1. to Dec. 31. & to fatten the hogs 8. acres of pumpkins should be planted on each side of the river, by the meadows.

NOTES to Page 92: Lucerne, Succory, Pumpkins

Other grasses.

ashes, while they are a fine manure for clover, destroy broomstraw. & are said to be the only thing which will do it. A. Stuart from J. Rose.

a milch cow (which would fatten to 700 lb) will require for the summer's food $1\frac{3}{4}$ a.s of grass which would mow to 3375 lb hay to the acre, or so as ground which would yield 3. ton of hay. [illegible]

Hay.

in a stack of hay a year & a half old, a cubic yard weighs 11. Dutchstone = 176 lb. Kaims 170.

NOTES to Page 93: Other Grapers, Hay

94. Artichokes. see page 88.

500. bushels to the acre made by mr Ben. Lewis.

½ bushel a day serves a hog.

Artichokes do better on clayey loams than either potatoes or carrots. the horsehoeing husbandry suits them best. double rows 18. I. apart, & intervals of 3½ f. the plants 1. f. in the row. when planted flush the rows should be 2. f. apart & the plants 1. f. in the row. average produce 481. bushels to the acre. but they do not leave the earth mellow. they thrive in almost any soil. 3. Young's exp. agr. 258.

Red beets. Carrots.

Beets are ameliorating. they suit clays better than carrots. should be substituted for unproductive fallows. they clean the grounds. plants should be hoed to 18 I. apart every way. average produce 346 bushels per acre. 3. Young's, exp. agric. 251.

to feed horses with carrots put 2 or 3. bushels at a time into a trough, and with water & a broom wash them. take them out, chop them with the edge of a shovel & give them in chaff to the horses. 2½ bushels are equivalent to a bushel of oats, and with a plenty of hay will serve a horse a week. 4. exp. agr. 409.

NOTES to Page 94: Artichokes, Red beets, Carrots

95

Cotton.

1000. hills of cotton will yeild from 10. to 15 lb of the common kind
the Nankeen cotton yeilds near the double, but it comes later & with more risk from frost.

a cotton warp & hemp filling make the best linen for negroes.

where cotton is to be divided with an overseer, it should be done weekly, not once in

Hemp & flax.

Dr. Logan does not approve of sowing flax with clover.
he does not think flax a great exhauster.

an acre of flax will make 50. lb
nothing will come immediately after flax except turnips.
ground once in flax takes 5. or 6. years before it will bring flax again.

hemp. plough the ground for it early in the fall & very deep. if possible plough it again in Feb. before you sow it, which should be in March.
a hand can tend 3. acres of hemp a year.
tolerable ground yields 500. lb to the acre. you may generally count on 100 lb for every foot the hemp is over 4. f. high.
a hand will break 60. or 70. lb a day, & even to 150. lb.
if it is to be divided with an overseer, divide it as it is prepared.

seed. to make hemp seed, make hills of the form & size of cucumber hills, from 4. to 6 f. apart, in proportion to the strength of the ground. prick about a dozen seeds into each hill in different parts of it. when they come up thin them to two. as soon as the male plants have shed their farina cut them up, that the whole nourishment may go to the female plants. every plant thus tended will yield a quart of seed. a bushel of good brown seed is enough for an acre.

NOTES to Page 95: Cotton, Hemp & Flack

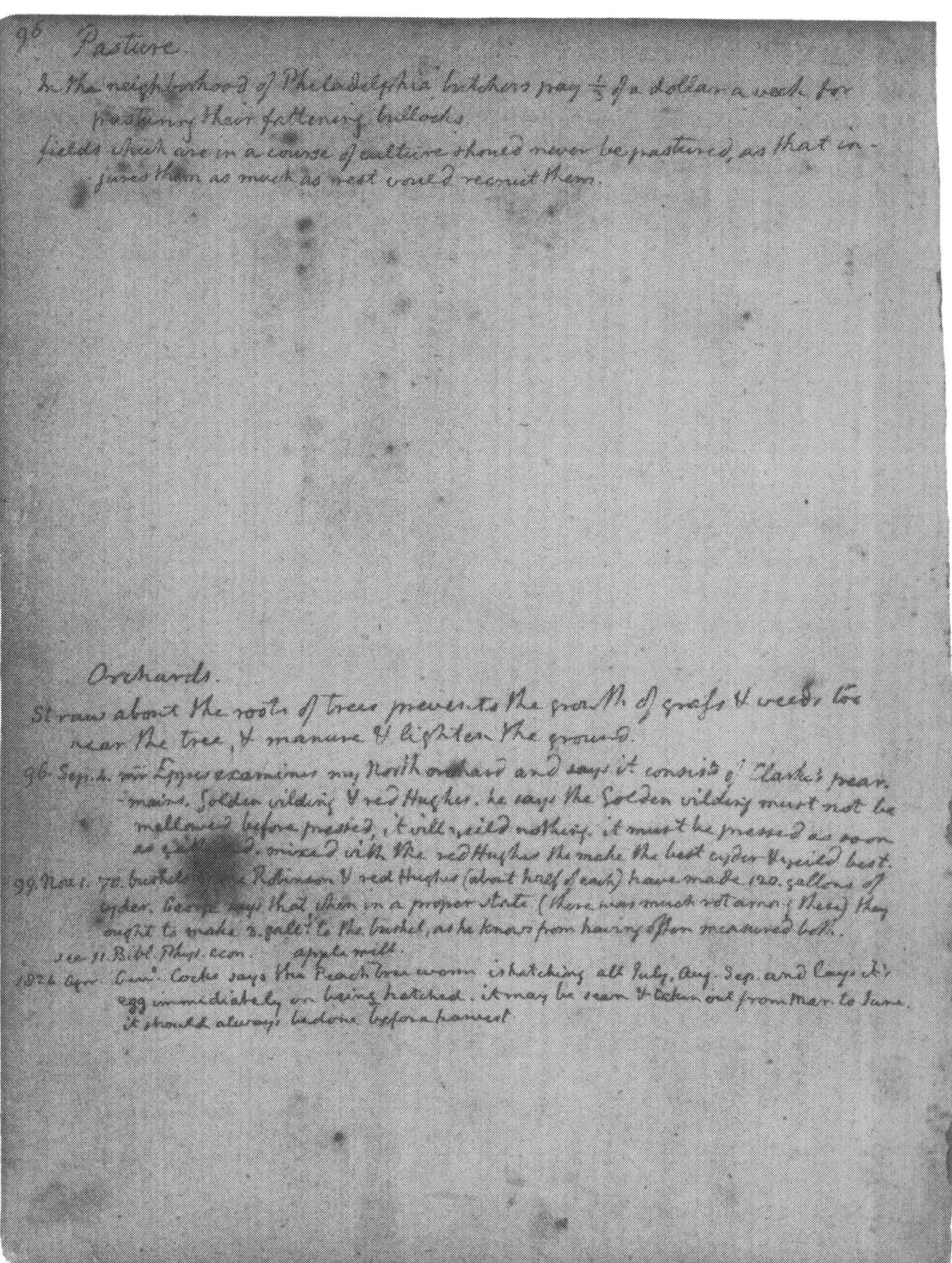

96. Pasture.

In the neighborhood of Philadelphia butchers pay 1/3 of a dollar a week for pasturing their fattening bullocks.

fields which are in a course of culture should never be pastured, as that injures them as much as rest would recruit them.

Orchards.

Straw about the roots of trees prevents the growth of grass & weeds too near the tree, & manure & lighten the ground.

96. Sep. 4. mr Eppes examines my North orchard and says it consists of Clarke's pearmains. Golden wilding & red Hughes. he says the Golden wilding must not be mellowed before pressed, it will yeild nothing. it must be pressed as soon as gathered. mixed with the red Hughes they make the best cyder & yeild best.

99. Nov. 1. 70. bushels of the Robinson & red Hughes (about half of each) have made 120. gallons of cyder. George says that when in a proper state (there was much rot among these) they ought to make 2. gall^s. to the bushel, as he knows from having often measured both.

see 11. Bibl. Phys. econ. apple mill.

1826. Apr. Genl. Cocke says the Peach tree worm is hatching all July, Aug. Sep. and lays it's egg immediately on being hatched. it may be seen & taken out from Mar. to June. it should always be done before harvest.

NOTES to Page 96: Pasture, Orchards

VIII. Rotation of crops.

97

	1	2	3	4	5	6	7	8.	9.
G. Washington's Rotation is	wheat	buckwheat	wheat	clover	clover	clover	potatoes		
						barley	corn		
Dr. Logan's. - - - - - - - -	wheat	barley	corn	potatoes flax	wheat	clover	clover	clo[ver]	X
a good one - - - - -	corn & pot[atoes] in balces	peas	wheat	clover	clover				

NOTES to Page 97: Rotation of Crops

NOTES to Page 98: Blank page retained in order to keep the left-right relationship of the book.

NOTES to Page 99: Blank page retained in order to keep the left-right relationship of the book.

NOTES to Page 100: Calendar of Work

NOTES to Page 101: Blank page retained in order to keep the left-right relationship of the book.

X. Building.

Brick. a demicord of earth [4.f. cube] makes 1000 bricks.

a man will turn up 4 such cubes, or even 5, a day. the price for turning up is 1/ (Maryland) the cube, or 1000 bricks, the labourer finding himself.

a cubic yard of earth in it's natural state weighs probably 1000. lb

a man moulds 2000. bricks a day. his attendance is a man to temper, one to wheel the mortar to him & a boy to bear off. (Philadelphia)

there are 3000. bricks to every eye of a kiln, sometimes 4000.

a cord of wood to every eye will suffice if there be a case of $2\frac{1}{2}$ bricks to the kiln; but if there be no case, $1\frac{1}{2}$ cord to each eye.

at George town in 1792. a brickmaker for $2\frac{1}{3}$ D. the thousand made the bricks, turning up the clay & finding himself every thing except wood to burn & plank to cover them.

the brickwork is about $\frac{1}{3}$ of the whole cost, the Carpenter's materials & ironmongery one third, & the Carpenter's work one third.

bricks cost at Philadelphia 4. D. per M. and laying them 1.67 exclusive of sand, lime &c.

brickwork requires 10. bush. of lime to the 1000. (Geo. town) but by Stephen Willis 15. bushels. this is exact from my own experiments

~~brick~~ mortar takes 3. hhds water to the 1000. bricks.

an acre of ground yields a million of bricks for every foot depth.

see page 3_

10. bushels of limestone make 15. bushels of lime & lay 1000 bricks, the inside mortar being half lime & half sand, & the outside mortar $\frac{2}{3}$ lime, & the walls grouted. from my own experience.

1796. Aug. 26. 32 cords of wood burnt a kiln of 9. eyes & 42 M. bricks.

1814 Chisolm & 2. apprentices (one of them a new beginner) lay 1600 bricks a day

1823. Apr. by accurate trial $7\frac{1}{2}$ lb white lead gives 3 coats to 1 square.

NOTES to Page 102: Building Brickwork

Stone. paving or other stone cut @ 8^d. the superficial foot, the block being found & provisions. 103

the price of a Corinthian column at Paris is 26^{lt} the inch of diameter;
an Ionic d^o. 6^{lt}. the inch. per Hallet.

good stone work, of unhewed stone, takes from 2. to 3 bush. of lime per perch.
the price for laying is 2/6 an 18 I. wall. in Augusta it is 2/
such stone work is cheaper than brick in the proportion of 1056 – 4 to 581 – 5
every thing calculated accurately by a workman at Georgetown, his brickwork comes to 9.6 per thousand, & his stonework 2. D. per perch, including the cost & carriage of every article, even of the rough stone.
a man lays generally 3. perch a day. & even 5. in very thick wall.
calculation of stone work at Monticello. the perch. laying [illegible] @ 2/9

~~[illegible]~~	0 – [illegible]
4. bush. lime @ 8^d - -	2 . 8
stone waggoning - -	5 . 0
attendance - -	4
	9 . 3

dry wall.

NOTES to Page 103: Stone, Stonework, paving or other stone cut

Wood. see page 37.

the sawmills over the mountains saw for 2/ the thousand, or one half for the other.

2 mawlers & 3. rivers will rive 750. pine slabs a day, of 14 f. long, and double that number 6 f. long. every slab clears about 4 d. that is to say 30. slabs properly lapped clear 10. f.

another estimate is that 3 men will get only 450. slabs a day of 6 f. long & 5. I. broad

to rive & draw 500 shingles is a common day's work.

a man may joint 3000. a day.

4. men got out and cut 600. chesnut pales a day, 7 f. long for the garden

a waggon brings in 300. of them at a Load

Paint. to a Square, i.e. 10. f. square, 1. ℔ Span. brown & 1. pint of oil gives 1. coat.

Venetian blinds. the Upholsterer's part costs 2. Doll. and the painting (by a coach-painter) a French crown.

Cost of sashes of Mahogany of 9. panes	12. I. 14.	26. f. runn^d measure, 16 joints	London @ .213 = 1.90	Philad^a @ .38 = 3.4
4. d^o.	18. I. 14.	19½ f. d^o . . . 9 d^o.	@ .34 = 1.35	@ .6 = 2.4

for sky lights the glass should lap 2½ I. or more, the parts which lap should not touch one another, because they will suck in the rain by capillary attraction. there should be a free passage between them for the air. Carstairs.

NOTES to Page 104: Wood, Paint, Venetian Blinds

Lime.

a bushel of limestone weighs 114. ℔ & makes 2. bushels of slacked lime.

1797. Aug. by a tolerably exact trial 1. hhd of unslacked limestone made 1½ hhd of slacked lime, wanting about ½ bushel. and 15½ bushels of slacked lime laid 1000. bricks in a wall of 1½ brick thick. we may say then that 10. bush. of limestone are required to 1000. bricks.

it takes a bushel of lime to give 3. coats of plaister to 4 square yards on brick wall.

a cord of limestone of 128. cub. feet or 102½ bushels make 6. waggon loads

Fresco painting. Schneider charges a dollar a yard, he finding paint &c. or 8/ ~~dollars~~ a day, paint &c. found him. he can do half a yard an hour.

the cost of iron pipes at Philada is as follows. 22. I. diam. is 6.25 pr foot. – 20 cost 5. 16. I. diam. cost 3⅓ – 10 = 2.40 – 8 = 1⅔ – 6 = 1.10 – 4 = .64 – 3 = .45 – 1½ = .40

Sheet iron. a square foot weighs 1. to 1½ ℔ & costs 20. cents. } Philadelphia
Sheet copper. costs about 40. cents the square foot. – – – – } 1792.

the largest sheet iron I have seen is 21. I. by 8 f. 3. I.

a box of tin contains 220 or 230 sheets 13¼ I. by 10⅛ = 11/12 of a foot and weighs 152. ℔. it costs 13. D. and will cover 1 square & a half of roof. a man puts on a square a day.

Bohemian glass costs	of the least thickness	.16 cents the square foot	} Donath. Philadelphia 1792
	1½ thickness – –	.20	
	double thickness for coaches	.30 – – – –	

Bringhurst supposes that no sheets of glass are made larger than 4. feet

a workman at Genoa to whom I shewed a draught of my chimney-pieces, gave me the following estimate of what they would cost in the different kinds of marble of which he gave me samples.

	price of the cubic foot of marble	architrave alone	architrave & entablat.	but if only a plain fascia 6 I. wide 1. I. thick
Common marble	4ᴸ – 10ˢ	90ᴸ	170ᴸ	2ᴸ – 1ˢ +
Marble of Carrara	12 –	105.	217–10	5 – 11 +
Jasper of Sicily	40 –	161 –	400 –	18 – 8 +
Verde antico.	270 –	620 –	1900 –	124 – 4 +

NOTES to Page 105: Lime, Fresco painting, Bohemian glass

106.

XI. Mill.

at Brandywine. 2 pr of stones rent for 266⅔ D.

100. bushels of wheat make 20. barr. flour at Brandywine & 22. in Maryland.

a millar's wages at Brandywine from 100. to 150. D. & found.

a head millwright's wages .86 cents, a journeyman's .67 per day & found.

the millwright's work of a mill of 2. pr stones, with boulting apparatus, fans, double wire screen, hopper boy, hoisting machine, screwpacker, is worth from 200. to 267 Doll.

a pair of millstones manufacture 10,000 bush. in the season. Dutton.

where the mill-wright is found, & every thing brought into place he should make a double armed waterwheel for 12/ the foot & the cog-wheel for 15/ the foot in diameter, & the shaft & gudgeon supporters into the bargain: and a single-armed water wheel for 20/ the foot. Gordon.

in Blowing much depends on the nature of the stone. but in very hard stone, a man striking for himself will bore about 8. holes of 12 I. depth a day. mr Cocke

1. ℔ of gun-powder will make about 20. charges. mr Cocke.

a man digs from 10. to 11. ~~square~~ cubic yards a day of canal work & throws it out. mr Cocke

a cooper's task is 4. flour barrels a day from the rough, i.e. from the stuff merely rived out into thickness for 2. staves. and 6. barrels a day when the staves are drawn.

1810. nov. the batteau with 8 hands collecting rock for the dam on the mountain side about ½ a mile above the dam, brings about 6. loads a day of 2. perch each. = 12. perch a day

a waggon collecting stone in the plantation from the E. side of the meadow branch brings 12 loads a day of ½ perch each = 6 perch a day. having it's driver & 2. of the nail boys to load & unload

12. hands get the long logs (60 f. long) and tyers (21. of 16 to 20. f. long) for a pen 12. f. wide in the clear, 50. f. long & 3. f. high, bring them into place by water, and lay them down in 3. days. the cost then of a pen 50. by 12. f. for the timber part is 18. D.

the stone 70. perch @ 4/ = 46.67

about 1.30 or 8/ a foot running measure 64.67

or 1. D. the cubic yard of the dam.

1811. June. compleated the new Pierhead. it's floor is 9 f. [illegible] I. below the spring of the brick arch, and 10 f. 2 I. below the crown of the arch.

1811. Jan. 8. by an accurate trial with the spirit level, I found the surface of the water above the dam 6 f. ⅛ I. higher than that at the mouth of the tail race of the saw mill.

1813. Mar. 25. fixed the bottom of the sawmill canal at 12. I. below the head of the dam by the spirit level.

1818. June. July. Aug. Sep. blowing on the road at the foot of the mountain on the river side, each borer uses ¼ ℔ powder a day and bores 3. holes of 12 I. each. which is 12. blasts to the ℔

1822. Aug. 24. by experiment at the Toll mill, the Peakstones ground 4. bushels wheat an hour
the Burr stones ground 4. bushels corn an hour
both then may be said to grind 200. bushels in 24. hours, half wheat, half corn.

NOTES to Page 106: Mill

1813. Jan. 7. a statement of the movement of the millworks at the foot of Monticello 107.
the water wheel is calculated to turn 8. times in a minute.

Saw mill. the greater cog wheel has . . . 144. cogs
and drives the balance wheel of 12. spurs
which gives 12. strokes of the saw for 1. of the waterwheel
or 12 × 8 = 96 strokes of the saw in 1'.

Threshing machine.
the lesser cog wheel has 112. cogs
drives a trundle of 14. rounds
which is 8. for 1.
the trundle has a horizontl cog wheel on same shaft of 48. cogs
which drives the shaft of the drum wheel carrying 12. spurs
which is 4. for 1.
both together give 8 × 4 = 32 revolns of the drum for 1. of the water wheel
or 32 × 8 revolns of the drum = 256 in 1'

Grist mill. the lesser cog wheel of 112. cogs
drives a wallower of 26. rounds
on the shaft of which is a cog wheel of 54 cogs
driving a trundle of . . . 16. rounds.
$\frac{112 \times 54}{26 \times 16} = \frac{6048}{416} = 14\frac{1}{2}$ revolns of the millstone for 1. of the water wheel
or $14\frac{1}{2} \times 8 = 116$ revolns of the stone in 1'.

mill stones grind in proportion to the squares of their diameters. therefore the work of a 5.f stone is to that of one of 6f. as 25 to 36.
their revolutions should be in the inverse ratio of their diameters, taking as a basis that a ~~[illegible]~~ 5f. stone turns 90. times in a minute. then for the revolns of a 6f. stone say as ~~[illegible]~~ 6 : 5 :: 90 : $\frac{90 \times 5}{6} = 75$
water wheels should also have their revolns in the inverse ratio of their diameters, taking for a basis that a 12f wheel should turn 13 times in a minute: then for a 20f. wheel say as 20 : 12 :: 13 : $\frac{13 \times 12}{20} = 7.8$
the best motion for a saw is to make 115 strokes in a minute.
the skirt of every millstone, of whatever size should move with the same velocity. per Gilmore. but qu? at 34 f. a second. to wit a 5f. stone shd make 2. revolutions in a second?

NOTES to Page 107: Movement of the millworks, Threshing Machine

XII. Still.

1812. Sep. 3. began to malt wheat. a bushel will make 8. or 10. gallons of strong beer
such as will keep for years, taking $\frac{3}{4}$ ℔ of hops for every bushel of wheat.

NOTES to Page 108: Still to make beer

NOTES to Page 109: Smith's shops

110. **Nails.**

Weight & measure of nails.

	Nails to ℔	℔ to the thousd.	Length
30d. British	....	56.	3. 8ths 4 - 1.23
24d. New York	29	34½	
20d. New York	45	22⅕	
Baltimore	50	20	
Richmond	50	20	
Fredsbg	54	18½	
British	....	23½	2 - 4.8
16d. Baltimore	59	17	
12d. New York	62½	16	
Baltimore	62½	16	
Fredsbg.	66⅔	15	2 - 6
10d. New York / Baltimore / Fredsbg / British	77	13	2 - 4
8d. New York	100	10	
Baltimore	100	10	
Fredsbg	111	9	2 -
Richmond	100	10	
British	....	10½	1 - 7
6d. Baltimore	125	8	
New York	140	7⅐	
Richmond	143	7	
Fredsbg	182	5½	
British	....	6.9	1 - 4
4d. New York	300	3⅓	
Baltimore	250	4	
Fredsbg	- -	- -	1 - 0
British	- - -	4.4	1 - 1
Mine.			
30d........	18	56	4d.
24d........	30	33⅓	3½
20d........	40	25	3
16d........	50	20	2¾
12d........	62½	16	2½
10d........	77	13	2¼
8d........	100	10	1⅞
6d........	143	7	1½
4d........	250	4.	1.

pr. Colo. Wadsworth. prices N.Y. curr. making alone.

Card. or 4 oz. tacks	2/6 pr. M.
12. oz. do.	2/6
clout do.	2/9
hob nails	2/9
2d. clouts	3/
3d do.	3/3
4d do.	3/9
6d do.	4/
½ inch brads	2/6
1. I. do.	2/6
1¼ do.	2/9
1½ do.	3/
1¾ do. / 2 I. do.	.... 3/3

		quoted by another
4d nails or brads	9d pr. lb	
6d do.	6d	6d
4d do. or trunk	3/3 pr. M	8d
8d nails	4d pr. lb	4½d
10d	3d pr. lb	3½d
12d.	do.	3d
20d	do.	2½d
24d	do.	2d

task per day

	man	boy	man Baltimore
24d	24. M		man
20d	20	- -	16 M
12d	16	12	15
10d	14	9	12
8d	10	7	8
6d	7	6	7
4d	5	4	3½
2d. brad	1000		
1¾ do.	1000		
1¼. 1½	1500		
4d nails	1500		
3d. clouts	1000		
2d, 1½d	1500		
card tack	1500		

Colo. Triplet.

	℔
the ton of rod is	2240
common loss 14. pr. c.	313.6
nails yielded	1926.4

a fire burns 6 to 7. bushels of coal a day

	nails
a boy after 6. months make	500
1. year	800
the best	884
a hired hand	1000

there are 4. sizes of nail rod the halfcrown, or 30d. is the largest. traces made of this a pair weigh 8. lb.

NOTES to Page 110: Nails

Estimate on the actual work of the autumn of 1792. 111.

Moses waste	15 in the C.
Shepherd	18.
Barnaby	22.
Davy	18.2
Jamey	29.83
Ben	28.
	131. in 600.
	22 in 100.
Joe	19
Wormeley	16.25
Burwell	29.
	64.25
	21.4 in 100

@ 22 ℔ waste in the 100. I get 1747 ℔ nails. ᵃ iron then costs 4.9ᵈ, say 5ᵈ pr ℔

the day's work of each	VI	VIII	X	XII
	℔	℔	℔	℔
Moses, Shepherd, Barnaby	4	4½	5	5½
Davey, Jamey, Ben, Joe, Wormeley	2½	3	3½	4

size	quantity	Market price	cost of iron	Clear profit
		£ s d	£ s d	£ s d
VIˢ	24½ ℔	1-4-6	0-10-2½	0-14-3½
VIIIˢ	28½	1-6-9½	0-11-10½	0-14-11
Xˢ	32½	1-9-9	0-13-6½	0-16-2½
XIIˢ	36½	1-11-1	0-15-2½	0-15-10½
average	30½	1-8-0	0-12-8½	0-15-4
290 days or a year	8845	406-0-0	184-5-5	222-7-0
deduct allowance to George of 3. per cent on the nails sold, or 6. per cent on the clear profits				13-6-8
				209-0-4

NOTES to Page 111: Estimate on the actual work of the autumn of 1792

NOTES to Page 112: Blank page retained in order to keep the left-right relationship of the book.

Coal.

at Millar's works, the negro men are tasked at 9. cords of coal wood a week, & are paid for whatever they do over that.

NOTES to Page 113: Coal

114. XIV. Carpenters, Wheelwrights. coopers.

staves for a tob°. hhd are by law to be 4f. 6 I. long. the head 36. I. in the clear with an allowance of 2. I. more for the pressing head.

1812. June. Johnny Hemings & Lewis make a set of Venetian blinds with fixed slats, i.e. 2. pair 3f. 3 I. square in 6. days, splitting out the slats from common plank with the handsaw. say a window a week.

1815. Mar. 21. Johnny Hemings began the body of a Landau Jan. 12. and finished it this day. being 9 weeks +5 days. he had not more help from Lewis than made up for his interruptions. the smith's work employed the 2 smiths perhaps 1/3 of the same time.

1818. Feb. 1. Johnny Hem. & Lewis began a dressing table & finished it in exactly 6. weeks, of which 4. weeks was such dreadful weather that, even within doors, nothing like full work could be done.

Apr 2. a 2d is finished, having taken only from Mar. 15. to wit 16. working days

7. a pannelled door is done in 5. days, all the stuff being previously planed up

1821. Apr. 14. the staves of a flour barrel are got 28. I. long & dressed to 27 I.
it takes 16. or 17. staves to a barrel & 6. heading pieces. 22. or 23. in all.
a cut of a middle sized tree yields 16. or 17. bolts, which give 4. staves each
such a tree, midling good will yield 18. or 20 cuts.
a cut will make 3. barrels, staves & heading
one tree with another will make 50. barrels.

NOTES to Page 114: Carpenters, Wheelwrights, coopers

NOTES to Page 115: Blank page retained in order to keep the left-right relationship of the book.

116. XV. Spinning, Weaving.

Estimate of what may be spun daily

	Length of Day. Hours	Linen task	Wool task	Cotton task
Jan. Dec.	9.	15. oz.	12. oz	6. oz.
Feb. Nov.	10.	16 2/3	13 1/3	6 2/3
Mar. Oct.	11.	18 1/3	14 2/3	7 1/3
Apr. Sep.	12.	20.	16.	8.
May. Aug.	13.	21. 2/3	17 1/3	8 2/3
June July	14.	23 1/3	18 2/3	9 1/3
Average	11½	19.	15 1/3	7 2/3

linen for laborers, 1. ℔ hemp makes 1. yd. warp & filling
Wool. for do. 2. yds to the ℔
Cotton for do. 3. yds to the ℔.

1813. June 17. Judge Holmes's statement of the cost of manufacturing superfine broadcloth at Winchester.

	s	d
spinning 1. ℔ clean wool. 20. cuts @ 2d.	3 -	4
carding. 10. cents pr. ℔		7½
weaving 1. yd. of 6/4 broadcloth weighing 1. ℔	4 -	0
fulling, dressing, dying 5/ pr. yard or ℔	5 -	0
	13 -	0 pr. yd. or ℔ of washed wool.

the wool unwashed yields from 1/3 to 1/2 it's weight of superfine cloth.
a yard of superfine 6/4 cloth weighs 1. ℔.
July 16. Judge Holmes writes that the workmen say it takes 2. ℔ washed Merino wool to make a yard of 6/4 cloth.
the 39. ℔ unwashed but on the sheep's back which I sent to Winchester has yielded 10. yds cloth.

NOTES to Page 116: Spinning, Weaving

XVI. Pot-ash. Pearl-ash.

117

a tree of 1½ f. diameter will yield 1. cord of wood.
2½ f. diam. - - - - - - 2. cords.
an acre of midling timbered land will yield 30. cord of wood.
of the heaviest timbered - - - - 100. cord.
a man will cut and burn 2½ cords a day.
a cord of wood yields 2. bushels of ashes. [neither pine nor chesnut will do.]
a bushel of ashes sells for 9. cents.
a bushel of ashes makes 6. ℔ of brown salts, which make from 3. to 5 ℔ Pearl ash in ye common way
5. ℔ of Pearl-ash in Hopkins's way.

there should be 15. or 16. tubs of 100. bushels each.
for a small work, 2 kettles suffice to boil the lie into brown salts
and 1. - - - - - to melt up the brown salts.
¼ cord of wood a day maintains one fire, which will do for 5. kettles.
to keep 3. kettles a going will require a man & boy to attend.
3. kettles will turn out 1000. ℔ of Pearlash a week.
consequently require 100. cords of wood a week & 7. cutters to keep them constantly at work.
each kettle costs 24. Dollars.
Pot-ash is worth in England the ton, & in America D. 114⅔ = .057 pr ℔.
Pearlash is worth in England £40. sterl. the ton, & in America 133⅓ D. .066 pr ℔.
or £40. lawful.

an estimate of the expence and profit of such a work @ 3. ℔ pearlash to the bush. ashes which would be 100. ℔ of Pearlash a day

	£ s d	
7. cutters, hired @ £12. a year, adding all other expences.	128-16-0	
a manager, hire & provisions - - - - - - - - -	50- 0-0	
a boy - - - - - - - - - - -	10- 0-0	
implements annually - - - - - - - -	10- 0-0	
a waggon & team & driver, all expences calculated - -	111-15-0	
@ 3. ℔ of pearlash from the bushel, instead of 5 ℔, and @ 5. days to the week, we should have 500 ℔ instead of 1000. ℔ a week, which would be 13. ton a year @ £40. Virga currency - - -	. . . . . .	520-0-0
clearing 150. acres of land a year, [illegible]? [whereon the ashes of an acre worth 40/ - the cutting & burng worth 15/]	. . . . . .	

NOTES to Page 117: Pot-ash, Pearl-ash

NOTES to Page 118: Blank page retained in order to keep the left-right relationship of the book.

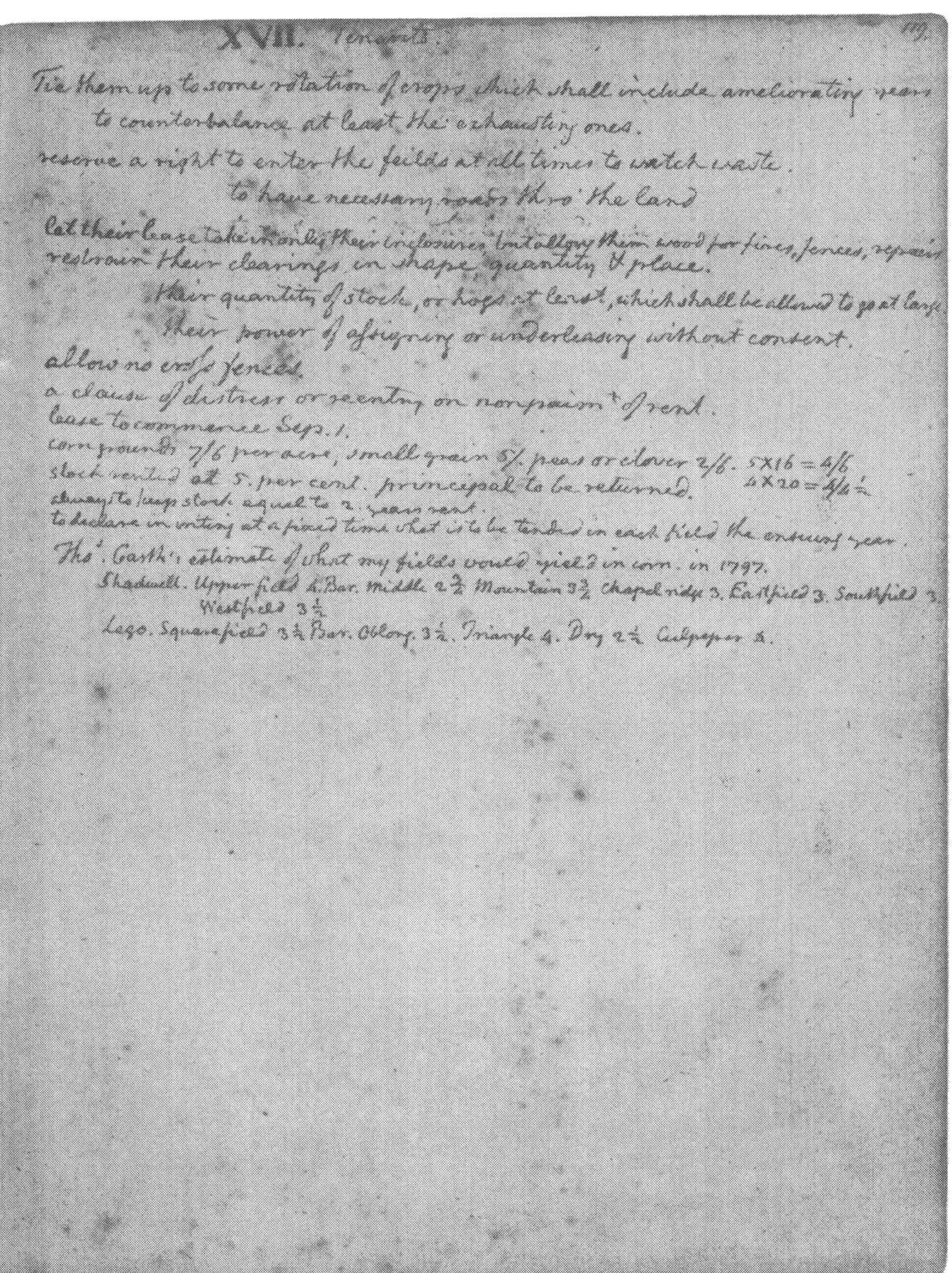

XVII. Tenants. 119.

Tie them up to some rotation of crops which shall include ameliorating years
to counterbalance at least the exhausting ones.
reserve a right to enter the feilds at all times to watch waste.
to have necessary roads thro' the land
let their lease take in only their inclosures but allow them wood for fires, fences, repairs
restrain their clearings in shape, quantity & place.
their quantity of stock, or hogs at least, which shall be allowed to go at large
their power of assigning or underleasing without consent.
allow no cross fences.
a clause of distress or reentry on nonpaimt. of rent.
lease to commence Sep. 1.
corn grounds 7/6 per acre, small grain 6/. peas or clover 2/6. 5×16 = 4/6
stock rented at 5. per cent. principal to be returned. 4×20 = 4/4½
always to keep stock equal to 2. years rent.
to declare in writing at a fixed time what is to be tended in each field the ensuing year.
Thos. Garth's estimate of what my fields would yield in corn. in 1797.
Shadwell. Upper field 4. Bar. Middle 2½ Mountain 3¾ Chapel ridge 3. Eastfield 3. Southfield 3. Westfield 3½
Lego. Squarefield 3½ Bar. Oblong. 3½. Triangle 4. Dry 2½ Culpeper 5.

NOTES to Page 119: Tenants

NOTES to Page 120: Blank page retained in order to keep the left-right relationship of the book.

Miscellanies

to bring the wheels of my Phaetons & chairs to an uniform measure, let the arms of the axles be always 10½ I. between the shoulder & linch pin, 1¾ I. diam. at the shoulder, & 1½ I. diam. at the inside of the linch pin, or washer.

1810. Jan. 9. running the rafter level through a field to guide the ploughs horizontally, Thruston makes a step of the level (10 f.) every minute, which is 600. f. = 200. yds an hour.

Jan. 9. in terrassing the new nursery in 4. f. terrasses, 2 men do 50 yds in length a day.

1811. Apr. 29. we find that in blowing rock it takes 2. oz. of powder to a blast, taking one depth of hole with another.*

1812. Aug. 5. 2 bars of tin weighing 12 oz. 8 or ¾ lb each have tinned 18. stewpans being our whole number. then it takes 1. lb to tin a dozen stewpans.

Oct. 20. 3 men & 3. lads get 550. bolts of stave timber for flour barrels in a day. each bolt makes 4. staves or heading pieces, & 25 staves & heading pieces make a barrel.

*1813. 1814. in blowing on the river road at the foot of Monticello, I found pretty accurately that each borer used ½ lb powder a day, & bored 3 holes of 12 I. each a day. this gives 1⅓ oz. to the blast

1817. Aug. 2. Colclaser says that a man saws & rives the timber & dresses compleatly for setting up [illegible] staves of 2½ barrels a day, 17. staves to a barrel.

NOTES to Page 123: Miscellaneous

1809.

Monticello farm

Divide it into 3. fields of 60. a^s. each. 1. for half corn, half oats, peas, or millet one for wheat 60. a^s. and one for clover 60 a^s. and aim at a 4th. for clo- -ver also as soon as we can.

the North field, to wit the 60. a^s. N. of the road leading through the farm will be one.

the Riverfield, to wit, the field on the River & up, between the road & Park branch to ye Ragged br.

Belfield, to wit the grounds ~~between~~ South of the same road, & between that, the N. & S. fence & the perpetual pasture, for a 3^d.

NOTES to Page 124: 1809 Monticello

125

Lego

plan for the crop of 1810

1810 clear the lowgrounds on the W. side of Secretary's ford (ab^t 12 or 15 a.) for tobacco
clean up the Square field for corn. 40. a.
Triangle & Oblong, put into oats. 80. a.
the belted grounds, not in wheat, put into oats.

1811. clear adjoining the Belted grounds for tob^o.
clean up Hickman's field for corn.
Square field. wheat
Culpeper. enlarge to 40 a^s. & sow wheat
Race [path] field wheat or oats & clover.
aim, as soon as possible at getting 3. fields of 80. a. each for this rotation, to wit,
1 field, half in corn, half in peas, oats or millet; & in the next rotation change the halves
1. in wheat 80. a.
1. in clover 80. a. and
a fourth field, as fast as we can, to be in clover also.
the △ and Dry field will be one
the Oblong & □ field another
Hickman's, and the Belted field a third.
Culpeper &c. a 4th.

NOTES to Page 125: Lego plan for the crop of 1810

NOTES to Page 126: Blank page retained in order to keep the left-right relationship of the book.

a. Land Roll. 1810. 127.

$1052\frac{3}{4}$ Monticello. viz. a. 1000. patented by Peter Jefferson. 1735. July 19.
$27\frac{1}{2}$ rec.d in exchange by Th: Jefferson from Nicholas Lewis } being part of acres
$25\frac{1}{4}$ purchased by Th:J. from Richard Overton } pat.d by Nich.s Meriwether
$1052\frac{3}{4}$

$574\frac{3}{4}$ Montalto. viz. $470\frac{1}{4}$ part of 483. purchased by Th:J. from Edw.d Carter the remaining $12\frac{3}{4}$ hav.g been conveyed to Nich.s Lewis in exchange
40. purchased by Th:J. from Thomas Walls
$61\frac{1}{2}$ purchased by Th:J. from Benj.n Brown Jr.
3. by estimation, being the bed of the public road 30. f. wide from Th:J's corner on it to it's crossing of Moore's creek
} being parts of 9350 acres patented by John Carter Sep. 28. 1730.

150. Tufton - - - - patented by Peter Jefferson 1753. Sep. 10

150. Portobello - - - - patented by Peter Jefferson 1740. Sep. 16.

$1162\frac{1}{4}$ Milton - - viz. $728\frac{1}{4}$ patented by
434. patented by Bennett Henderson } purchased by Th:J. from the representatives of Bennet Henderson.
$1162\frac{1}{4}$

222. on Mc.Gehee's road & Henderson's branch patented by Th: Jefferson 1788. Apr. 12.

196. Ingraham's. on the waters of Buckisland creek. patented by Th: Jefferson 1788. Apr. 12.

$819\frac{1}{4}$ Lego. purchased by Th:J. from Tho.s Garth, being Edwin Hickman's fourth part of 3277. a. patented by Smith, Hickman, Graves and Clarke. 1730. May. 26.

485. on the Shadwell mountain, patented by Th: Jefferson. 1789. July 23.

400. Shadwell. purchas.d by Peter Jefferson from Wm. Randolph, part of 2400. a. pat.d by him 1735. July 1.

5212. in one contiguous body.

400. Pouncey's. pat.d by Peter Jefferson, whereof 100. a. having been sold to Wm. Spears was repurchased from his son John Spears by Th: Jefferson

4. Limestone quarry on Plumbtree branch, purchased by Th:J. of Robert Sharpe, being part of 400. acres patented by Crawford.

$66\frac{2}{3}$ Limestone on the waters of Hardware, an undivided sixth of 400. a. pat.d by Philip Mayo 1749. Sep. 1.

$5682\frac{2}{3}$ whereof $3574\frac{5}{12}$ are in St. Anne's parish
$2108\frac{1}{4}$ are in the parish of Fredericksville.
$5682\frac{2}{3}$

$4164\frac{1}{2}$ acres. Poplar Forest. viz. $2558\frac{1}{2}$ part of 4000. a. pat.d by William Stith Mar. 5. 1747. and Sep. 10. 1755. [$1441\frac{1}{2}$ a. the residue thereof, with $8\frac{1}{2}$ a. adjoining patented by Th:J. Mar. 27. 1797. having been conveyed to T. M. Randolph & Martha his wife.]

$2558\frac{1}{2}$

800. a. on a branch of Buffalo creek patented by Th: Jefferson May 23. 1797.

183. purchased of John Robertson by John Wayles

380. purchased of the same John Robertson by John Wayles, having been pat.d by Rich.d Callaway May 12. 1759.

214. purchased of Daniel Robertson by John Wayles by whom they were patented Aug. 1. 1772.

29. rec.d in exchange from Benj. Johnson for 32. a. of the preceding tract by deed of

$4164\frac{1}{2}$

157. Natural bridge, in Rockbridge. patented by Th:J. July 5. 1774.

$10,004\frac{1}{6}$ in the whole

4. lots in Beverley town, Henrico. viz. No. 57. at the foot of the hill, 107. & 108. on the public road, and 151. includes the ferry landing, being the uppermost lot of the town on the river.

a moiety of lot 335. in Richmond, containing 825. square yards purchased by Th: Jefferson of William Byrd. sold to D. Higginbotham

NOTES to Page 127: Land Roll 1810

Roll of Negroes. 1810. Feb. in Albemarle.

Monticello.

House &c.

Burwell. 83.
Edwin 93.
Edy. 87.
~~James~~ Jan. 7. 05
Maria. Oct. 27. 07.
Patsy. 10. May 11.
Fanny. 88
Ellen. 09. Aug. 22.
~~[illegible]~~
James. 11. Nov.
Critta. 69
Sally 73.
Harriet. 01. May
Madison 05. Jan.
Eston 08. May 21.
Betty Brown. 59
Robert. 99. Dec.
Mary. 01. Oct.
Peter Hemings. 70.
Nance. 61.
Mary. perhaps ab^t 80.
William 01. Mar.
Davy. 03. Feb.
Celia. 06.
Ursula. 87. Tucker 10. Apr.
Joe. 05. Jan.
Anne 07. Feb.
Dolly 09. Feb.
Cornelius 11. Apr. 1.
Cretia. [illegible] 99
John 1800.
Randal. 02.
Henry 05.
Milly 07.
Lilburn 09.
Sucky. Jerry's. 96.
Bec. Bagwell's. 97
Indridge 97. Mar. 30
Evelina. Lewis' 97. Oct. 24
Lavinia Rach's. 97. Mar. 22.
37

Tradesmen

John Hemings. 75
Lewis. ab^t 60
Davy. 55.
Shepherd. 82.
Abram. ab^t 1740.
Joe. 80
Moses. 79.
~~Davy.~~ Isbel's 84. Sep.
Thruston. 9[illegible] July 5.
James. Lewis's 95 Apr.
Phill. 96. (Sucky's.
Nace. 96. Aug. Maria's.
Jameo. 97. Eve's.
Beverley. 98. Apr. 1.
~~James Hubbard 83.~~
Jerry. 77.
Jame. 76.
Barnaby. 83.
Wormley 81.
John 53.
Ned 60.
James (Ned's) 96. [illegible]
22

farm

John Bedf^d 85.
Bartlet. 86
Isaac. ab^t 68.
Isabel. prob^a ab^t 58
Thrimston. ~~[illegible]~~ 1792 June 22
Lovilo. 01. Oct. 27
~~[illegible]~~
Amy. John prob^a ab^t 56.
Jenny. Ned's. 66.
Israel. 1800. Dec. 28.
Moses. 03. Jul. 28
Sucky. 06. Dec. 21
Jenny. Lew's. 68.
Isabel. 1800. May.
Doll. 57.
~~Molly 89.~~
~~Mary~~ Jerry's. 76. Q. 13
Isaiah. 1800. Dec. 31.
Jerry. 02. Jan. 14
Jupiter 04. Jan. 15.
~~[illegible]~~ d. 1810
~~Phill [illegible]~~ d. 1810
~~Squire. 27.~~ d. 1810.
19

Tufton

Bagwell. 68.
Caesar. 49
Ben. 85.
Phill Hub^d 86.
Ned. 86.
Dick. 90.
Gill. 92.
~~Lewis. 90.~~
Abram. 94.
Minerva. 71.
~~Virginia.~~ 93
Esther. 95. Mar. 19
Nanny. 00. Apr. 10
Willis. 06. Jan. 6
Archy. 08. Feb. 3
Jordan. 10
Mary Bagwell. 85
Washington 05. Mar.
Rachael. 76.
Eliza. 05. Sep. 30
Ellen. 08. Dec. 18
Nancy. 91.
Thenia. 93.
Dolly. 94.
Lilly. 91.
d. ~~Anderson ab^t July 30~~
Stannard. 09. June 2
Lucy. 11. Mar. 12.
26

Lego

Charles. ab^t 85
Lewis. 86.
Davy Bedf^d 85.
Aggy. 89
Polly. 10 Aug.
Sally Lew's. 92.
Scilla. Ned's. 94
James. 11. Sep.
7

37
22
22
26
7
114

NOTES to Page 128: Roll of Negroes 1810 Feb. in Albemarle

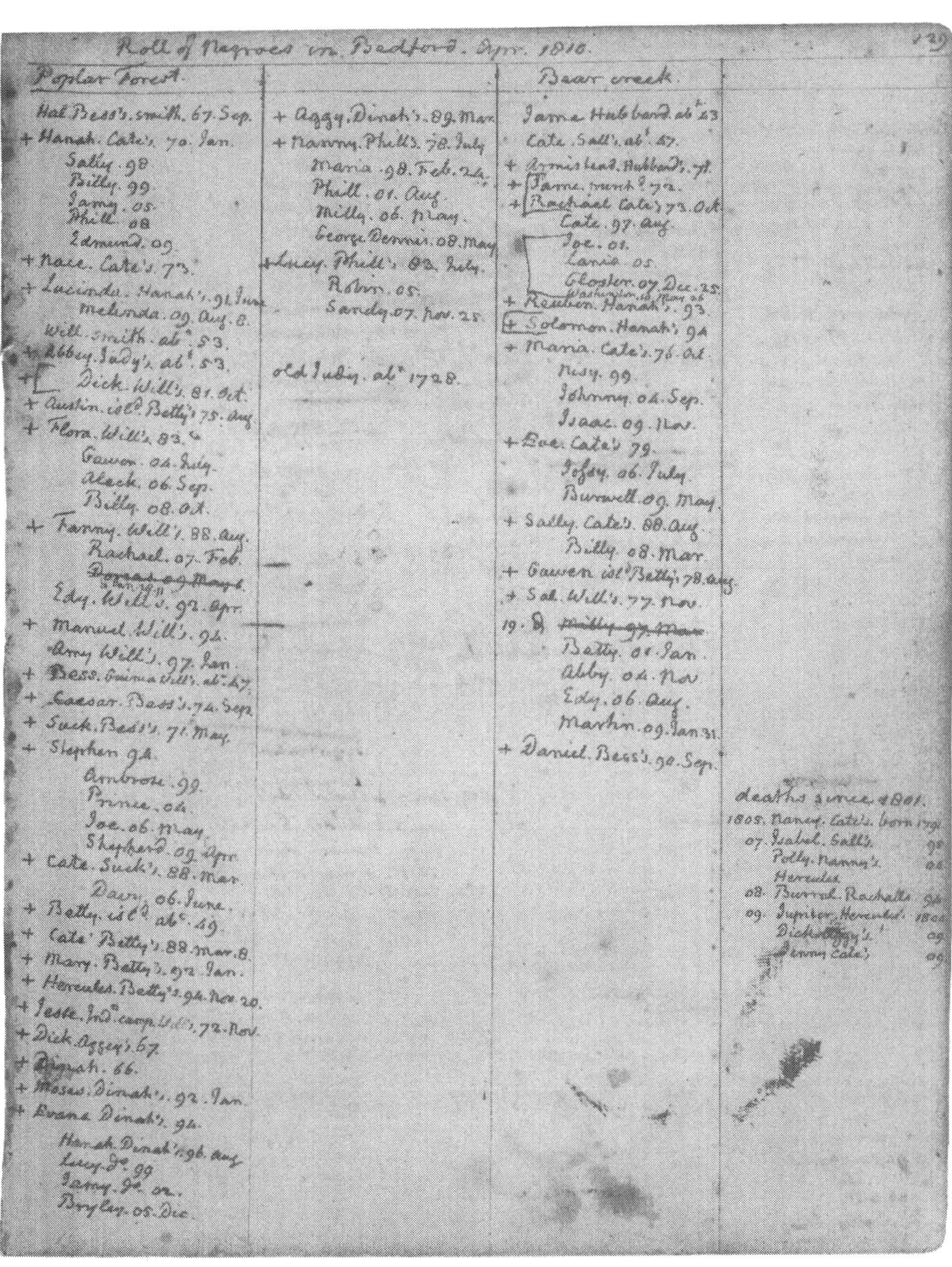

Roll of Negroes in Bedford. Apr. 1810.

Poplar Forest.

Hal. Bess's. smith. 67. Sep.
+ Hanah. Cate's. 70. Jan.
Sally. 98
Billy. 99
Jamy. 05.
Phill. 08
Edmund. 09.
+ Nace. Cate's. 73.
+ Lucinda. Hanah's. 91. June
melinda. 09. Aug. 8.
Will. smith. ab^t. 53.
+ Abby. Judy's. ab^t. 53.
+ Dick. Will's. 81. Oct.
+ Austin. isl^d. Betty's. 75. Aug.
+ Flora. Will's. 83.
Gawen. 04. July.
Aleck. 06. Sep.
Billy. 08. Oct.
+ Fanny. Will's. 88. Aug.
Rachael. 07. Feb.
~~Dorcas. 09. May 6.~~ Stanley 10
Edy. Will's. 92. Apr.
+ Manuel. Will's. 94.
Amy. Will's. 97. Jan.
+ Bess. Guinea Will's. ab^t. 47.
+ Caesar. Bess's. 74. Sep.
+ Suck. Bess's. 71. May.
+ Stephen. 94.
Ambrose. 99.
Prince. 04.
Joe. 06. May.
Shepherd. 09. Apr.
+ Cate. Suck's. 88. Mar.
Davy. 06. June.
+ Betty. isl^d. ab^t. 49.
+ Cate. Betty's. 88. Mar. 8.
+ Mary. Betty's. 92. Jan.
+ Hercules. Betty's. 94. Nov. 20.
+ Jesse. Ind^n. camp Will's. 72. Nov.
+ Dick. Aggey's. 67.
+ Dinah. 66.
+ Moses. Dinah's. 92. Jan.
+ Evans. Dinah's. 94.
Hanah. Dinah's. 96. Aug.
Lucy. do. 99
Jamy. do. 02.
Bryley. 05. Dec.

+ Aggy. Dinah's. 89. Mar.
+ Nanny. Phill's. 78. July
Maria. 98. Feb. 24.
Phill. 01. Aug.
Milly. 06. May.
George. Dennis. 08. May
+ Lucy. Phill's. 83. July.
Robin. 05.
Sandy. 07. Nov. 25.

old Judy. ab^t. 1728.

Bear creek.

Jame. Hubbard. ab^t. 43
Cate. Sall's. ab^t. 47.
+ Armistead. Hubbard's. 71.
+ Jame. smith's. 72.
+ Rachael. Cate's. 73. Oct.
Cate. 97. Aug.
Joe. 01.
Lania. 05
Gloster. 07. Dec. 25.
Washington. 10. May 26
+ Reuben. Hanah's. 93.
+ Solomon. Hanah's. 94
+ Maria. Cate's. 76. Oct.
Nisy. 99.
Johnny. 04. Sep.
Isaac. 09. Nov.
+ Doe. Cate's. 79.
Josey. 06. July
Burwell. 09. May.
+ Sally. Cate's. 88. Aug.
Billy. 08. Mar.
+ Gawen. isl^d. Betty's. 78. Aug.
+ Sal. Will's. 77. Nov.
19. ~~Milly. 97. Mar.~~
Betty. 01. Jan.
Abby. 04. Nov.
Edy. 06. Aug.
Martin. 09. Jan. 31.
+ Daniel. Bess's. 90. Sep.

deaths since 1801.
1805. Nancy. Cate's. born 1791
07. Isabel. Sall's. 90
Polly. Nanny's. 04
Hercules
08. Burrel. Rachael's. 96
09. Jupiter. Hercules'. 1800
Dick. Aggy's. 09
Jenny. Cate's. 09

NOTES to Page 129: Roll of Negroes in Bedford 1810

Roll of the negroes according to their ages.
Albemarle.

1727. ~~Squire~~ d. Mar. 20. 1810
31. ~~Goliah~~ d. May 5. 1810
~~Abram~~
~~Phill~~ d. Sep. 1810.
~~Caesar~~ d. 1820
~~Molly~~ d. Apr. 21. 1811
53. John
55. Davy
56. Amy
57. Doll
~~Isabel~~ d. 1819.
59. Betty Brown
60. Ned.
Lewis
61. Nance
64. Jenny Ned's
68. Isaac
Bagwell
Jenny. Lewis's
69. Critta
70. Peter Hemings
71. Minerva
73. Sally
75. John Hemings
76. Jamey
~~Mary~~ Jerry's d. 13
Rachael
77. Jerry
79. Critta
~~Moses~~
80. Mary, Moses's
Joe
81. Wormley
82. Shepherd
83. ~~Phill~~
Barnaby
Burwell
84. Davy. Isabel's
85. Charles
Ben
John Bedf.
Davy Bedf.
86 ~~Phill Hubbard~~ m'd 1812
Bartlet
Ned. jr
87. Ursula
Edy
88. Lewis
Mary. Bagwell's
Fanny
~~89 Aggy~~ Charles's d. 15
90. Dick
~~Isaac~~ July 16. 15.
Abram
91. Nanny. Rach's
Lilly
92. Gill
Sally. Lewis's
Moses, Dinah's

1793. Edwin
Virginia. Bagw's
94. Scilla. Ned's
Dolly. Doll's
95. Thruston
James. Lew's
Esther
96. Philip
Nace
James. Ned's
Sucky. Jerry's
97. Sanco
Indridge
Evelina
Maria
Bec.
98. Beverly. run away 22.
Aggy Ned's
1800.
Nanny. Bagw's
Isabel. Lew's
Thrimston. Isabel's
Israel. Ned's
Isaiah. Jerry's
01. William. Moses's; Bedf.
Harriet. Sally's. run. 22
Mary. Bet's
d. 16 ~~Louisa Isabel's~~ 1815
02. Jerry. Jerry's
Randal. Cretia's
03. Davy. Moses's
Moses. Ned's
04. Jupiter. Jerry's
05. James. Edy's
Madison. Sally's
Joe. Ursula's
Henry. Cretia's d. 21
Washington. Mary's
Eliza. Rachael's
06. Willis. Bagw's
~~Anderson Lilly's~~ d. Oct. 1811
Celia. Moses's
Suckey. Ned's
07. Anne. Ursula's
Milly. Cretia's
Maria. Edy's
08. Archy. Bagw's
Eston. Sally's
Ellen. Rach's. Dec.
09. Dolly. Ursula's
Stannard. Lilly's
Kilburn. Cretia's
Ellen Fanny's
10. Tucker Mary's. Apr.
Patsy Edy's May 11.
[illegible] Sep
Polly [illegible] Aug
11. Lucy. Lilly's Mar. 12.

1811. Apr. 1. Cornelius Ursula's
Sep. Jamey. Scilla's
Dec. Jenny. Fanny's
Oct. Matilda. Cretia's
Dec. 25. Robert. Virginia's
1812. Oct. 27. Zachariah. Moses's
Dec. 6. Betsy-Ann. Edy's
1813. January. Lindsay. Esther's
May. Edmund. Rachael B.
~~Sep. Fanny. Scilla's~~ d. Mar. 1814. } whoop's cough
~~Sep. 10. Mary. Cretia's~~ d. Mar. 1814
Oct. 1. Thomas. Ursula's
1814. May Marshal. Maria's [i.e. Lavania's]
d. June ~~Moses Fanny's~~
1815 June 5. Peter. Edy's
July. James Band. Cretia's
Aug. Patsy. Moses's
Sep. Amanda. Virginia's
1816. Jan. 21. Louisa. Ursula's
April 15. Marlin. Maria's
July Miles. Scilla's
Jennet. Sally's
Lindsay. Rachael's B.
1817. July 11. ~~Malinda Fanny's~~
Aug. Fossett. Moses's
1818. Jackson Milly's
Lucy Scilla's
James Hamilton Maria's
Caroline. Ursula's
Lorenzo. Sally's
1819. Jan. 7. Isabella. Edy's
Apr. 3. Indridge. Fanny's
Aug. Nancy. Cretia's
Oct. 15. Fontaine. Mary Moses
1820. Jan. 27. Critta. Ursula's
Mar. Martha. Beck's
July. Amy. Isabel's
1821. Apr. Aggy Scilla's
May. Sally's
William Edy's
Nov. Virginia's
1822. Sep. Melinda. Fanny's
Dec. Gilly. Aggy's
1823 Martha. Maria's (Rachael's)
Manuel. Eve's
May Isabella. Sally's; Cha's wife
girl Virginia's
George. Ursula's
1824. Aug. another

NOTES to Page 130: Roll of the negroes according to their ages Albemarle

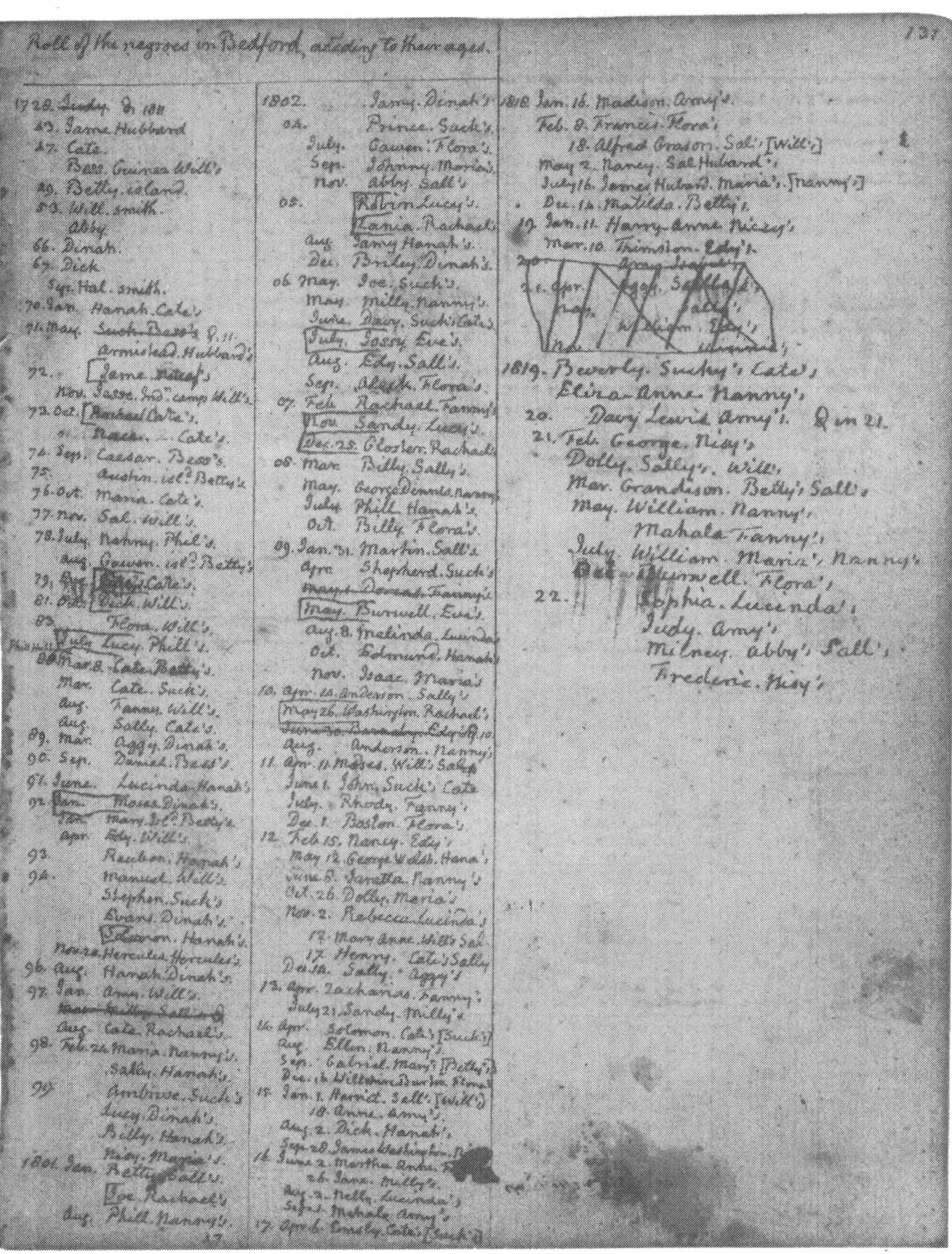

131

Roll of the negroes in Bedford, according to their ages.

1728. Jenny. d. 1811
43. Jame Hubbard
47. Cate.
Bess. Guinea Will's
49. Betty. island.
53. Will. smith.
Abby
66. Dinah.
67. Dick
Sep. Hal. smith.
70. Jan. Hanah. Cate's
71. May. Suck. Bess's d. 11.
Armistead. Hubbard's
72. Jame. Hubbard's
Nov. Jesse. Ind^n. camp Will's.
73. Oct. Rachael Cate's.
Nace. Cate's.
74. Sep. Caesar. Bess's.
75. Austin. isl^d. Betty's.
76. Oct. Maria. Cate's.
77. Nov. Sal. Will's.
78. July. Nanny. Phil's.
Aug. Gawen. isl^d. Betty's
79. Aug. [illegible] Cate's.
81. Oct. Dick. Will's.
83. Flora. Will's.
July Lucy. Phill's.
Mar. 8. Cate. Betty's.
Mar. Cate. Suck's.
Aug. Fanny. Will's.
Aug. Sally. Cate's.
89. Mar. Aggy. Dinah's.
90. Sep. Daniel. Bess's.
91. June. Lucinda. Hanah's
92. Jan. Moses. Dinah's.
Feb. Mary. Isl^d. Betty's
Apr. Edy. Will's.
93. Reuben. Hanah's
94. Manuel. Will's.
Stephen. Suck's
Evans. Dinah's.
Solomon. Hanah's.
Nov. 22. Hercules. Hercules's
96. Aug. Hanah. Dinah's.
97. Jan. Amy. Will's.
[illegible] Sallie's
Aug. Cate. Rachael's.
98. Feb. 24. Maria. Nanny's.
Sally. Hanah's.
99. Ambrose. Suck's
Lucy. Dinah's.
Billy. Hanah's.
Nisy. Maria's.
1801. Jan. Betty. Sall's.
Joe. Rachael's
Aug. Phill. Nanny's.

1802. Jamy. Dinah's
04. Prince. Suck's.
July. Gawen. Flora's.
Sep. Johnny. Maria's.
Nov. Abby. Sall's.
05. Robin. Lucy's.
Kania. Rachael's
Aug. Jamy. Hanah's.
Dec. Briley. Dinah's.
06. May. Joe. Suck's.
May. Milly. Nanny's.
June. Davy. Suck's Cate's
July. Jossy. Eve's.
Aug. Edy. Sall's.
Sep. Aleck. Flora's
07. Feb. Rachael. Fanny's
Nov. Sandy. Lucy's.
Dec. 25. Gloster. Rachael's
08. Mar. Billy. Sally's.
May. George Dennis. Nanny's
July. Phill. Hanah's.
Oct. Billy. Flora's.
09. Jan. 31. Martin. Sall's.
Apr. Shepherd. Suck's
May. Dorcas. Fanny's
May. Burwell. Eve's.
Aug. 8. Malinda. Lucinda's
Oct. Edmund. Hanah's
Nov. Isaac. Maria's
10. Apr. 16. Anderson. Sally's
May 26. Washington. Rachael's
June. Barnaby. Edy's d. 10.
Aug. Anderson. Nanny's
11. Apr. 11. Moses. Will's Sally
June 1. John. Suck's Cate
July. Rhody. Fanny's
Dec. 1. Boston. Flora's
12. Feb. 15. Nancy. Edy's
May 12. George Webb. Hana's
June 8. Joretta. Nanny's
Oct. 26. Dolly. Maria's
Nov. 2. Rebecca. Lucinda's
17. Mary Anne. Will's Sal.
17. Henry. Cate's Sally
Dec. 16. Sally. Aggy's
13. Apr. Zachariah. Fanny's
July 21. Sandy. Milly's
14. Apr. Solomon. Cate's [Suck's]
Aug. Ellen. Nanny's.
Sep. Gabriel. Mary's [Betty's]
Dec. 16. William Burton. Flora's
15. Jan. 1. Harriet. Sall's [Will's]
18. Anne. Amy's.
Aug. 2. Dick. Hanah's.
Sep. 28. James Washington. [illegible]
16. June 2. Martha Anne. [illegible]
26. Jane. Milly's.
Aug. 2. Nelly. Lucinda's
Sep. 1. Mahala. Amy's
17. Apr. 6. Emsly. Cate's [Suck's]

1818. Jan. 16. Madison. Amy's.
Feb. 8. Francis. Flora's
18. Alfred Grason. Sal's [Will's]
May 2. Nancy. Sal Hubard's
July 16. James Hubard. Maria's [Nanny's]
Dec. 14. Matilda. Betty's.
19. Jan. 11. Harry. Anne. Nicey's
Mar. 10. Thruston. Edy's.
[illegible]
1819. Beverly. Suckey's Cate's
Eliza-Anne. Nanny's
20. Davy Lewis. Amy's. d. in 21.
21. Feb. George. Nisy's
Dolly. Sally's. Will's
Mar. Grandison. Betty's Sall's
May. William. Nanny's
Mahala. Fanny's
July. William. Maria's Nanny's
Oct. Burwell. Flora's
22. Sophia. Lucinda's
Judy. Amy's
Milney. Abby's Sall's
Frederic. Nisy's

NOTES to Page 131: Roll of the Negroes in Bedford, according to their ages

		winter of 1809.10	11.12	12.13	13.14	14.15	15.16	16.17	17.18	18.19	20.21	21.22	22.23
Monticello plantation	work horses	2.	3	2	2	1	1	1	1	1			
	mules	10	10	13	11	6	9	11	9	6			
	breeding mares		1	2									
	colts	1.	1	3	1	1	1						
	steers		2.4.	2	3	2	2	2+1	4	6			
	cows.	6	8	6	8	9	13	11	12	12			
	cattle. 3 y. old male												
	female		1		4	2			3				
	2. y. o. male				1								
	female				2	1		3					
	yearlings	3.		4	4		3			4			
	calves.		1	1	1				2	1			
	Ewes above 6 y.o. & rams	16	2 ram	4	[illegible]	[illegible]	13	14+11	14+7				
	Ewes from 1. to 6. y. o	11		40	29	27	27	24	42	63			
	lambs of last year	8		20		20	11	27					
	Sows	9.	4+1	4+1	5	6	6+2	8	10				
	shoats	42.	16	11	14	37	46+16	42	35	97			
	pigs	9	18		30	38	46	53.	65				
	bacon hogs killed	40.	34	14	13	29.	66	62	70	84			
	beeves killed	[illegible]	19	2				3	3				
Tufton	work horses	8.	9	10	9	8	6+3	7					
	mules						1	2					
	breeding mares												
	colts												
	steers	9.	4+1	4+1	6+1	8	10	8					
	cows above 3 y. old	9.	14	10	10	12	11	9					
	cattle. 3. y. o. male		2	2	6		1	1					
	female	5	4			2							
	2. y. o. male	4		2	9		1	1					
	female			5		4	4						
	yearlings			8	3	3	9	6					
	calves.	9.	7	2		8		1					
	ewes abv. 6. wethers. rams		7+2+1	..1.1	11.6.		14						
	ewes from 1. to 6	14.	50	55	41	46	31	40					
	lambs of last year			10	24	12	19	11					
	sows	8.	10	7	4	8	9	8					
	shoats	8.	46	18	33	29	44	39					
	pigs	42.	16		37	40	24	38					
	bacon hogs killed	13.	62	20	29	29	49	33					
	beeves killed		4	3		3	2						
Lego.	work horses	3.		4	4	4	4	3					
	mules			2	1	2	2	2					
	breeding mares												
	colts												
	steers			5+1	4+1	4	4	5					
	cows above 3. y. old			7	6	6	5	5					
	cattle 3. y. o. male			1	1	2							
	female				2			2					
	2. y. o. male			2	2	2	6	2					
	female			2		2	4	2					
	yearlings			2	5	4	3	5					
	calves			3		2	2						
	ewes abv. 6. wethers. rams			~~2+4~~	7	4.5.5	6+1	4					
	ewes from 1. to 6. y. o.			10	3	16	13	16					
	lambs of last year				8	7	8	5					
	sows			5+1	4	5	5	4					
	shoats			21	17		16	17					
	pigs					15	16						
	bacon hogs killed			15	14	16	10	18					
	beeves killed			1		2	2						

NOTES to Page 132: Lego, Tufton, Monticello plantation

	09.10	10.11	11.12	12.13	13.14	14.15	15.16	16.17	17.18	18.19	19.20
Poplar Forest											
work horses	7	6		6	5	5	5	8	8	8	6
mules											
breeding mares											
colts					7+1			1	1	1	1
steers & bulls 6+	6+1	4+1	11	8+1	"	4+2	3	4	8	11+1	8
cows	25	8	21 heifers	8	9	7	8		7	7	8
cattle 3 y.o. male	3								4		2
female	6		[illegible]	10	4	2	1		1	2	3
2 y.o. male	5			4			}4				1
female	6										4
yearlings	2				2	3	4		3	3	
calves	9	1	5	5	5	4	3		5	5	4
ewes abv 6. wethers. rams	16	4	2 rams		6 & 12	8+6	}21	11	18	18	23
ewes from 1. to 6. y.o.	17	27	37	26	30	12		21	31	32	48
lambs of this year	13			26	18	3	16	23	21	21	21
sows & boars	11	10+2	81	11+1	9+1	5	8	11		8+1	9
shoats	84	45		50	50	7		58		45	[illegible]
pigs	10	59				28	45			34	[illegible]
bacon hogs killed	32	50	47	40	43+	21	20	47		43	38
beeves killed	7	3	4	2	1	2	1				
Bear Creek											
work horses	4	4		8	6	5	4	6		8	8
mules											
breeding mares	1	1									
colts	1	1				2	2				1
steers & bulls	3+2	4+1		6	4	2	2	4		6.2.1	4+1
cows	5	7+8	5	5	8	7	5			8	9
cattle 3 y.o. male		6									2
female	3	4		7		2	3			1	3
2 y.o. male		5									
female		2		2							4
yearlings	4	8			4	2				4	
calves	5		5	4	3	4	3			5	7
ewes abv 6. wethers. rams		10	[illegible]	8	2+1	7	}24	8		11	15
ewes from 1. to 6. y.o.				14	11	18		12		19	9
lambs of last year		15			4	3	6	8		11	4
sows & boars	9	8+2	64	9+1	10+1	6	5	10		8.1	8
shoats	55	37		25	35	13	18	29		57	36
pigs	25	13		5		16	24	34		37	22
bacon hogs killed	18	34	28	32	32+	34	6	35		46	37
beeves killed					2	2		1			

sows and boars . . . 6.
shoats . . . . . . 31.
pigs . . . . 8.
bacon hogs killed

NOTES to Page 133: Bear creek, Poplar Forest

Bread list. Feb. 1810.

Monticello House.

- Burwell & fam. 6
- Edy, James, Maria, Lovilo, Amy, Thruston } 6
- Davy, Fanny, Ellen, Aggy } 4
- John Hemings et ux. 2
- Critta 1
- Sally, Beverly, Harriet, Madison, Eston } 5
- Betty Brown, Edwin, Robert, Mary } 4
- Wormley, Ursula, Joe, Anne, Dolly, the dogs } 7
- Peter Hem. & fam. 7
- Moses, Mary, William, Davy, Celia } 5
- Nance 1
- Joe 1
- John 1
- Lewis 1
- Tilla 1
- 2 shoemakers 2
- house 2
- 56

Farm

- James, Cretia, John, Randal, Henry, Milly } 6
- Jerry, Mary, Suckey, Isaiah, Jerry, Jupiter, Squire, Bec } 8
- Davy, Isabel, Indridge, Thrimston, ~~[illegible]~~ } 4
- Jenny Ned's, James, Moses, Suckey } 4
- Jenny Lew's, Evelina, James, Isabel, Goliah } 5
- Amy John's 1
- Abram, Doll, Lazaria, Shepherd } 4
- Phill, Molly, Bartlet } 3
- John Bedf.d 1¼
- Jame Hubb.d 1¼
- Barnaby 1¼
- Philip 1
- Nace 1
- Sancho 1
- Tom 1¼
- Edmund 1¼
- Frederic 1¼
- Tom lee 1¼
- mr Bacon 6
- mr Starke 8
- 60¾

Tufton

- Bagwell, Minerva, Virginia, Esther, Nanny, Willis, Archy } 7
- Mary Bagw.'s, Washington } 2
- Caesar 1¼
- Ben 1¼
- Phill Hubbard 1¼
- Ned 1¼
- Dick 1¼
- Gill 1¼
- Jesse 1¼
- Abram, Rachael, Nanny, Eliza, Ellen } 5
- Thenia 1
- Dolly 1
- Lilly, Anderson, Stannard } 2
- 26¾

Lego

- Charles, Aggy } 2¼
- Isaac 1¼
- Davy Bedf.d 1¼
- Lewis 1¼
- Sally Lew's 1
- Scilla Ned's 1
- Nancy, child, Israel } 2¾
- Tom Buck 1¼
- Goodman 6
- 18

NOTES to Page 134: Bread list, Feb. 1810

1810.

June 25. began the wheat harvest at Monticello.

Nov. 9. 10. there fell in the course of 48. hours about 4 3/8 I. of rain. it raised the river to the brim of the bank between the milldam & ford on this side and carried away the middle of the dam, & tore very much to pieces the Eastern 1/3. it barely entered the lowest part of the low grounds there & at Milton. the water was about 4. f. deep in the lowest floor of the manufacturing mill.

July. 11. rec^d. from Pop. Forest as follows

68. hams	
81. shoulders	
75 midlings	
224	
24. pieces beef	
248	

224. pieces equivalent to 37 1/3 hogs
252 sh^d have come from 42 hogs
252

Hogs killed Dec. 1810.

Bacon. mill }	58	
McGehee	32	90.
Bedford		85.
		175.

	Overseers	Negroes	House		
Bacon	4			Albemarle	
McGehee	5				
Goodman	5				
Carden	3				
Starke	5				
negroes		36			
Mont^o. House			32		
do.			*36	→	90
Pop. For. H.			*10	Bedford	
Griffin	10.				
Roberts	4.				
negroes		25.			85
	36	61	78		175

*changed to 42. & 4

in the distribution 4. children count as 1. grown person
the spinning girls count as 1/2
the nails boys count as 1.
once a month to the House list 134 viz. 30 rations

House list	134	30
Bacon's	116	26
McGehee's	100	23
Goodman's	50	11
	400	90

Monticello.

House	grown + children		Farm			Tufton			Lego		
Burwell	2 + 5	13	James, Cretia	2 + 5	13 1/2	Bagwell, Minerva	3 + 3	18	Charles, Aggy	2	9
Edwin	1.	4 1/2	Suckey, Bec, Indridge, Evelina, Lazaria	2	10	Caesar	1.	4 1/2	Lewis	1.	4 1/2
Joe, Edy	2 + 3	12	L's Jenny	1 + 1	5	Ben	1.	4 1/2	Davy Bedf.	1.	4 1/2
Davy, Fanny	2 + 1	9	Davy, Isabel	2 + 1	11	Phill Hub.	1.	4 1/2	Solomon	1.	4 1/2
Amy	1.	4 1/2	Shepherd	1.	4 1/2	Ned jr.	1.	4 1/2	Moses	1.	4 1/2
Critta	1.	4 1/2	Abram, Doll	2.	9	Dick	1.	4 1/2	Sally	1.	4 1/2
Sally	2 + 3	12	Thruston	1.	4 1/2	Gill	1.	4 1/2	Scilla	1.	4 1/2
Bet	1 + 2	6 1/2	L's Jame	1.	4	Jeste	1.	4 1/2	Eve	1 + 2	6 1/2
R. A. Hem.	2 + 5	13	Philip	1.	4	Abram jr.	1.	4 1/2	Lucy	1 + 2	6 1/2
Nance	1	4 1/2	Nace	1.	4	Virginia	1.				50
Moses, Mary	2 + 3	12	Sanco	1.	4	Esther	1.				
Wormly, Ursula	2 + 3	12	Jerry, Mary	2. + 3	12	Mary	1 + 1	6			
John Hem.	2.	9	John Bedf.	1.	4 1/2	Rachael	1 + 2	8			
Lewis	1.	4 1/2	Bartlet	1.	4 1/2	Nanny	1 + 1	6			
James	1.	4	Isaac	1.	4 1/2	Thenia	1				
John Gard^r.	1.	4 1/2	Amy	1.	4 1/2	Dolly	1				
Ned	1.	4 1/2	R's Jenny	1. + 3	8	Lilly	1 + 2	8			
		134	Molly	1.	4 1/2			100			
			Tom		116						
	25 + 28			23 1/2 + 13			19 + 11			10 + 4	

NOTES to Page 135: 1810 harvest at Monticello

1810. Dec.		linen	pl.	cotton	blank.	bed	hat	stockings
Burwell								
Edwin		7	5½				1	
Joe		7	5½				1	
Edy		homespun						
James	05							
Maria	07							
Davy		7	3	2½			1	
Fanny								
Ellen	09							
Amy								
Critta								
Sally								
Beverly	98	4⅔	2	1¾				
Harriet	01							
Madison	05							
Eston	08							
Betty Brown					1			
Robert	99							
Mary	01							
Peter Hemings		7	3	2½	1			
Nance					1			1
Moses		7	3	2½			1	
Mary								
William	01							
Davy	03							
Celia	06							
Wormly		7	3	2½			1	
Ursula								
Joe	05							
Anne	07							
Dolly	09							
James		7	3	2½			1	
~~[illegible]~~								
John	00							
Randal	02							
Henry	05							
Milly	07							
Lilburn	09							
John Hemings		7	5½		1		1	1
Lewis		7	3	2½			1	
Jenny		7	2	3				1
James	95	5⅔	2½	2	1		1	
Evelina	97				1			
Isabel	00	4		3½	1			
Davy		7	3	2½	1		1	
Isabel		7	2	3	1	1		1
Indridge	97				1			
Thrimston	99	4⅓		3½ }	1			
Lovilo	01	3⅓		3 }				
Shepherd		7	3	2½				
Abram		7	3	2½	1		1	
Doll		7	2	3	1	1		
Thruston	98	5⅔	2½	2				
Philip	96	5⅓	2⅓	2				
Nace	96	5⅓	2⅓	2				
Sanco	97	5	2⅓	1¾				
Jerry		7	3	2½	1			
Mary					1	1	1	
Sucky	96				1			
Isaiah	00				}			
Jerry	02				} 1			
Jupiter	04				}			

1810		linen	plains	cotton	blank.	bed	hat	stockings
Barnaby		7	3	2½			1	
Lilly		7	2	3		1	1	1
Anderson	06	2		1¾ }	1			
Shannon	09	1		1 }				
John		7	3	2½	1		1	
Amy		7	2	3				1
Ned		7	3	2½			1	
Jenny		7	2	3			1	1
Aggy	98	4⅔		3¾				
Israel	00	4		3¼ }				
Moses	03	3		2½ }	1			
Sucky	06	2		1¾ }				
Molly		7	2	3		1		
Bagwell		7	5½				1	
Minerva		7	2	3			1	1
Bec.	97				1			
Nanny	00	4		3¼ }				
Willis	06	2		1¾ }	1			
Archy	08	1⅓		1¼ }				
Mary		7	2	3	1		1	
~~Washington~~	05	2⅓		2				
Virginia		7	2	3			1	
Esther	95	5⅔	2	3			1	
Caesar		7	3	2½			1	
Ben		7	3	2½	1		1	
Phil Hubd.		7	3	2½			1	
Ned		7	3	2½				
Dick		7	3	2½				
Gill		7	3	2½				
Jesse		7	3	2½				
Abram		7	3	2½				
Rachael		7	2	3		1		1
Lazaria	97				1			
Eliza	05	2⅓		2 }				
Ellen	08	1⅓		1¼ }	1			
Nancy		7	2	3		1	1	
Thenia		7	2	3			1	
Dolly		7	2	3			1	
Isaac		7	3	2½			1	
Charles		7	3	2½				
Aggy		7	2	3		1		1
Lewis		7	3	2½				
Sally		7	2	3			1	1
Scilla		7	2	3				
Davy Bedfd.		7	3	2½			1	
John Bedfd.		7	3	2½			1	
			3¾ great coat					
Bartlet		7	3	2½				
James Ned;	96	8	4½		1			
James Hubard								
hired								
Tom		7	3	2½				
Tom Buck		7	3	2½				
Tom Lee		7	3	2½				
Frederic		7	3	2½				
Nancy		7	2	3				
child		1		1				
		303						
		175						
		478						

R's James & Bedfd. John great coats

1811. June 10. Summer clothes
Joe.
Davy jr.
Moses
Wormley
James
John Hem.
Lewis.
Davy
Shepherd
Abram
Thruston
Philip.
Nace
Sanco
Beverly
James jr.
Jerry
Barnaby
John gardr.
Ned
Bagwell
Caesar
Ben
Phil Hubd.
Ned jr.
Dick
Gill
Jesse
Abram jr.
Isaac
Charles
Lewis jr.
Davy Bedfd.
John Bedfd.
Bartlet
James Ned;
Tom.
2½ y. Irish @ 39
Jenny Li.
Isabel
Doll
Mary Jer.
Lilly
Amy
Jenny N.
Minerva
Mary Ba.
Virginia
Esther
Rachael
Nancy
Thenia
Dolly
Aggy
Sally
Scilla
3 y. Irish 20
Eve
Lucy
Solomon
Moses Bedfd.

NOTES to Page 136: 1810 slaves list

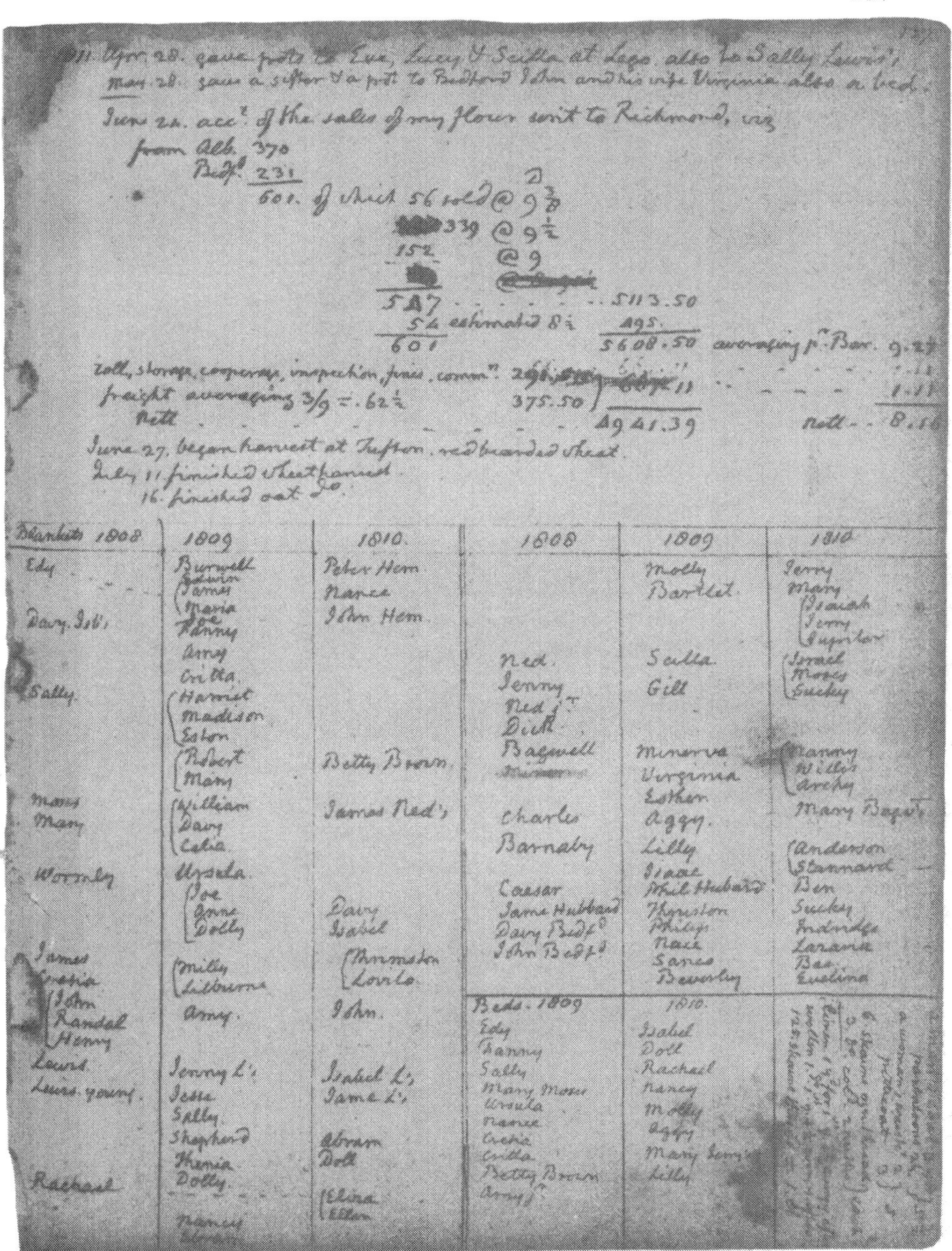

1811. Apr. 28. gave pots to Eve, Lucy & Scilla at Lego. also to Sally Lewis's;
May 28. gave a sifter & a pot to Bedford John and his wife Virginia. also a bed.

June 22. acc^t. of the sales of my flour sent to Richmond, viz

from Alb. 370
Bedf^d. 231
601. of which 56 sold @ 9 7/8 D
339 @ 9 1/2
152 @ 9
547 . . . . 5113.50
54 estimated 8 1/2 . . 495.
601 . . . . 5608.50 averaging p^r. Bar. 9.27

toll, storage, cooperage, inspection, fees, comm^n. . . . 667.11 . . . 1.11
freight averaging 3/9 = .62 1/2 . . . 375.50 . . . 1.11
nett . . . . 4941.39 . . . nett . . 8.16

June 27. began harvest at Tufton. red bearded wheat.
July 11. finished wheat harvest
16. finished oat do.

Blankets 1808	1809	1810.	1808	1809	1810.
Edy Davy. Isb's Sally. Mary Mary Wormly James Critta John Randal Henry Lewis Lewis. young. Rachael	Burwell Edwin James Maria Joe Fanny Amy Critta Harriet Madison Eston Robert Mary William Davy Celia Ursula Joe Anne Dolly Milly Lilburne Amy. Jenny L's Jesse Sally Shepherd Maria Dolly. Nancy	Peter Hem. Nance John Hem. Betty Brown. James Ned's Davy Isabel Thrimston Lovilo John. Isabel L's James L's Abram Doll Elina Ellen	Ned. Jenny Ned j^r. Dick Bagwell ~~Minerva~~ Charles Barnaby Caesar Jame Hubbard Davy Bedf^d. John Bedf^d.	Molly Bartlet Scilla Gill Minerva Virginia Esther Aggy. Lilly Isaac Phil Hubbard Thruston Philip Nace Sanco Beverly	Jerry Mary Isaiah Jerry Jupiter Israel Moses Suckey Nanny Willis Archy Mary Bagot Anderson Stannard Ben Suckey Indridge Lavania Bec Evelina

Beds. 1809	1810.
Edy Fanny Sally Mary Moses Ursula Nance Cretia Critta Betty Brown Amy j^r.	Isabel Doll Rachael Nancy Molly Aggy Mary Bery's Lilly

NOTES to Page 137: Blankets 1808-1810

Estimate of corn necessary for Monticello from Jan. 15. to Nov. 1. 1812.

		Bar
bread. 100. pecks = 25 bushels a week for 40. weeks (from 1st. Sat. of Jan. to last Sat. of Oct. 40. weeks) — —	200	
to be drawn from the rent of the toll mill @ 5. Bar. a week		200.
the Stable. suppose 7. horses @ 2. gall^s. a day is 2½ bar. a week 25. weeks	62½	
to be drawn at a waggon load of 7½ Bar. [illegible] weeks from Tufton		62

Stock. 3. horses @ 6. gall^s. & 10. mules @ 3. gall^s a day. for 90. days }
the same at half allowance after grass comes 90. days more } — 65.
a mare & colt @ 2. gall^s. between them 90. days — — 4½
23. grown hogs @ 1. ear a piece a day 75. days — — 4½
60. sheep @ ½ pint of meal a day 75. days — — 7
2. beeves @ 1½ gallon a day each for 30. days — — 2½
2. do. — — 75. — — 5½
heretofore rec^d from Tufton 27 Bar — 89
to be still brought from thence 33
to be bought — — 29 — — 89

3 milch cows @ 1. peck of bran a day. pr. week 21. pecks
2 oxen @ 1. peck of bran a day besides chaff 14
3. other cows — — 35 = 8. 3 (B. P.)
21

Estimate for Tufton	B.
bread @ 31. pecks a week. 40. w.	62.
9 horses. at the above rates	60.
56. hogs as above — —	10½
3. beeves as above at 50. days	5½
60. sheep as above 75. days	7
	145.
the gage of the corn in the barn	125
deficiency to be economised	20
7. milch cows at the above rates	147. b
4. oxen at do. both for 12 weeks	84
	231.

of the 95. [illegible] to 27. B. from Tufton
33. to be deliv^d to E. Bacon
62. for the stable
95

Estimate for Lego.	B.
bread. 27. pecks a week for 40. weeks	54.
2 horses & 2. mules as above	22½
35 hogs as above — —	6½
3. beeves as above for 60. days	6¾
16. sheep as above — —	2.
	91¾
the corn gaged at — —	69.
deficiency to be economised	22¾
2. milch cows — —	42 bush. bran
2. oxen — —	42
	84.

NOTES to Page 138: Estimate of corn from Monticello

NOTES to Page 138: Estimate of corn from Monticello

Lucy	7	5						
Robin 03.	3-1	2-3						
Sandy 07.	2-2	2-1						
Moses.	7	$5\frac{1}{2}$						
Solomon	7	$5\frac{1}{2}$						
Tom[hired]	7	$5\frac{1}{2}$		1.				

NOTES to Page 140: continuation of slave list

NOTES to Page 141: Blank page retained in order to keep the left-right relationship of the book.

Distribution of Blankets

Dec. 1811.14.17

Burwell
Edy
~~Edwin~~
Davy. jr.
Sally
~~Robert~~ 99. ma'd 1815
Mary 01
x Moses. smith
Mary
Wormley
James
Cretia
x John 00
Randal 02
Davy
Lewis
~~Lewis jr.~~
~~Sally L's~~
x Rachael
Ned
Jenny
x Ned jr. 86
x Dick. 90
x Scilla. 94
x Jenny. 11
x Burwell
x Archy 00
x [illegible]
x John Bedf.

1812.15.18

Joe
x Jamesy 05 / Maria 07 Edy's
Fanny
Critta
Harriet 01
Madison 05
Eston 08
Beverly. 98
William 01
Davy 03
Ursula
Joe 05
Anne 07
~~Henry 03~~
~~Milly 07~~
~~Thruston~~ 95
Amy
Jenny L.
~~Jesse~~
Shepherd
x Thenia
Dolly
x Nancy
x Abram jr.
x Bartlet
x Aggy. 98
Gill. 92
x [illegible]
x Virginia
x Esther

1813.16.19

Peter Hemings
John Hemings
Patsy 10 / Betsy 12 Edy's
Ellen 09
Jenny. 11
Nance
~~Billy B.~~
Betty Brown
~~x Robert~~
Celia. 06
Tucker. 10
Dolly 09
Cornelius. 11
Lilburn 07
Matilda. 11
~~Isabel~~
Thrimston 99
~~Lovila~~ 01
Indridge. 97
John
Isabel L's. 00
James. L's 95
x Evelina. 97
~~Abram~~
Doll
x Eliza 05 / Ellen 08
x Lazaria. 97
Jerry
~~Mary~~
x Isaiah 00
Jerry 02
Jupiter 05
Israel. 00
Moses 03
Suckey 06
n. James. 96
x Nanny. 00 / Willis 06
x Mary Bagw's
~~Dec.~~ 97

1811.14.17

x Charles
Barnaby
Caesar
x Davy. Bedfd.
x Joe 01 / Lany 05
x Gloster 07 / Washington. 10
x Jossy 06 / Burwell 09
x Robin. 05 / Sandy. 07
x Dick. Bedfd.
Phill. Bedford

1812.15.18

~~Aggy~~
Polly. 10
x Lilly
Isaac
x Philip 96
Nace 96
Sanco. 97
x Rachael Bedfd.

1813.16.19

Stannard. 09
x Lucy. 11
x Ben
x Suckey. 96
x James Bedfd.
x Eve
x Lucy
x Moses B. 92
x Solomon. 94

Beds. 1811.14.17

x Minerva
Jenny. Ned's
Amy John's
Jenny L's
~~Sally L's~~
x Scilla
Ursula
x Rachael Bedfd.
x Virginia
Indridge
~~Isabel~~

1812.15.18

Edy
Fanny
Sally
Mary. Moses
Nance
Cretia
Critta
Betty Brown
x Esther
x Suckey

1813.16.19

~~Isabel~~
Doll
x Rachael
~~Nancy~~
~~Aggy~~
~~Mary. Jenny's~~
x Lilly
x Eve
x Lucy
x Mary Bagw's
x Maria
x Milly

NOTES to Page 142: Distribution of Blankets

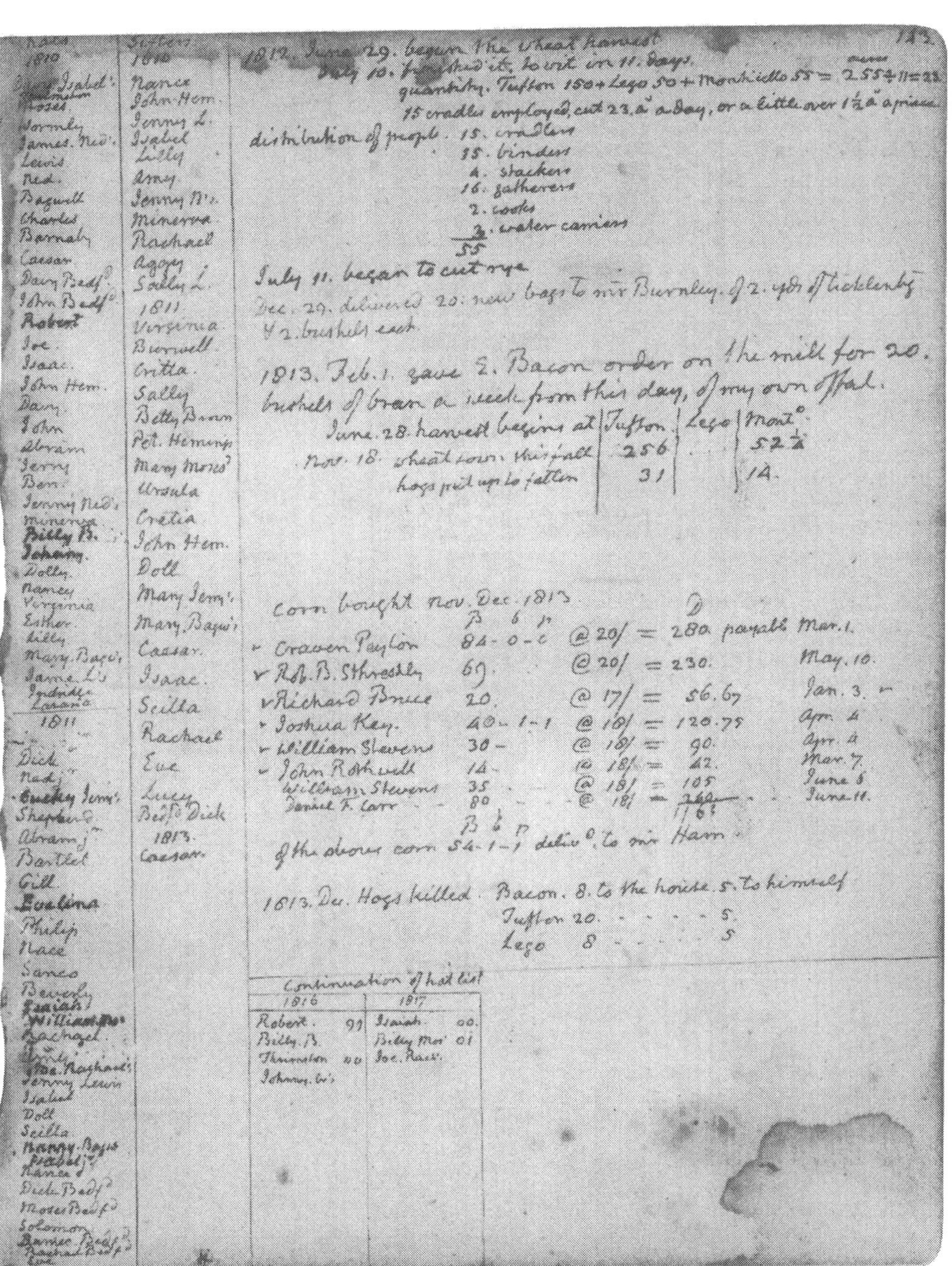

1812. June 29. began the wheat harvest
July 10. finished it, to wit in 11. days.
quantity. Tufton 150 + Lego 50 + Monticello 55 = 255 ÷ 11 = 23
15 cradles employed, cut 23. a. a day, or a little over $1\frac{1}{2}$ a. a piece.

distribution of people. 15. cradlers
15. binders
4. stackers
16. gatherers
2. cooks
3. water carriers
55

July 11. began to cut rye
Dec. 29. delivered 20. new bags to mr Burnley. of 2. yds of ticklenburg & 2. bushels each.

1813. Feb. 1. gave E. Bacon order on the mill for 20. bushels of bran a week from this day, of my own offal.

	Tufton	Lego	Mont°
June. 28. harvest begins at			
Nov. 18. wheat sown this fall	256		$52\frac{1}{2}$
hogs put up to fatten	31		14.

Corn bought Nov. Dec. 1813

	B. b. p.		D	
Craven Peyton	84 - 0 - 0	@ 20/ =	280	payable Mar. 1.
Rob. B. Sthreshley	69.	@ 20/ =	230.	May. 10.
Richard Bruce	20.	@ 17/ =	56.67	Jan. 3.
Joshua Kay.	40 - 1 - 1	@ 18/ =	120.75	Apr. 4
William Stevens	30 -	@ 18/ =	90.	Apr. 4
John Rothwell	14 -	@ 18/ =	42.	Mar. 7.
William Stevens	35	@ 18/ =	105	June 8
Daniel F. Carr	80	@ 18/ =	240	June 11.

B. b. p.
of the above corn 54 - 1 - 1 deliv^d. to mr Ham

1813. Dec. Hogs killed. Bacon. 8. to the house. 5. to himself
Tufton 20. - - - - 5.
Lego 8 - - - - 5

Continuation of last list

1816		1817	
Robert.	99	Isaiah.	00.
Billy. B.		Betty Mo.	01
Thruston	00	Joe. Rasv.	
Johnny.			

Births 1810
Isabel's
Moses
Wormly
James. Ned's
Lewis
Ned.
Bagwell
Charles
Barnaby
Caesar
Davy Bedf^d.
John Bedf^d.
Robert
Joe
Isaac
John Hem.
Davy
John
Abram
Jerry
Ben.
Jenny Ned's
Minerva
Billy B.
Johnny.
Dolly
Nancy
Virginia
Esther
Lilly
Mary. Bag's
Jame L's
Indridge
Lovana
1811
Dick
Ned jr
Shepherd
Abram jr
Bartlet
Gill
Evelina
Philip
Nace
Sanco
Beverly
Isaiah
Rachael
Isabel
Doll
Scilla
Nanny
Dick Bedf^d
Moses Bedf^d
Solomon
Rachael Bedf^d

Sisters 1810
Nance
John Hem.
Jenny L.
Isabel
Lilly
Amy
Jenny N's.
Minerva
Rachael
Aggy
Sally L.
1811
Virginia
Burwell
Critta
Sally
Betty Brown
Pet. Heming
Mary Moses'
Ursula
Cretia
John Hem.
Doll
Mary Jen's
Mary Bag's
Caesar
Isaac
Scilla
Rachael
Eve
Lucy
Bedf^d Dick
1813.
Caesar

NOTES to Page 143: Slaves 1810 to 1812

1813. Dec	[illegible]	[illegible]	[illegible]	[illegible]	[illegible]	[illegible]	socks
Abram old	7	3	2½	1			
Doll	7	2	3	1	1	1	
Abram junr.	7	3	2½		1		✓
Aggy. Ned. 98	5⅔		4½				
Bagwell	10	6	6		1		✓
Minerva	7	2	3				
Willis 6	3		2½				
Archy 8	2½		2				
Jordan 11	1⅔		1¼				
Barnaby	7	3	2½				
Bartlet	7	3	2½		1		✓
Ben	7	3	2½	1	1		✓
Betty Brown	7		3	1			
Robert 99	5⅓		4½				
Mary 01	4⅔		3¾				
Beverly	7	3	2½		1		
Billy Bedf. 99	5½	2¼	2		1		
Burwell							
Caesar	7	3	2½				
Charles	7	3	2½				✓
Aggy (Isabel's)	7	2	3		1	1	
Polly 10	1⅔		1½				
Critta	7		5				
[illegible]	7	3	2½				
Isabel	7	2	3	1	1	1	
Davy junr.	7	3	2½				
Fanny	7		5				
Ellen 9	2		1¾ }	1			
Jenny 11	1⅓		1½ }				
Davy Bedf.	7	3	2½				✓
Dick Bedf.	7	3	2½		1		✓
Dick. Ned.	7	3	2½		1		✓
Dolly 94	7		5				
Edwin	7		3½				
Edy	7		5				
James 5	3⅓		2¾				
Maria 7	2⅔		2¼				
Patsy 10	1⅔		1½				
Betsy 12	1		1				
Esther	7	2	3			1	
Lindsay 13	-	-	-	-	-	-	-
Eve	7	2	3	1	1	1	
Joshua 6			2¾				
Burwell 9	[illegible]		1¾				
Evelina 97	7		5	1			
Gill	7	[illegible]	2½		1		gr. coat
Indridge	7	2	3	1	1		
Isaac	7	3	2½				gr. coat

Name		[illegible]	[illegible]	[illegible]	[illegible]	[illegible]	[illegible]	socks
Israel	0	5	2½	1½	1			gr. coat ?
James. Ss		7	3	2½				
Cretia		7	3	5				
John	0	5	.	4				
Randal	2	4⅓		3½				
Henry	5	3⅓		2¾				
Milly	7	2⅔		2¼				
Lilburn	9	2		1¾				
Matilda	11	1⅓		1¼				
Mary	13	-	-	-				
James Bedf.		7	3	2½	1	1		✓
Rachael		7	2	3		1		
Joe	[illegible]	4⅔		3¾				
Lania	[illegible]	3⅓		2¾				
Glaster	[illegible]	2⅔		2¼				
Washington	10	1⅔		1½				
Edmund	13	-	-	-				
James. Lewis's		7	3	2½	1			
James Ned.		7	3	2½	1	1		gr. coat
Jerry		7	3	2½	1			gr. coat
Isaiah	0	5		4 }				
Jerry	2	4⅓		3½ }	1			
Jupiter	4	3⅓		3 }				
Jesse		7	3	2½		1		✓
Joe		7	3	2½				
John Bedf.		7	3	2½				✓
Virginia		7	2	3				baby cl.
Robert	11	1⅓		1¼				
John Gorder		7	3	2½	1			
Amy		7	2	3		1		
John Hemings		7	3	2½	1			
Lazaria		7	2	3	1	1		baby cl.
Lewis		7	3	2½				
Jenny		7	2	3		1		
Isabel	0	5		4	1			
Lilly		7	2	3			1	
Stannard	9	2		1¾ }	1			
Lucy	11	1⅓		1¼ }				
Lovilo	1	4⅔	2	3¾	1			
Lucy		7	2	3	1	1	1	
Robin	5	3⅓		2¾				
Sandy	7	2⅔		2¼				
Mary. Bagw.		7	2	3	1		1	
Washington	5	3⅓		2¾				
Moses. smith		7	3	2½				
Mary		7	3	5				
William	1	4⅔	.	3¾				
Davy	3	4	.	3½				
Caelia	6	3	.	2½ }	1			
Tucker	10	1⅔		2½ }				
Zachariah	12	1		1				
Moses. Bedf.		7	3	2½		1		✓

NOTES to Page 144: Slaves 1813 Dec.

Nace		7	3	2½		1		
Nance		7		5	1	1		
Nancy		7	2	3				
Nanny. Bagw's.	0	5		4	1			
Ned		7	3	2½				
Janey		7	2	3				
Moses	3	4		3¼	}1			
Sucky	6	3		2½				
Ned junr.		7	3	2½		1		✓
Peter Hemings		7		5½	1			
Philip		7	3	2½		1		✓
Rachael		7	2	3		1	1	
Eliza	5	3⅓		2¾	}1			
Ellen	8	2⅔		2				
Sally		7		5				
Harriet	1	4⅓		3¾				
Madison	9	3⅓		2¾				
Eston	8	2⅔		2				
Sanco		7	3	2½		1		
Scilla		7	2	3		1		
Jamy	11.	1⅓		1¼				
Q Fanny	13							
Shepherd		7	3	2½		1		✓
Solomon		7	3	2½	1	1		✓
Sucky		7	2	3	1	1		
Thenia	93.	7	2	3				
Thrimston	99	5⅓	2¼	2	1			
Wormly		7	3	2½				
Ursula		7		5				
Joe	5	3⅓		2¾				
Anne	7	2⅔		2¼				
Dolly	9	2		1¾	}1			
Cornelius	11	1⅓		1¼				
Thomas	13							
hired								
Lewis. Bacon's		7	3	2½		1		
Peter		7	3	2½		1		

	shirting all Cotton	dble cloth wool & cotton	single cloth wool & cotton	shirting cotton & thread
41. men	287. yds.	226. yds		
32. women	224	160.		
61. children	. . .	. . .	137 yds	180 yds
134.	511	386	137	180 = 1214.

	cotton lb	wool lb	thread lb
511. yds, all cotton	256		
386. cotton & wool dble	103	206	
137. do. . . single	36	54	
180. cotton & thread	45	. .	45
	440	260	45

Summer clothes. all cotton
42 men @ 2½ yds = 105
21 women @ 3. yds = 63
168 yds requir.s 84 cotton

1816. Feb. 3. a kiln of 27. cords yields 605 b. = 22½ b. to a cord.
Feb. 5. ordered distribution of 147. b. shipstuff & 252 b. bran now dece me at the mill as follows

	b. bran	b. shipst.		
mr Ballard	9.	+ 12		weekly
Ham	7.	10		
Bacon	6.	8.	for the plantation	
Jerry	2		for the house	

the bran will thus last 10. weeks
the shipstuff 5. weeks, by which time we shall have a screw to crush & grind corn & cobs together.

		Tufton	Lego	Mont.	Total	
wheat sowed autumn 13.		260	109	50	419.	wheat
oats	spring 14.	40	50	20	110	oats
rye		–	–	–	50	rye

June 27. began wheat harvest
July 15. finish it.
21. finished rye & oats

NOTES to Page 145: Slaves continued

1814. Dec. 16.

Offal allowed at the mill this year is 2. bush. bran } for every barrel of flour
½ bush. shipstuff

gave orders for Tufton 16. bush. bran + 4. bush. shipstuff weekly
Mont° 13 3
Lego 11 3
making 40 + 10 which if continued 15 weeks will be
600. b. bran 150. b. shipstuff.

1814. Dec.	shirting	woollen	blankets	beds	hose	[illegible]
Abram	7.	5½			1	
Doll	6.	5			1	
Abram junr.	7.	5½			1	
Aggy Ned's. 98	[illegible]	4½			1	
Bagwell	7.	6	1		1	
Minerva	6	5		1	1	1
Willis 6.	3⅓	2¾				
Archy 8.	2⅔	2¼	1			
Jordan 11.	1⅔	1½				
Barnaby	7.	5½	1		1	1
Bartlet	7.	5½			1	
Ben	7.	5½			1	
Betty Brown	6	5			1	
Robert 99	5⅔	4½	1		1	1
Mary 01.	5	4			1	
Beverly	7.	5½			1	
Billy Bedf. 99.	5⅔	4½			1	
Burwell	7.		1.		1	
Caesar	7.	5½	1		1	
Charles	7.	5½	1		1	1
Aggy (Isbel's)	6.	5			1	
Polly 10.	2	1¾				
Critta	6	5			1	
Davy senr. Isabel	6⅔	[illegible]	1		1.1.	1 Davy
Davy jr.	7	5½	1		1	1
Fanny	6	5			1	
Ellen 9.	2⅓	2				
Jenny 11.	1⅔	1½				
Moses 14.						
Davy B.	7.	5½	1		1	1.
Dick B.	7.	5½	1		1	
Dick. Ned's	7.	5½	1		1	
Polly	6	5			1	
Edwin	7.	5½	1		1	
Edy	6	5	1.		1	
James 5.	3⅔	3				
Maria 7.	3	2½				
Patsy 10.	2.	1¾				
Betsy 12.	1⅓	1¼				
	212	187	13		29	

	shirting	woollen	blankets	beds	hose	[illegible]
Esther	6	5			1	1
Lindsay 13.	1	1				
Eve	7.	5½			1	
Joshua 6.	3⅓	2¾	1			
Burwell 9.	2⅓	2				
Evelina 97.	6	5			1	
Gill	7.	5½			1	
Indridge	6	5			1	
Isaac	7	5½			1	1
Israel 0	5⅓	4¼			1	
James. foreman	7.	5½	1		1	1
Cretia	6	5	1		1	
John 0.	5⅓	4¼	1		1	
Randal 2.	4⅔	3¾				
Henry 5.	3⅔	3				
Milly 7.	3.	2½				
Lilburne 9.	2⅓	2				
Matilda 11.	1⅔	1½				
James. B.	7	5½			1	
Rachael	7	5½		1	1	
Joe 1.	5	4	1		1	
Lania 5.	3⅔	3				
Gloster 7.	3	2½	1			
Washington 10.	2	1¾				
Edmund 13.	1	1				
James. Lewis	7	5½			1	1
James. Ned's	7	5½			1	
Jerry	7	5½			1	1
Isaiah 0.	5⅓	4¼			1	
Jerry 2.	4⅔	3¾				
Jupiter 4.	4	3¼				
Jesse	7	5½			1	
Joe	7.	5½			1	1
John. B.	7.	5½	1		1	1
Virginia	6	5		1	1	1
Robert 11.	1⅔	1½				
John. gardener	7.	5½			1	1
Amy	6 [illegible]	5 [illegible]	[illegible]	1	[illegible]	

NOTES to Page 146: Slaves 1814 December

	Shirting	woollen	blankets	beds	hose	[illegible]
John Hemings	7.	5½			1	1
Lewis	7.	5½	1		1	1
Fanny	6	5		1	1	
Isabel 0	5⅓	4½			1	
Lilly	6	5			1	1
Stannard 9.	2⅓	2				
Lucy 11.	1⅔	1½				
Lovilo 1.	5	4			1	1
Lucy	6	5			1	
Robin 5	3⅔	3	1			
Sandy 7.	3	2½				
Molly 12						
Maria [Lavaria]	6	5			1	
Marshal 14.						
Mary Bagwell	6	5			1	1
Washington 5	3⅔	3				
Moses smith	7	5½	1		1	1
Mary	6	5	1		1	
William 1.	5	4			1	
Davy 3.	4⅓	3½				
Celia 6.	3⅓	2¾				
Tucker 10.	2	1¾				
Zachariah 12	1⅔	1½				
Moses B.	7	5½			1	
Nace	7	5½			1	
Nance	6	5			1	
Nancy	6	5			1	1
Nanny Bagwell 0	5⅓	4½			1	
Ned	7	5½	1		1	1
Jany	6	5	1	1	1	1
Moses 3.	4⅓	3½				
Suckey 6.	3⅓	2¾				
Ned jr	7	5½	1		1	
Peter Hemings	7	5½			1	
Philip	7	5½			1	
Rachael	6	5	1	1	1	
Eliza 5.	3⅔	3				
Ellen 8.	2⅔	2¼				
Sally	6	5	1		1	
Harriet 1.	5	4			1	
Madison 5.	3⅔	3				
Eston 8.	2⅔	2¼				
Sanco	7.	5½			1	
Scilla	6.	5	1	1	1	
Jamy 11	1⅔	1½				
~~Fanny~~						
Shephard	7	5½			1	
Solomon	7	5½			1	
Sucky	6	5			1	
Thenia	6 242	5 196	10		1 31	1

	Shirting	woollen	blankets	beds	hose	[illegible]
Thrimston 0	5⅓	4¼			1	1
Wormly	7	5½	1		1	1
Ursula	6	5		1	1	
Joe 5.	3⅔	3				
Anne 7	3	2½				
Dolly 9	2⅓	2				
Cornelius 11	1⅔	1½				
Thomas 13	1	1				
hired. Lewis. Bat.	7	5½			1	1
Peter	7 44	5½ 36	1		1 5	1
	212	167	13	8	29	
	190	154	7		23	
	242	196	10		31	
	44	36	1		5	
	688	553	31		88	

Estimate of corn from Jan. 17. to Aug. 1. 1815.

			Monticello	Bar.	Farm	Bar.	Tufton	Bar.	Lego	Bar.
Bread		28 weeks to Aug. 1.	60.	84	34.	51	30.	42	26.	40
workhorses	@ 1½ b. a week	15 weeks to May 1.			1		8		4	
	@ 3 pecks a week	10 weeks more to July 10.								
mules	@ 1. b. a week	15 weeks to May 1.			7	37	2	56	2	32
	@ ½ b. a week	10 weeks more to July 10.								
other horses					2		0		0	
sheep	@ ½ pint a day	8 weeks to Mar 15.			58.	5	64.	6	33.	3
breeding sows	@ ½ pint a day	15 weeks to May 1			16		8		5	
shoats	@ ½ pint a day	10 weeks more to July 10			37	27	29	26	0	5
pigs	@ ½ pint a day	20 w. from wean'g to July 10			38		40		15	
beeves	@ 1. gallon a day				1.	1.	3.	4	1.	1½
the Stable	@ 2. b. a day, deducting my absences	to July 10	8.	62						
				146		128		134		81½

steers. cows & other cattle to be fed on shucks, tops, chaff, bran & straw

Jan. 17. 1815. Mont° grain used to this day B.
made at Monticello 30
recieved from Tufton 102.
from Lego
from the mill

from Jan. 18. to Aug. 1. to be recieved from Tufton 36.
oats from Lego 10
from mill to Aug. 1. 56
to be bought 165
267

NOTES to Page 147: Slaves list continued 1814

Bread lists for 1815

Monticello	farm	Tufton	Lego	weight of hogs killed: Monticello	Lego
Betty Brown	Abram	Bagwell	Charles	190	137
Edwin	Doll	Minerva	Aggy	185	92
Robert	Shepherd	Willis	Polly	185	84
Mary	Barnaby	Archy	James B.	184	84
Sally	Stannard	Jordan	Rachael	176	76
Beverly	Bartlet	Mary	Joe	165	76
Harriet	Davy senr.	Washington	Lania	165	71
Madison	Isabel	John B.	Gloster	156	71
Eston	Indridge	Virginia	Washington	153	70
Billy B.	Thrimston	Robert	Edmund	133	67
Burwell	Lovilo	Esther	Eve	125	65
Caesar	Jenny L's	Lindsay	Joshua	123	65
Critta	James L's	Rachael	Burwell	120	65
Davy jr.	Philip	Elina	Lucy	120	62
Fanny	Jenny B's	Ellen	Robin	120	62
Ellen	Moses	Nancy	Sandy	117	60
Jenny	Sucky	Abram jr.	Molly	113	16)1207(75½
Moses	Gill	Maria	Scilla	112	Bedford
Ned	Isaac	Marshal	Jarry	112	
James	Jerry	Lilly	Davy B.	110	101
Israel	Isaiah	Lucy	Moses B.	106	99
Aggy	Jerry	Sucky	Solomon	103	91
Thenia	Jupiter	Dick B.		102	91
Dolly	Amy	Dick Ned's		101	80
Joe	Nace	Ned jr.		100	76
Edy	Sanco	Jesse		100	67
James	Lewis	Ben.		94	67
Maria	Peter			92	67
Patsy				90	61
Betsy				29)3752.	56
James foreman				average 130	55
Cretia				Tufton.	47
John				9) 1069 (119	13)958(73¾
Randal					
Henry					
Milly					
Lilburn					
Matilda					
John Gordon					
John Hemings					
Lewis					
Evelina					
Isabel					
Moses					
Mary					
William					
Davy					
Caelia					
Tucker					
[illegible]					
[illegible]					
[illegible]					
[illegible]					
Cornelius					
Thomas					
59	28.	26	21.		

Crop of 1814.

Tufton.

	B.
corn furnishd Monticello	138
used at Tufton to Jan. 17.	125
left there for use	132
the whole made	395

Lego

	Bar.
corn. used at Lego to Jan. 17.	60
left there for use	65
the whole made	125
wheat. eaten to Jan. 17.	20
left to be eaten	50
furnd Tufton. used	9
sowed at Lego	80
delivd. at mill	440
	599

rye. eaten 58.6.
sowed 12.6.
made 70.

for the plantn from Jan. 17. to Aug. 1

corn left on hand	65. Barrels
wheat do.	10
oats to be used	10
	85. Barrels

Oats

NOTES to Page 148: Bread lists for 1815

1815. June 26. Wheat harvest begins.

	wheat	cradlers	assistants
Mr. Bacon's	60 a.	3	6.
Ham's	120	6	12
Ballard's	200	10	20
	380	19	38

Wheat sowed in autumn 1814.

	bush.
Monticello	50
Lego	80
Tufton	290
	420

for 19. cradlers & their assistants provide 19. muttons
to wit 3. muttons for mr Bacon's people } ½ a mutton a day between them.
6 . . . . Ham's
10 . . . Ballard's ½ a mutton a day.
19

for 19. cradlers & their assistants provide 38. gall^s. whiskey. or 2 gall. every cradler & assist^t.
to wit 6. gall^s. for mr Bacon. about 2½ pints a day
12. . . . Ham 5. pints
20. . . . Ballard . 1. gall^n. a day.

Monticello		Lego		Tufton	
James	Isabel	Charles	Rachael B.	Dick. B.	Minerva
Shepherd	Jenny N^s.	James B.	Eve	Ben.	Mary
Bartlet	Jenny L.	Davy B.	Lucy	John B.	Virginia.
Lewis B^s.	Indridge	Moses B.	Scilla.	Abram j^r.	Esther.
Thrimston	Doll	Solomon.	×Billy B.	Dick N^s.	Rachael
	Amy.	×Moses smith.	×Billy Mos^s.	×Barnaby	Nancy
11. in all.		×Beverly	×Johnny	×Nace	Maria
		×Wormly	×Lovilo	×James L.	Lilly
		×Robert.	×Peter.	×Sanco	Sucky
			Joe.	×Davy j^r.	×Evelina
		19. in all		×Lewis	×Isabel
				×Ned.	×Aggey
				×Gill	×Nanny
				Ned j^r.	
				×Israel	
				Isaiah	
				Wash^n.	30. in all.

Jerry. Jenny. Randal. Critty. Davy. Moses. Ned. Peter. Jupiter. Scon. } were added.

The corn at Tufton being now (June 29. 15) entirely out, I give an order on the mill as follows.

			D	
for bread, ~~1. bu. peck~~, 8 bushels midlings	@ .50	=	4.	a week
8. horses @ 1½ gall. a day. 14 bush. Shipstuff	@ .20	=	2.80	
for the hogs @ bush. add^l. Bran	@ .10	=	1.	
			7.80	a week

Tufton,

			D	D
8. bush. a week for bread for 14. weeks to Sep. 30	is 112. midlings @ .50	=	56.	
1½ gall. a day for 8. horses is 1½ bush. a day to d^o.	140. shipstuff @ .20	=	28.	
3. bush. a day for hogs . . .	300. bran @ .10	=	30	114
Lego.				
1½ gall a day for 6. horses & ½ gal. for 2 mules to Oct. 8	100. shipstuff . . .		20	
1. bush. bran for hogs, a day to d^o.	100. bran		10	30
				144. D

Corn bought for 1815		D
T. J. Randolph	49. B. @ 15/	122.5
C. L. Bankhead	13. d^o.	32.5
Drury Wood	28 . 18/	84.
C. L. Bankhead	37. wheat 15/	92.5
Shadwell mills	400. midd^s. 15/	200.

Oats.	b	D
Drury Wood	180. 2/	60.
David Carr	105. 2/3	39.37
Th. J. Randolph	125 2/	41.67
		141.04
Ship stuff.		
Shad. mills.	240. b @ .20	48.
bran d^o.	400. b @ .10	40.
		229

D
587.75
229.04
816.79

NOTES to Page 149: Wheat harvest in1815 and slave workers.

1815. Dec.	wool	shirts	socks	blankets	beds
Abram	5½	7			
Doll	5	7			
Abram j"	5½	7		1	
Aggy 98. 8	5¼	6⅔			
Bagwell	6	10			
Minerva	5	7		1	
Willis 6	3½	4			
Archy 8	2¾	3⅓			
Jordan 11	2	2⅓			
Barnaby	5½	7			
Bartlet	5½	7		1	
Ben	5½	7			
Betty Brown	5	7			1
Robert 99	5	6⅓			
Mary 01	4½	5⅔			
Beverly	5½	7		1	
Billy Bedf 99	5	6⅓			
Burwell					
Caesar	5½	7			
Charles	5½	7			
Polly 10	2¼	2⅔			
Critta	5	7		1	1
Davy	5½	7			
Isabel	5	7			
Davy j"	5½	7			
Fanny	5	7		1	1
Ellen 9	2½	3			
Jenny 11	2	2⅓			
Moses 14	1¼	1⅓			
Davy B.	5½	7			
Dick B.	5½	7			
Dick Ned	5½	7			
Dolly	5	7		1	
Edwin	5½	7			
Edy	5	7			1
James 5	3½	4⅓			
36	[illegible]	[illegible]		[illegible]	

	wool	shirts	socks	blankets	beds
Maria 7	3	3⅔			
Patsy 10	2¼	2⅔			
Betsy 12	1¾	2			
Peter 15					
Esther	5	7		1	1
Lindsay 13	1½	1⅓			
Eve	5	7			
Joshua 6	3¼	4			
Burwell 9	2½	3			
Evelina	5	7			
Gill	5½	7		1	
Indridge	5	7			
Isaac	5½	7		1	
Israel 0	4¾	6			
James foreman	5½	7			
Cretia	5	7			1
John 0	4¾	6			
Randal 2	4¼	5⅓			
Henry 5	3½	4⅓		} 1	
Milly 7	3	3⅔			
Lilburne 9	2½	3			
Matilda 11	2	2⅓			
James Band 15					
James Bedf	5½	7			
Rachael	5	7		1	
Joe 1	4½	5⅔			
Lewis 5	3¼	4⅓			
Gloster 7	3	3⅔			
Washington 10	2¼	2⅔			
Edmund 13 (Lindsay Sub…)	1½	1⅓			
James Lewis	5½	7			
James Ned	5½	7			
Jerry	5½	7			
Isaiah 0	4¾	6			
Jerry 2	4¼	5⅓			
Jupiter 4	3¾	4⅔			
36	135	172¾		5	2

NOTES to Page 150: Slave list 1815 Dec.

	woolen	shirts	socks	blankets	beds
Joe	5½	7		1	
John B.	5½	7			
Virginia	5	7		1	
Robert 11	2	2⅔			
Amanda 15					
John gardener	5½	7			
Amy	5	7		1	
John Hemings	5½	7			
Lewis	5½	7			
Jenny	5	7		1	
Isabel	4¾	6			
Lilly	5	7		1	
Stannard 9	2½	3			
Lucy 11	2	2⅓			
~~[illegible]~~ 0	4½	5⅔			
Lucy	5	7			
Robin 5	3½	4⅓			
Sandy 7	3	3⅔			
Molly 14	1¼	1⅓			
Maria (Malinda July 16)	5	7			
Marshal 14 ([illegible] Apr 15.15)	1¼	1⅓			
Mary. Bagw's.	5	7			
Washington 5	3½	4⅓			
Moses. smith	5½	7			
Mary	5	7		1	1
William 1	4½	5⅔		] 1	
Davy 3	4	5			
Celia 6	3¼	4			
Tucker 10	2½	2⅔			
Zachariah 12	1¾	2			
Patsy 15					
Moses. Bedf.	5½	7			
Nace	5½	7		1	
Nance	5	7			1
Nancy	5	7		1	
Nanny. Bagd's 0	4⅔	6			
36	142⅔	186		9	1

	woolen	shirts	socks	blankets	beds
Ned	5½	7			
Jenny	5	7			
Moses 3	4	5			
Sucky 6	3¼	4			
Ned jr.	5½	7			
Peter Hem.	5½	7			
Philip	5½	7		1	
Rachael	5	7			
Eliza 5	3½	4⅓			
Ellen 8	2¾	3⅓			
Sally	5	7			1
Harriet 1	4½	5⅔		1	
Madison 5	3½	4⅓		] 1	
Eston 8	2¾	3⅓			
Sanco	5½	7		1	
Scilla	5	7			
Jamey 11	2	2⅓			
Shepherd (Miles July 16)	5½	7		1	
Solomon	5½	7			
Sucky	5	7			
Thenia	5	7		1	
Thrimston	4¾	6			
Wormly	5½	7			
Ursula	5	7		1	
Joe 5	3½	4⅓		] 1	
Anne 7	3	3⅔			
Dolly 9	2½	3			
Cornelius 11	2	2⅓			
Thomas 13	1½	1⅔			
29. Louisa Jan. 21.16					
Lewis. Bacon's	5½	7		1	
Peter	5½	7		1	
	133⅓	172⅔		10	7
	162¼	212⅔		8	4
	135	172⅔		5	2
	142⅔	186		9	1
	573½	743⅓		32	8

NOTES to Page 151: Continuation of Slave list

Monticello		Tufton		Lego		Tradesmen		Factory	
James	Doll	Bagwell	Minerva	Charles	Rachael B.	John Hem.	Abram	Cretia	spin cotton
Bartlet	Isabel	John B.	Mary	James B.	Eve	Lewis	Barnaby	Harriet	wool
Shepherd	Jenny N's	Dick B.	Virginia	Davy B.	Lucy	Billy B.	Nace	Aggy	hemp
Davy jr.	Jenny L's	Dick Ned	Esther	Moses B.	Scilla	Lovilo	Beverly	Nanny	
Gill	Amy	Ben	Rachael	Solomon	Evelina			Isabel	
Robert	Indridge	Abram jr.	Nancy			Davy	Joe	Johnny	carders
Lewis	Ursula	Philip	Maria			Sanco	Moses	Randal	
Peter		Ned jr.	Lilly			James L.	John	Isaiah	
Isaac			Sucky			Thrimston	Wormly	Israel	
						James	Ned	Dolly	weavers
						Israel		Mary	
Billy Mos. 01.		Jerry jr. 02.		Joe. 01.				Eliza	quilter
								Kitty	

we require annually 600. yds of woollen & cotton. viz. 300. wool + 150 cotton
800. yds of linen. viz. 400. hemp.
300 wool may be spun by 1. spinner in a year.
150. cotton by 1. spinner in 3. months. remain 9. months for fine cotton.
400. hemp. by 3. spinners in 26. weeks. remains half the year.
300. wool } should employ 4. carders but 6. months. remains ½ time for interruption.
150 cotton }
1400. yds of cloth @ 60. yds a week would employ 2. weavers 6. mo. the rest for fine work

	1816	17	18	19	20	21	22
Tufton							
Meadowfield	wh.	cl.	cl	cl.	wh.	corn	p.o
Poggio	p.o.	wh.	cl	wh	corn	p.o	wh.
Barn	*	cl	wh	corn	p.o	wh.	cl
Indian	*	wh	corn	p.o	wh.	cl	cl
Morgan	wh.	corn	p.o.	wh.	cl	cl	wh.
Milton	corn	p.o	wh	cl	cl.	wh	corn
Lego							
Mountain	p.o	wh	cl.	cl	wh.	corn	p.o.
Culpeper	wh.	cl.	cl.	wh.	corn	p.o	wh.
△	cl	cl	wh.	corn	p.o.	wh.	cl
Oblong	cl	wh	corn	p.o.	wh.	cl	cl
Barn	corn	p.o	p.o	wh.	cl	cl	wh.
Hickman	wh.	corn	wh	cl	cl	wh	corn
Monticello							
Ragged	p.o.	corn	p.o	wh	cl	cl	wh.
Meadow	wh.	p.o.	wh.	cl	cl	wh	corn
Cooper's	corn	wh	cl.	cl	wh.	corn	p.o.
Knob.	wh.	cl.	cl.	wh	corn	p.o.	wh.
North	cl.	cl.	wh.	corn	p.o.	wh.	cl.
Belfield	cl.	wh	corn	p.o.	wh.	cl	cl.

	1816	17	18	19	20	21	22
Poplar Forest							
Tomahawk	wh.	cl	cl.	wh.	corn	p.o.	wh.
Fork	cl	cl.	wh.	corn	p.o.	wh.	cl
Ridge	clov.	wh.	corn	p.o.	wh.	cl	cl
Belted	corn	p.o.	p.o.	wh.	cl	cl	wh.
Early's	wh.	corn	wh.	cl	cl	wh	corn
McDaniel's	p.o.	wh.	cl	cl	wh.	corn	p.o.
Bear creek							
Holloway.	corn	p.o.	p.o.	wh.	cl.	cl	wh.
Halbard.	wh.	corn	wh.	cl.	cl	wh.	corn
△	p.o.	wh.	cl.	cl	wh	corn	p.o.
Upper	wh.	cl.	cl.	wh.	corn	p.o.	wh.
Middle	cl.	cl.	wh.	corn	p.o.	wh.	cl.
Lower	cl.	wh.	corn	p.o.	wh.	cl.	cl.

carding, spinning, weaving per day

	hours	spind.	spin lb	weave yds	
Jan.	9.	10.oz.	1 ¼	3 ¾	Dec.
Feb	10.	12.	1 ½	4 ½	Nov
Mar.	11.	14.	1 ¾	5 ¼	Oct
Apr.	12.	16.	2.	6	Sep.
May	13.	18.	2 ¼	6 ¾	Aug.
June	14	20	2 ½	7 ½	July.

NOTES to Page 152: Slaves and wool 1816-1822

Crop of 1816.		Tufton	Lego	Mont°.	Sown [illegible]
wheat made	- -	998.	713½		
rye	- -	278			
oats					
tob°					
for 1817 wheat sown		248	130½		
rye					
oats					
wheat deliv^d at mill		709–32	583		

NOTES to Page 153: Crop of 1816

1816	Woollen 1816	due 15	Shirting 1816	due 15	[illegible]	[illegible]	[illegible]	[illegible]
Abram	5½		7	7	1			1
Doll	5		7	7	1	1		
Abram jr. ✓	5½		7	3½				
Aggy. Ned's	5		7	6⅓				
Bagwell ✓	7		10½	7				1
Minerva	5		7	3½	-			1
Willis 6	3½		4⅓	4				
Archy 8	3		3⅔	3⅓				
Jordan 11	2¼		2⅔	2⅓				
Barnaby	5½		7	...				1
Bartlet	5½		7	3½				
Ben ✓	5½		7	3½	1			1
Betty Brown	5		7	7	1			
Beverly	5½		7	3½				
Billy B.	5½		7	3⅓	1			1
Burwell								
Caesar	5½		7	3½				1
Charles ✓	5½		7	3½				1
Polly 10	2½		3	2⅔				
Critta								
Davy	5½		7	7	-	-	-	1
Isabel	5		7	7	1	1		1
Davy jr.	5½		7	3½				
Fanny								
Ellen 9								
Jonny 11					1			
Davy B.	5½		7	3½	-	-	-	1
Dick B. ✓	5½		7	3½				
Dick Ned's ✓	5½		7	3½				
Dolly	5		7	7				
Edwin	5½		7	3½	-	-	-	1
Eve ✓	5½		7	3½	1	1		
Joshua 6	3½		4⅓	4				
Burwell 9	2¾		3⅓	3				
Evelina ✓	5		7	3½	1			
Gill			7	3½				
Esther	5		7	3½		-	-	1
Lindsay 15	1¾		2	1⅓				
38	154¼		209	136	9	3		13

	Woollen 1816	due 15	Shirting 1816	due 15	[illegible]	[illegible]	[illegible]	[illegible]
Isaac	5½		7	3½	-	-	-	1
Sucky	5		7	3½	1			
Israel			8½	...	1			
James forem.	5½		7	3½				
Cretia	5		7	7				
Johnny 0 ✓	5		6⅓	3	-	-	-	1
Randal 2 ✓	4½		5⅔	2½				
Henry 5	3¾		4⅔	4⅓				
Milly	3½		4	3⅔				
Lilburn	2¾		3⅓	3				
Matilda	2¼		2⅔	2⅓	1			
Bond	1¼		1⅓	...				
James B. ✓	5½		7	3½	1			
Rachael ✓	5½		7	3½				
Joe 1 ✓	4¾		6	5⅔				
Lewis 3	3¾		4⅔	4⅓				
Gloster 7	3¼		4	3⅔				
Washingt. 10	2½		3	2⅔				
Edmund 13	1¾		2	1⅔				
Lindsay 16								
James L.	5½		7	3½	1	-	-	1
James H.	5½		7	3½	1	-	-	1
Jerry ✓	5½		7	3½	1	-	-	1
Isabel	5		7	6	1			
Isaiah 0 ✓	5		6⅓	3	1			
Jerry 2 ✓	4¼		5⅔	2½	1			
Jupiter 4	4		5	2⅓				
Joe	5½		7	3½	-	-	-	1
Edy								
James 2								
Maria 7								
Patsy 10								
Betsy 12								
Peter 15								
John B. ✓	5½		7	3½	-	-	-	1
Virginia	5		7	3½	-	-	-	1
Robert 11	2¼		2⅔	2⅓				
Amanda 15	1¼		1⅓	...				
38	125		167⅔	98½	[illegible]	0		8

NOTES to Page 154: Slaves 1815 and 1816

	Woollen 1816	due 15	Shirting 1816	due 15	[illegible]	[illegible]	[illegible]	[illegible]
Johnfoord	5½	......	7	3½	1	-	-	1
Amy	5	......	7	7				
John Hem.	5½	......	7	3½	1	-	-	1
Louis	5½	......	7	......				1
Jenny	5	......	7	3½				
Lilly	5	......	7	3½	-	1	-	1
Stannard 9	2¾	......	3⅓	3	}1	}1		
Lucy 11	2¼	......	2⅔	2⅔				
Lucy	5	......	7	3½	1	1		
Robin 5	3¾	......	4⅔	4⅓				
Sandy 7	3¼	......	4	3⅔				
Molly 14	1½	......	1⅔	1⅓				
Melinda 16	......	......	......	......				
Maria	5	......	7	3½	1	1	-	1
Marshal 14	1½	......	1⅔	1⅓				
Martin 16		......	......	......				
Mary Bag.	5	......	7	3½	1	1	-	1
Washingtn 5	3¾	......	4⅔	4⅓				
Mary Bet. 1	4¾	......	6	5⅔				
Milly, Sandy Moses smith	5½	......	7	3½	-	-	-	1
Mary	......	......	......	......				
William 1	4¾	......	6	5⅔				
Davy 3	4¼	......	5⅓					
Caelia 6	......	......	......	......	}1			
Tucker 10	......	......	......	......				
Zacharia 12	......	......	......	......				
Patsy 10	......	......	......	......				
Moses B.	5½	......	7	3½	1			
Nace	5½	......	7	......				
Nance	5	......	7	7	1			
Nancy	5	......	7	3½	.	.	.	1
Nanny Dy. 0	5	......	6⅓	6	1			
Ned	5½	......	7	3½	.	.	.	1
Fanny	5	......	7	7	.	.	.	1
Moses 3	4¼	......	5⅓	5	}1			
Sucky 6	3½	......	4⅓	4				
Ned jun.	5½	......	7	3½				
Peter Hem.	5½	......	7	3½	1			
38	139¾		182	113	12	4		10

	Woollen 1816	due 15	Shirting 1816	due 15	[illegible]	[illegible]	[illegible]	[illegible]
Philip ✓	5½	......	7	3½				
Rachael	5	......	7	7	.	1		
Eliza 5	3½	......	4⅔	4⅓	}1			
Ellen 8	3	......	3⅔	3⅓				
Robert	5½	......	7	3	1	-	-	1
Sally	......	......	......	......				
Harriet 1	4¾	......	6	......				
Madison 4	......	......	......	......				
Eston 8	......	......	......	......				
Sancho ✓	5½	......	7	3½				
Scilla	5	......	7	3½				
Jamy 11	2¼	2	2⅔	2⅓				
Miles 16	......	......	......	......				
Shepherd	5½	......	7	3½				
Indridge	5	......	7	3½	1	-	-	1
Solomon	5½	......	7	3½	1			
Thenia	......	......	......	......				
Thruston ✓	5½	......	7	3	1	-	-	1
Wormly	5½	......	7	3½	-	-	-	1
Ursula	5	......	7	7				
Joe 5	3¾	......	4⅔	4⅓				
Anne 7	3½	......	4	3⅔				
Dolly 9	2¾	......	3⅓	3	}1			
Cornelius 11	2¼	......	2⅔	2⅓				
Thomas 13	1¾	......	2	1⅔				
Louisa 16	......	......	......	......				
26	86		110⅔	69½	6	1		4
Woollen	154¼	shirting 1816		209	9	3		13
~~Shirting~~	125			167⅔	10	0		8
	139¾			182	12	4		10
	86			110⅔	6	1		4
	505			669⅓	37	8		35
			1817	136				
				98½				
				113				
				69½				
				417				

NOTES to Page 155: Slaves list continued read list 1817 Monticello

Bread list for 1817.

Monticello

Betty Brown.
Mary.
Billy B.
Burwell
Caesar.
Critta
Davy junr.
Fanny.
Ellen
Jenny.
Ned
Gill
Israel
Dolly
Joe
Edy
~~James~~
Maria
Patsy
Betsy
Peter.
John Hemings
John gardener.
Lewis.
Moses
Mary
William.
Davy
Caelia
Tucker
Zacharia
Patsy

Nance
Peter Hemings
Sally
Beverly
Harriet
Madison
Eston.
Wormly
Ursula & Louisa
Joe
Anne
Dolly
Cornelius
Thomas.

the farm.

Abram.
Doll.
Barnaby
Stannard
Davy.
Isabel
Thrimston.
Polly. Charles's.
Isaac.
James
Critta
Johnny.
Randal
Henry
Milly
Lilburne
Matilda.
Band
James Lewis's.
James. Ned's
Jerry
Isabel
Jupiter.
Amy.
Jenny. L's
Jenny. Ned's
Moses
Sucky
Nace.
Sanco.
Shepherd
Indridge
Sally. mrs Marks's
Fernit. 6.
Nancy 9.
Charlotte 15
35.

Tufton

Abram junr.
Bagwell
Minerva
Willis
Archy
Jordan
Ben
Lilly
Lucy
Dick B.
Dick. Ned's
Esther
Lindsay
Sucky
Isaiah
Jerry. junr.
John B.
Virginia
Robert
Amanda.
Maria & Martin
Marshal.
Mary. Bagwell's
Washington.
Nancy
Ned junr.
Philip
Rachael
Eliza
Ellen.
30.

Lego

Bartlet
Charles
[illegible]
Davy B.
Eve.
Joshua
Burwell
Evelina.
James B.
Rachael & Lindsay
Joe
Lania.
Gloster
Washington
Edmund
Lucy & Melinda
Robin
Sandy
Molly
Milly & ~~[illegible]~~
Sandy.
Moses. B.
Nanny Bagw's.
Robert
Scilla & Miles
Jamy.
Solomon.
29.

a woman suckling a child has 1½ peck
a man having neither wife nor mother 1½
all others a peck.

NOTES to Page 156: Slaves list continued read list 1817 Monticello

1817. Dec. & Jan. 1818 - hogs killed

Monticello.

210
209 828
133
125.
133
140
185
133
129
148
112
153
175
191
140
187
150
135
103
128
143
133
149
118
125
100
170
102
123
175
110
113
158
131
130
105
146
97
101
170
41 127
5823
600. Pours
5223

220.
133
167
188
167
185
172
175
135
156
133
171
91
67
84
109
117
104
118
147
168
132
169
143
153
123
108
183
28=4040
41=5823
69/ 9863/143

Tufton.

138
132
136
142
98
116
94
78
106
60
108
60
78
104
118
98
114
92
60
82
110
59
80
86
60
25/2409(96

Lego.

106
114
108
124
152
120
80
132
60
90
102
11/1188(108

Bedford.

℔ ℔
16. hogs = 2000 or 125 average

9263
2409
1188
2000
14860

NOTES to Page 157: 1817 Dec. & Jan. 1818 hogs killed

1817.	woollen	shirting	blankets	beds	hats
Abram	5½	7			
Doll	5	7			1
Abram jr.	5½	7			1
Bagwell	7	10½	1		
Minerva	5	7		1	
Willis 6	3¾	4⅔			
Archy 8	3¼	4	} 1		
Jordan 11	2½	3			
Barnaby	5½	7	1		
Milly	5	7			
Sandy 13	2	2⅓			
Bartlet	5½	7			1
Ben	5½	7			
Lilly	5	7			
Stannard 9	3	3⅓			
Lucy 11	2½	3			
Betty Brown	5	7			
Beverly	5½	7			1
Billy B.	5½	7			
Burwell	- -	- -	1		
Caesar	5½	7	1		
Charles	5½	7	1		
Polly 10	2¾	3⅓			
Critta					
Davy	5½	7	1		
Isabel	5	7			1
Davy jr.	5½	7	1		
Fanny					
Ellen 9					
Jenny 11					
Melinda 17					
Davy B.	5½	7	1		
Dick B.	5½	7	1		1
Dick Ned's	5½	7	1		1
Dolly	5	7			
Eve	5½	7			1
Joshua 6	3¾	4⅔	} 1		
Burwell 9	3	3⅓			
Evelina	5	7			1

	woollen	shirting	blankets	beds	hats
Gill	- -	7			
Esther	5	7			
Lindsay 13	2	2⅓			
Isaac	5½	7			
Sucky	5	7			1
Israel		7			
James forem.	5½	7	1		
Cretia	5	7	1		
Johnny 0.	5¼	6⅔	1		
Randal 2.	4¾	6	1		
Henry 5.	4	5			
Milly 7	3½	4⅓			
Lilburn 9.	3	3⅔			
Matilda 11.	2½	3			
Band 15	1½	1⅔			
James B.	5½	7			1
Rachael	5½	7		1	1
Joe 1	5	6⅓	} 1		1
Lania 5	4	5			
Gloster 7	3½	4⅓	} 1		
Washington 10	2¾	3⅓			
Edmund 13	2	2⅓			
Lindsay 16	1¼	1⅓			
James Lewis	5½	7			
James Ned's	5½	7			
Jerry	5½	7			
Isabel	5	7		1	1
Isaiah 0.	5¼	6⅔			1
Jerry 2.	4¾	6			
Jupiter 4.	4¼	5⅓			
Joe	5½	7			
Edy		- -	1		
Maria 7					
Patsy 10					
Betsy 12					
Peter 15					
John B.	5½	7	1		
Virginia	5	7		1	
Robert 11	2½	3			
Amanda 15	1½	1⅔			

NOTES to Page 158: 1817 slave list

	age	woollen	shirting	blankets	beds	hats
Jim gardener		5½	7			
Amy		5	7		1	1
John Hemings		5½	7			
Lewis.		5½	7	1		
Jenny		5	7		1	1
Lucy		5	7			1
Robin	5	4	5	1		
Sandy	7.	3½	4⅓			
Molly	14	1¾	2			
Melinda	16	1¼	1⅓			
Maria		5	7.			
Marshal	14	1¾	2.			
Martin	16	1¼	1⅓			
Mary Bagwell		5	7.			
Washington	5.	4.	5.			
Mary. Bett.	1	5	6⅓	1		
Moses. smith.		5½	7	1		
Mary		- -	- -	1		
William	1	5	6⅓			1
Davy	3	4½	5⅔			
Caelia	6	3¾	4⅔			
Tucker	10					
Zacharia	12.					
Patsy	15					
Fossett	17					
Moses. B.		5½	7			1
Nace		5½	7			1
Nance		5	7			1
Nancy		5	7.			
Nanny Bagg.	0.	5	7.			1
Ned		5½	7.	1		
Jenny		5	7.	1	1	
Moses	3	4½	5⅔			
Sucky	6	3¾	4⅔			
Ned jr		5½	7	1		1
Peter Hem.		5½	7			
Philip		5½	7			1
Rachael		5½	7	1		1
Eliza	6	4	5			
Ellen	8	3¼	4			

	age	woollen	shirting	blankets	beds	hats
Robert		5½	7			
Sally Hem.				1		
Harriet	1	5	6⅓			
Madison	9					
Eston	8					
Sancho.		5½	7			1
Scilla		5	7	1	1	1
Jamy	11.	2½	3			
Miles	16.	1¼	1⅓			
Shepherd		5½	7			1
Indridge		5	7		1	
Solomon		5½	7			1
Thrimston		5½	7			
Wormly		5½	7	1		
Ursula		5	7		1	1
Joe	5	4.	5			
Anne	7	3½	4⅓			
Dolly	9	3	3⅔			
Cornelius	11	2½	3			
Thomas	13	2	2⅓			
Louisa.	16	1¼	1⅓			
140.		523½	690⅓	32	10.	

NOTES to Page 159: 1817 slave list continued, Sally has three children

negroes leased to Th. J. Randolph

Bagwell
Minerva
Willis 06.
Archy 18.
Jordan 11.
Ben
Lilly
Lucy 11
~~[illegible]~~
Dick. B.
Dick. Ned's
James. Ned's
Abram
Esther
Lindsay. 13.
Sucky
Isaiah 1800
Jerry jr. 02.
John. B.
Virginia
Robert 11.
Amanda 15.
Maria
Marshal 14
Martin 16
Mary. Bag's
Washington 05
Nancy
Ned jr.
Philip
Rachael
Elina 05.
Ellen 08.

Bartlet
Charles
Davy B.
Eve
Joshua 06
Burwell 09.
Evelina
James B.
Rachael
Joe 01.
Lania 05.
Gloster 07.
Washington 10.
Edmund 13.
Lindsay 16.
* ~~Lucy~~ Sally 92
Robin Cary Amm[illegible]
Sandy James 16
Molly Lorenzo 18
Melin[illegible] Beck 97
~~[illegible]~~
~~Milly~~ d. 19.
Sandy 13.
Moses. B.
Nanny. Bag's
~~Robert~~
Silla
Jamy 11
Miles 16
Solomon
29 + 31 = 60

Negroes retained

~~Abram~~
Doll 57
Barnaby 83.
Stannard 09
Betty Brown
Beverly
Burwell
Caesar
Polly. Charles's 10.
Critta
Davy
~~Isabel~~ d. 19.
Davy jr.
Fanny
Ellen 9.
Jenny 11.
Melinda 17.
Dolly
Gill
Isaac
Israel 00.
James
Cretia
~~Johnny~~ 0.
Randal 2.
Henry 5.
Milly 7
Lilburn 9.
Matilda 11.
Band 15
30.

James L's
James N's
Jerry
Isabel
Jupiter 04.
Joe
Edy
Maria 7.
Patsy 10.
Betsy 12.
Peter 15.
John. gardener
Amy
John Heming
Lewis
Jenny
Mary Bet's 1
~~Moses smith~~
Mary
William 1.
Davy 3.
Caelia 6.
Tucker 10.
Zachariah 12
Patsy 15.
Fossett 17.
Nace
Nance
28

Ned
Jenny
Moses 3.
Sucky 6
Peter Hemings
Phill. Nanny's
Sally Hemings
Harriet 1.
Madison 5.
Eston 8.
Sancho
Shepherd
Indridge
Thrimston
Wormly
Ursula
Joe 5
Anne 7
Dolly 9
Cornelius 11
Thomas 13
Louisa 16

given to Th. J. Randolph
1812. Lewis Sally
Thruston Bec
Aggy
1816 Edwin Maria
James
1819. Moses
Johnny

30 + 28 + 22 = 80

NOTES to Page 160: Negroes leased to Tho. Randolph - Negroes Retained

1718
Summer clothes

Abram
Doll h
Barnaby
Beverly h
Caesar
Davy
Isabel
Davy j
Isaac
James
Johnny
Randal
Henry
James L.
James N.
Jerry
Jupiter
Joe
John gardener
Amy h
John Hern
Lewis
Jenny h
Moses
William h
Davy
Nace h
Ned
Jenny
Moses h
Phill
Madison h *
Sancho h
Shepherd h
Indridge
Thrimston
Wormley
Ursula h
Joe
Mary Bacon

Note 1.lb spun cotton, 5 yds to the lb will make 5. yds tble woollen cloth
or 1 1/3 lb raw cotton
and 1.lb spun cotton will make 5. yds of shirting mixed with hemp.
1818. Oct. 80 people little & big require 300 yds outer clothing, require 60 lb spun cotton
400. inner do. require 80
140 lb

Pork. Dec. 1818.

	hogs		lb	D	
Monticello.					
sold to Craven Peyton	11	weighing	1283	@ 8.50 =	109.05½
Larkin Powers	4		618		52.53
Jas. Dinsmore	4		500		42.50
Saml. O. Minor	10		1067		90.69½
Mary Bacon	2		250 = 3718		21.25
					316.03
furnished E. Bacon	5		600		
Young Carden	2.		255	855	
the House	46			7292	
	84 x 141½ =			11865	

from Th. J. R. sold him 450 . . . 38.25
furnished him 400
to the house 35. hogs 3865. averag 102 lb
3965

hogs from Bedford Jan. 1809.

	Tomahawk		Bearcreek		Total	
Overseer	2		2		4	
people	10+9		10		20+9	
my use there	6		6		12	
Monticello	25	2562	27	2747	52	
	43+9	3762+	45	4584	88+9	8346

Note that on the 9th. of April 1820. I gave to Th. J. Randolph Lucy and her children, Robin, Sandy, Molly, Melinda, and Nicholas in exchange for Sally & her 3. children Cary-anne, Jennet, and Lorenzo and Beck and her two children Fleming and Lilburne

NOTES to Page 161: 17-18 Summer clothes for slaves spun cotton

1818.—19	woolen	shirting	blankets	beds	[illegible]	Summer clothes
Barnaby	5½	7			1	2½ r
Stannard 9.	3¼	4				
Betty Brown	5	7		1		3. o
Beverly	5½	7	1.			2½ r.
Burwell						
Caesar	5½	7				2½ r.
Polly. Charles 10	3	3⅔				
Critta.	5	7	1.	1.		3. o
Davy senr.	5½	7			1	2½ r
Davy junr.	5½	7			1	2½ r
Fanny.	5.	7	1.	1.		3. o
Ellen 9	3¼	4				
Jenny 11	2¾	3⅓				
Melinda 17	1½	1⅓				
Doll	5.	7				3. r
Dolly	5.	7.	1			3. o
Gill.	4	7	1			
Isaac	5½	7	1.		1	2½ r
Israel		7				
James	5½	7			1	2½ r
Critta	5.	7		1.		3. o
~~Johnny~~	5½	7				
Randal 2	5	6⅓			1	2½ r
Henry 5	4½	5⅓	1.		1	2½ r
Milly 7	3¾	4⅔				3 r
Lilburn 9	3¼	4				
Matilda 11	2¾	3⅓				
Bagwell 15 / Lovila 18	1¾	2				
James L's	5½	7			1	2½ r
James N's	5½	7			1	2½ r
Jerry	5½	7			1	2½ r
Isabel	5.	7			1	3 r
Jupiter 4.	4½	5⅓			1	2½ r
Joe.	5½	7	1		1	2½ o
Edy	5	7		1.		3. o
Maria 7	3¾	4⅔	1			3 r
Patsy 10	3	3⅔				
Betsy 12	2½	3.				
Peter 15	1¾	2				
John gardr.	5½	7			1	2½ o
Amy.	5	7	1			3. r.
John Hem.	5½	7			1	2½ o
Lewis	5½	7			1	2½ r.
Jenny.	5	7	1			3
44	182½	250	11			

	woolen	shirting	blankets	beds	[illegible]	summer clothes
Mary Beti	5	7				3. o
~~Moses~~	5½	7				
Mary	5.	7		1.		3. o
~~Bridget~~ 1.	5½	7	1.		1	2½ r
Davy 3	4¾	6	1.		1	2½ r
Caelia 6	4.	5.				3.
Tucker 10	3.	3⅔				
Zachariah 12	2½	3				
Patsy 15	1¾	2.				
Fossel 17	1¼	1⅓				
Nace	5½	7	1.			2½ r
Nance	5.	7.		1		3. o
Ned	5½	7			1	2½ o
Jenny	5.	7			1	3 r
Moses 3.	4¾	6.				2½ r
Sucky 6.	4	5.				3.
Peter Hem.	5½	7				2½ o.
Phill B. 1.	5½	7	1.?		1	2½ r
Sally Hem.	5.	7.		1.		3. o
Harriet	5.	7.	1.			3. o
Madison 5.	4½	5⅓	1			2½ o.
Eston 8.	3½	4⅓				2½ r
Sancho	5½	7	1.			2½ r
Shepherd	5½	7	1.			2½ r
Indridge	5.	7.			1	3 r
Thrimston	5½	7			1	2½ r
Wormly	5½	7			1	2½ o
Ursula	5.	7.	1.			3 r
Joe 5	4¼	5⅓	1		1	2½ r
Anne 7	3¾	4⅔				3.
Dolly 9.	3¼	4				
Cornelius 11	2¾	3⅓				
Thomas 13	2¼	2⅔				
Louisa 16	1½	1⅔				
Caroline 18						
35	146½	189⅓	10	8		
44	182½	250	11			
79	11¼	14⅔				
	340	453⅔				
Mrs. Marks's						
Sally	5	7				3 r
Ferril 10	2¾	3⅓				
Nancy 12	2¼	2⅔				
Charlotte 16	1¼	1⅓				
4	11¼					

NOTES to Page 162: Slave list for 1818

Estimate of corn from Jan. 1. 1819.

			Bar
for 90 persons from Jan. 1. to Nov. 1. 44. weeks @ 4½ Barrels a week			200.
9. breeding sows to May 1. 120. days @ 1. pint a day each		{	3½
62. shoats to July 10. 191. days @ ½ pint a day	28½		18½
26. pigs from weaning to July 10. suppose 160. days @ ½ pint a day			6½
2. beeves	231½		3
for the Stable to July 1. (deducting 1. month absence) 150. days @ 1¾ [salt] a day			52½
for the plantation horse & 6. mules to July 1. 180. days @ 1½ bush a day			54.
for 63. sheep to Mar. 15. 75. days @ ½ pint a day			7½
for 4. oxen to May 15. 135. days @ 6. gall. a day	134.		20
			365½

(margin: these are proper subjects of ... reduction)

corn on hand	65.	
expected from the mill in 44. weeks @ 2. B. a week	88	153
to be bought		212½

3. milch cows to be fed with bran, shipstuff &c.
the other cattle on stalks, tops, shucks, chaff, straw &c.

1819. Oct. 1. to July 7. 1820. Estimate in corn, but its equival. in offal to be used in all possible cases

	Bar
90 persons from Oct. 1. 19. to July 7. 20. 40 weeks @ 4½ B. a week	180
fattening hogs 70. @ 1½ B. each	105.
9. breeding sows @ 1. pint a day each from Dec. 1. to Mar. 10. 100. d.	3
60. shoats @ ½ p. a day 100. d	9½
pigs	5¼
6. beeves @ 2. g. a day Dec. 1. to Mar. 1. [killing off 1. a fortnight] say 60. d. on the whole	23
Stable @ 14. g. a day. Oct. 1. to July 1. [—mo. Bedfd] say 7. mo.	73½
1. plantn horse & 6. mules Oct. 1. to July 1. @ 1½ b. 270. d	81.
sheep. suppose 80. @ ½ pint each from Dec. 15. to Mar. 15. 90 d.	11
4 oxen. @ 6. g. a day. Dec. 1. to May 15. 165. d.	25.
1. milch cow at the stable @ 1. peck a day 165. d.	8¼
	520

the other cattle to live on stalks, tops, shucks, chaff, straw &c.

		B.		
Resources.	corn on hand	80.		
	from Thos. J. R.	200		
	mill @ 2. B. a week 40 weeks	80	360	360
*	offal of 350. B. flour @ 25. per B. 8750 lb		35	
	do. to be bot at the mill. suppose		65	100
				460
	corn or wheat to be bought or wheat			60 = 340. b.
				520

for every barrel of flour is allowed
2. b. bran. ½ b. shipstuff

NOTES to Page 163: Estimates of corn from Jan 1 1817

1819—20	woollen	shirting	blankets	beds	hats	summer clothes
Barnaby	5½	7.				
Stannardo	3¼	4				
Betty Brown	5	7	1			
Beverly	5½	7				
Burwell						
Caesar	5½	7.				
Polly. Chas. 10	3.	2⅔				
Critta	5	7				
Davy senr.	5½	7.				
Davy jr.	5½	7.				
Fanny	5	7				
Ellen 9	3¼	4.	} 1.			
Jenny 11	2¾	3⅓				
Melinda 17	1½	1⅓	} 1			
Indridge 19						
Doll	5	7.	1.	1		
Dolly	5.	7.				
Gill	5½	7				
Isaac	5½	7.				
Israel	5½	7.	1			
James	5½	7.				
Critta	5	7.		1		
Randolph 2	5.	6⅓				
Henry 5	4½	5⅓				
Milly 7	3¾	4⅔				
Lilburn 9	3¼	4.	} 1.			
Matilda 11	2¾	3⅓				
Band 15	1¾	2.				
Lovila 18	1.	1.				
Nancy 19						
James L's	5½	7.	1.			
James Ned's	5½	7.	1.			
Jerry	5½	7.	1.			
Isabel	5	7.	1.	1.		
Lyilon 4	4½	5⅔				
Joe	5½	7.				
Edy	5.	7.		1		
Maria 7	3¾	4⅔	} 1			
Patsy 10	3	3⅓				
Betsy 12	2½	3	} 1			
Peter 15	1¾	2				
Isabella 19	165¾	215	[illegible] 12			

	woollen	shirting	blankets	beds	hats	summer clothes
John gardener	5½	7.	1.			
Amy	5.	7.				
John Hem.	5½	7	1.			
Lewis	5½	7.				
Jenny	5	7				
Mary. Bet's	5.	7.				
Mary. Moses'	5.	7.		1.		
Davy	5½	7.				
Caelia 6	4	5	} 1.			
Tucker 10	3	3⅔				
Zachariah 12	2½	3				
Patsy 15	1¾	2.				
Forrest 17	1¼	1⅓				
Fontaine 19						
[illegible]	5½	7				
[illegible]	5.	7.	1.			
Ned	5½	7.				
Jenny	5	7				
Moses 3	4¾	6	1			
Sucky 6	4.	5				
Peter Hem.	5½	7.	1.			
Phill Bedfd.	5½	7.				
Sally Hem.	5.	7.				
Harriet	5	7.				
Madison 5	4½	5⅓				
Eston 8	3½	4⅓				
Sancho	5½	7.				
Shepherd	5½	7.				
Indridge	5	7	1.			
Thrimston	5½	7.	1.			
Wormley	5½	7.				
Ursula	5	7				
Joe 5	4¼	5⅓				
Anne 7	3¾	4⅔				
Dolly 9	3¼	4				
Cornelius 11	2¾	3⅓	} 1			
Thomas 13	2¼	2⅔				
Louisa 16	1½	1⅔				
Caroline 18	1.	1.				
Sally 37	5	7				
Ferrel 10	3.	3⅔				
Nancy 12	2½	3.				
Charlotte 16	1½	1⅔				
	170⅓	220⅔	9	5		
	165¾	215	12			
	336[illegible]	435⅔	21			

NOTES to Page 164: Slaves 1819-22

Rotation of blankets

1817.8.	1818.9.	1819.20.	Roll Beds 1817.8.
20 / 23	21 / 24	22 / 25	Amy.
Barnaby.	Stannard.	Betty Brown.	Jenny L's
Burwell	~~Bernaby~~	Ellen. / Jenny	Jenny N's
~~Caesar~~	Critta.	Melinda / Indridge	Indridge
Davy senr.	Fanny	Doll.	Ursula
Davy jr.	Dolly.	Israel	Sally H.
James	Gill.	Lilburn	
		Matilda	1818.9.
Cretia.	Isaac.	James L's	Betty Brown.
Jupiter.	~~Henry~~	~~James Hr~~	Critta
Edy / Isabella / William / ~~Lewis~~	Milly	Jerry / ~~Isabel~~	Fanny.
	Band	Maria	Nance.
Mary Bett's	Lovila	Patsy	Sally Hem.
Mary. Mose	Joe	Betsy / Peter	
Zachariah	Amy	John	
Patsy	Jenny L's	John Hem.	
Thomas	Davy. cooper.	Celia.	1819.20.
Louisa	Fossett	Tucker	Doll
Ned.	Fontaine	Nance.	Cretia.
Jenny N's	Nace	Moses.	Isabel.
~~Phill. P.~~ / Polly (Charles)	~~Harriet~~	Peter Hem.	Edy
Randal.	Madison	Indridge	Mary Mose.
Sally Hem.	Eston / Sanco.	Thrimston	
Sucky (Nance, Charlott)	Shepherd / Ursula / Sally H.	Dolly	
Wormly (Caroline, Esther)	Joe / Anne	Cornelius	

Nov. 16. rec'd linen 134. yds
70. lb. cotton yarn No. 5

	yds	cotton	wool
~~women~~ woollen	138	64 lb	128 lb
~~women~~	100		
38. children	100.	20	40
45. grown. shirt'	315	158	
38 young	120	24.	hemp 36
		266	36 / 168.

Outer clothing. Men. 137½ yds
Women 95 } 232½. if 180. yds are wove by Xmas we must get from the store 52½ yds
Children 105½ this may be all woven by Jan. 31.
338

Shirting. Men 175
Women 133 } 308. if 270. yds are woven by Jan. 31. we must get from the store 38
children 127⅔ this must be linen from the store 128
435⅔ 166

285½ yds of outer clothing @ 8. lb cotton to 30. yds will require 76 lb cotton yarn
270. yds of shirting @ 16. lb to 30. . . . . 144.
220. lb spun cotton No. 5.

NOTES to Page 165: Blankets, roll beds

Tomahawk 19	woolen	shirting	blankets	beds
Hanah	5	7		1
Billy 99	5 1/2	7		
Jamy 5	4 1/4	5 1/3		
Phill 8	3 1/2	4 1/3	1	
Edmund 9	3 1/4	4		
George Webb 12	2 1/2	3		
Lucinda	5	7		
Melinda 9	3 1/4	4		
Rebecca 12	2 1/2	3		
Nelly 16	1 1/2	1 2/3		
Sally Hana's	5	7		
Maria nanny's	5	7		
James Hub 18	1	1		
Nace	5 1/2	7	1	
Hanah Dinah's	5	7	1	
Dick 18	1 3/4	2		
Abby	5	7	1	1
Will	5 1/2	7	1	
Manuel	5 1/2	7		
Amy	5	7		
Anne 15	1 3/4	2		
Mehala 16	1 1/2	1 2/3		
Madison 18	1	1		
23	88 3/4	110	5	2

Tomahawk 19	woolen	shirting	blankets	beds
Edy	5	7		
Nancy 12	2 1/2	3		
Thurston 19	baby clothes			
Gawen	5 1/2	7		
Sal. Will's	5	7	1	1
Betty	5	7		
matilda 18	1	1		
Abby 4	4 1/2	5 2/3		
Edy 6	4	5	1	
Martin 9	3 1/4	4		
Moses 11	2 3/4	3 1/3		
Mary Ann 12	2 1/2	3		
Harriet 15	1 3/4	2	1	
Alfred Crasby	1	1		
Dick	5 1/2	7		
Dinah	5	7		
Lucy	5	7	1	
Jamy 2	5	6 1/3		
Billy 5	4 1/4	5 1/3		
Evans	5 1/2	7		
Prince	5 1/2	7	1	
Betty	5	7		
Hercules	5 1/2	7		
Jesse	5 1/2	7		
24	95 1/2	123 2/3	5	1

NOTES to Page 166: Slaves Woolen shirts blankets

Bear cr. 1819	woolen	shirting	blankets	beds
Jame Hubard	5½	7.		
Cate	5	7.		
Armstead.	5½	7		
Aggy. Dick's	5.	7.	1.	
Sally 12.	2½	3.		
Cate. Rachael's	5.	7.		
Maria. Cate's	5	7	- - -	1.
Johnny 4.	4½	5⅔		
Isaac. 9.	3¼	4.		
Nisy.	5.	7.	1	
James Heth^n 15	1¾	2.	1.	
Harry-anne 19	baby clothes			
Sally. Cate's	5.	7.	1.	
Billy 8.	3½	4⅓	1.	
Anderson 10	3.	3⅔		
Henry 12	2½	3.	1.	
Nancy. 18.	1	1		
Reuben	5½	7.		
Austin	5½	7.		
Flora	5.	7.	- - -	1.
Gawen 4.	4½	5⅔	1.	
Aleck 6	4.	5.		
Billy 8	3½	4⅓		
Willis Burwell 18	1¾	2.		
Francis 18	1	1		
25	93¾	121⅓	7.	2.

Bear cr. 1819	woolen	shirting	blankets	beds
Fanny.	5.	7.		
Rachael 7.	3¾	4⅔	1	
Rody 11.	2¾	3⅓		
Zachariah 13	2¼	2⅔		
Martha Ann 16	1½	1⅓		
Joe 6	4½	5.		
Shepherd 9	3¼	4.		
Cate. Suck's	5.	7.		
Davy 6	4.	5	1	
John 11	2¾	3⅓		
Solomon 14	2.	2⅓	1	
Elmsly 17	1¼	1⅓		
Daniel	5½	7		
Nanny.	5.	7.	- - -	1.
Milly 6	4.	5		
George Donny 8	3½	4⅓		
Janetta 12	2½	3.	1.	
Ellen. 14.	2.	2⅓		
Stephen	5½	7		
Cate. Betty's	5	7.		
Mary. Betty's	5.	7.	- - -	1
Gabriel 14	2.	2⅓		
22.	78.	99⅓	4	2.

wheat. eaten 558. bush.
sowed 324.

wool 16. men at 5½ yds 88) 210. dble cloth woollen — cotton 58 lb — wool 116 lb
26 women 5 130)
52 childn . . . . . 138. single . . . . . 28 — 56
shirt 42. grown . . . 294 147
92 children . . . 101 . . . . . 32 . . . . . hemp 48 lb
265 — 172 — 48

5. yds double cloth, wool & cotton, weigh 4. lb
30. yds require 8. lb cotton & 16. lb wool.
30. yds cotton shirting weigh 15. lb
30. yds cotton & hemp weigh 15. lb
the 30. yds require 6 lb cotton & 9 lb hemp.

NOTES to Page 167: Bear cv Woolen Shirting blankets beds

Distribution of blankets at Poplar Forest.

1819.

Jamy 5. } Phill 8. } Hanah's

Nisy.

James Washington 15 } Harry-Anne 19 }

Sal. Will's.

Abby 2. } Edy 6. }

Mary-Ann 12. } Harriet 15 } Alfred 18 }

Sal. Cate's.

Billy 8. } Anderson 10 }

Henry 12. } Nancy 18 }

Nace

Will.

Abby.

Gawen 6. } Aleck 6 } Flora's

Rachael 7. } Rody 11. } Fanny's

Aggy

Hanah. Dinah's

Lucy. Dinah's

Prince.

Davy 6. } John 11 } Solomon 14 } Elmsly 17 } Suck's (Cate's)

Janetta 12 } Ellen 14 } Nanny's

1820.

Jame Hubard.

Edmund 9 } George Welsh 12 } Hana's

Cate. Rachael's

Johnny 5 } Isaac 9 } Maria's

Lucinda. Hanah's

Reuben. Hanah's

Billy. Hanah's

Betty. Sal's

Martin 9. } Moses 11. } Sal's

~~[illegible]~~ } ~~[illegible]~~ } Francis 18 } Flora's

Zacharias 13 } Martha Ann 16 } Fanny's

~~[illegible]~~ Will's

Manuel.

Evans.

Jamy 2 } Billy 8 } Dinah's

Cate Suck's

Daniel. Suck's

Stephen. Suck's

Mary. Betty's

Hercules. Betty's

Nanny.

1821.

Cate.

Hanah.

Sally. Hannah's

Armstead.

Maria. Cate's

Melinda 9 } Rebecca 12 } Nelly 16 } Lucinda's

Gawen.

Austin

Flora. Will's

Fanny. Will's

Anne 15 } Michala 16 } Madison 18 } Amy's

Edy. Will's.

Nancy 12 } Thimston 19 }

Dick.

Dinah.

Betty

Cate. Betty's

Joe 6 } Shepherd 9 }

Jesse

Maria. Nanny's

Milly 6 } George Dennis 8 } Nanny's

	wool	blk
The Men require	88	112
Women	125	175
young under 17.	129	153⅔
	342	440⅔
on hand	200	100
to be bought	142	340

Distribution of beds at P. F.

1819	1820.	1821.
Hanah.	Sal. Cate's	Cate.
Abby.	Fanny	Lucinda
Maria. Cate's	Cate. Suck's	Edy.
Sal. Will's	Hanah Dinah's	Dinah.
Flora	Amy Will's	Betty
Nanny	Nisy.	Aggy
Mary Betty's		Maria Nanny's

Hogs. 1819. P. F.

People. 20.

Th. J. at P. F. 12.

Overseers &c. 8.

Monticello $\frac{35}{75}$

NOTES to Page 168: Distribution of blankets at Poplar Forest 1819 1820 1821

1822. Dec. 1825.	1823 Dec. 1826	1824. Dec. 1827
Celia	Barnaby	Stannard
Tucker	Burwell	Critty.
Nance	Davy sen[r]	Davy Moses'
Moses	Davy j[r]	Fanny
Pet. Hem	James	Gill
Indridge.	Cretia	Israel
Thrimston	Jupiter	Joe.
Dolly	Edy	Amy
Cornelius	Isabella	Nace
Thomas	William	Jenny
Betty Brown.	Mary Bet's	Madison
Ellen	Mary Moses'	Eston
Jenny	Zachariah	Shepherd.
Doll	Ned	Ursula.
Israel	Jenny	Anne
Lilburn	Suckey	Sally Marks.
Matilda	Polly	
James Carp[r]	Randal	
Jerry.	Sally Hem.	
Maria	Wormley	
Patsy	Thomas	
Betsy	Louisa	
Peter	Caroline	
John.	Critta	
John Hem.	Nancy	
	Charlotte	

NOTES to Page 169: Blankets 1822 Dec. 1825 1823 Dec. 1826 1824 Dec. 1827

NOTES to Page 170: Blank page retained in order to keep the left-right relationship of the book. Doodle

		woollen	shirting	
outer clothing.	24. Men.	132	168	made 115. yds dble cloth for outer clothing else.
	19. women	95	133	
	42. children	130½	160	
		357½	461.	

26. blankets
8. beds. = 54. yds

Estimate of corn from Jan. 21. 1821. — Bar.

				Bar.
86. persons @ 5. B. a week. 27. weeks to July 30.				135.
fattening hogs				3.50
9. breeding sows @ 1. pint a day each	to Mar. 10.	70. days		2.
44. shoats @ ½ pint a day		70. days		4.80
70. pigs @ ½ pint a day	to July 10.	190. days		36.
2. beeves 3. gall. a day	to Mar. 10.	70. days		20.
Stable 6. horses & a mule 14. gall. a day	to July 1.	150. days		52.50
Plantn 1. horse & 6. mules @ 1½ bush. a day	to July 1.	180. days		54.
93. sheep. @ ½ pint a day	to Mar. 15.	74. days		10.60
5. oxen @ 1. bushel a day	to May 15.	120. days		24.
				342.40

Resources.

Jan. 1. due of rent . . . . 170.

Mill [to Sep. 30. wd be 150. B. but] to July 1.

Offal of 350. B. flour. [for milch cows. 700. bush. bran. +] 175. b. shipstuff . . . 22.

60. do. of Monticello [120. b. bran +] 30. b. shipstuff . . . 6

250. b. oats rent 50

Bacon's	the House	
Barnaby	Betty Br.	Peter Hem.
Shammond	Mary	Phill B.
Davy senr.	Burwell	Sally Hem.
Doll	Critta	Beverly
Isaac	Davy jr.	Harriet
James	Fanny	Madison
Critta	Ellen	Eston
Hardy	Jenny	Thrimston
Milly	~~[illegible]~~	Wormly
Lilburne	Indridge	Ursula
Matilda	Dolly	Joe
Bard	Gill	Anne
Laila	Israel	Betty
Nancy	Joe	Cornelius
Samuel L.	Edy	Thomas
Jerry	Maria	Louisa
Isabel	Patsy	Caroline
Lapeter	Betsy	Critta
Amy	Peter	
Anne	Isabella	
Polly Chas.	John Hem.	
Jonny L.	Johnson	
Jenny	Lewis	
Moses	Mary Mo.	
Suckey	Davy	
Rae	Celia	
Shepherd	Tucker	
Frederick	Zachariah	
Sally Davy	Patsy	
Fernal	Russel	
Nancy	Fontaine	38 persons
Charlotte	Nance	29 p. House
3[illegible]	Ned	52 p. 13[illegible]

NOTES to Page 171: Outer clothing house slaves resources

1821. 2	woolen	shirting	blankets	beds	hats
Barnaby	5 1/2	7.			1
Stannard. 9	3 3/4	4 2/3	1		1
Betty Brown	5.	7.		1.	
Burwell					
Critta.	5.	7.	1.	1.	
Davy senr.	5 1/2	7.			
Davy j.	5 1/2	7.			1
Fanny	5.	7.	1.	1.	
Ellen 9	3 3/4	4 2/3			
Jenny 11	3 1/4	4			
Indridge 19	1 1/4	1 1/3			
Doll.	5.	7.			1
Dolly	5.	7.	1		1
Gill		7.	1.		
Isaac.	5 1/2	7.	1.		1
Israel		7			
James.	5 1/2	7.			1
Cretia.	5.	7.			1
Milly 7.	4 1/4	5 1/3	1		1
Lilburne 9	3 3/4	4 2/3			1
Matilda. 11	3 1/2	4			1
Band 15	2 1/4	2 2/3	1		
Louisa. 18.	1 1/2	1 2/3			
Nancy 19.	1 1/4	1 1/3			
James L.	5 1/2	7			1
Jerry	5 1/2	7			1
~~[illegible]~~ B. 22	5.	7			1.
Jupiter 4	5.	6 1/3			1
Amy. 20	1.	1.			
Joe.	5 1/2	7.	1.		1
Edy	5.	7.			
Maria 7.	4 1/4	5 1/3			
Patsy 10.	3 1/2	4 1/3			
Betsy 12.	3.	3 2/3			
Peter 15	2 1/4	2 2/3			
Isabella 19.	1 1/4	1 1/3			
William 21.	baby clothes				
John gardr.	5 1/2	7			1
Amy	5	7	1		1
John Hem.					1
Lewis	5 1/2	7			1
Jenny	5	7	1		1
42					

1821. 2	woolen	shirting	blankets	beds	hats
Mary Bet.	5	7			1
Mary. Mos.	5	7			1
Davy 3	5 1/4	6 2/3	1		1
Celia. 6	4 1/2	5 2/3			1
Tucker 10	3 1/2	4 1/3			1
Zacariah. 12	3	3 2/3			
Patsy 15	2 1/4	2 2/3			
Fossett 17	1 3/4	2	1		
Fontaine 19	1 1/4	1 1/3			
Nace	5 1/2	7.	1.		1
Nance	5	7		1	1
Ned.	5 1/2	7			1
Jenny	5	7			1
Moses 3.	5 1/4	6 2/3			1
Sucky 6.	4 1/2	5 2/3			1
Peter Hem.	5 1/2	7			
Phill B.	5 1/2	7			
Polly. Chas. 10.	3 1/2	4 1/3			1
Sally Hem.	5.	7		1	
Madison 5	4 3/4	6	1		1
Eston 8	4	5	1		1
Shephord.	5	7	1		1
Indridge	5	7			1
Thrimston	5 1/2	7	1		1
Wormly	5 1/2	7	1		1
Ursula	5	7	1		1
Joe 5	4 3/4	6	1		1
Anne 7.	4 1/4	5 1/3	1		1
Dolly 9.	3 3/4	4 2/3			1
Cornelius 11	3 1/4	4			1
Thomas 13	2 3/4	3 1/3			
Louisa 16	2	2 1/3			
Caroline 18	1 1/2	1 2/3			
Critta. 19	1 1/4	1 1/3			
34.					
Sally. M.	5	7			1
Nancy 12	3	3 2/3			
Charlotte 16	2	2 1/3			
	wool	linen			
men	93 1/2	259	20	5	
women	95				
children	120 1/2	147 2/3			
	309	406 2/3			

NOTES to Page 172: Slave list 1821-2

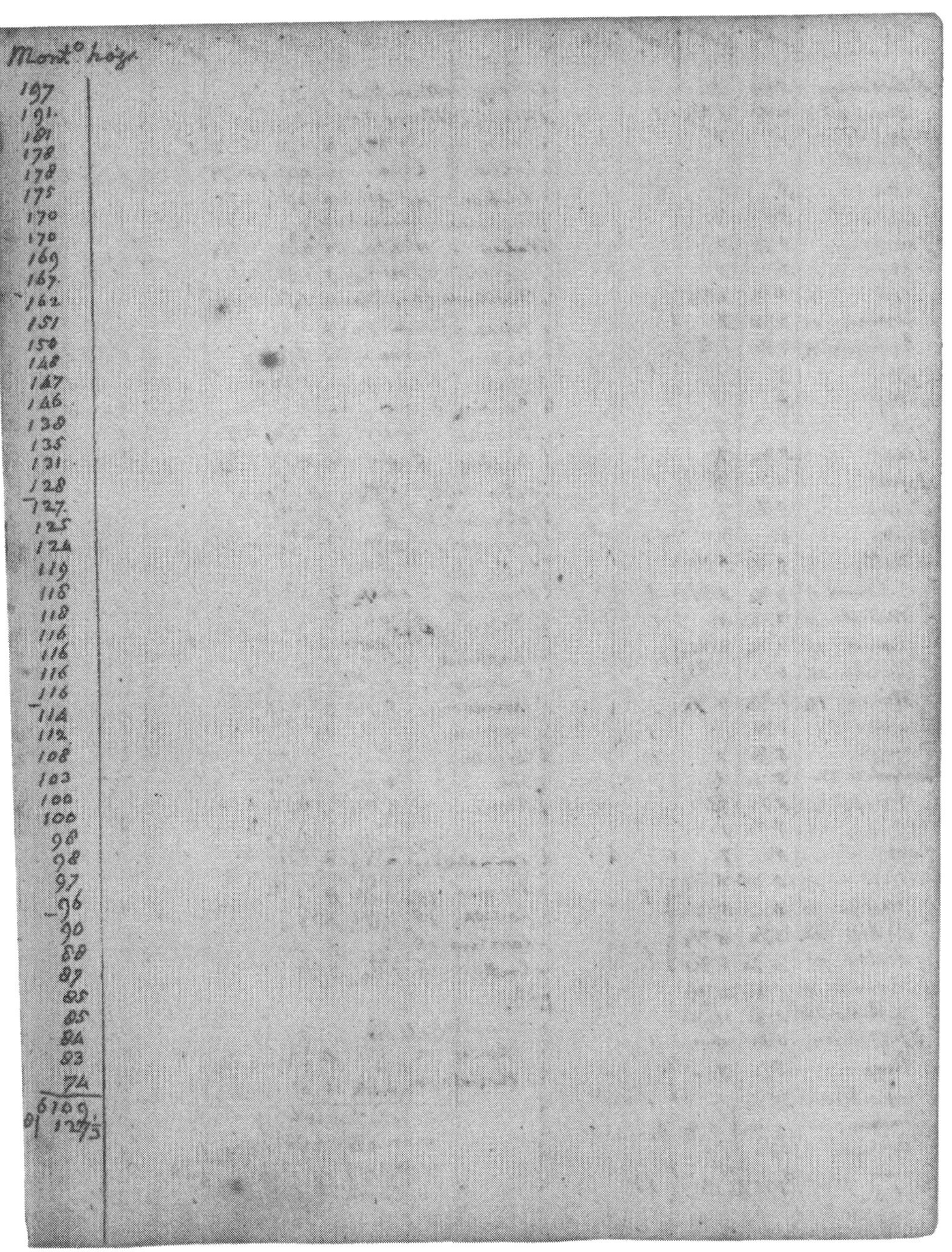

Mont° hogs

197
191.
181
178
178
175
170
170
169
167.
162
151
150
148
147
146
138
135
131
128
127.
125
124
119
118
118
116
116
116
116
114
112
108
103
100
100
98
98
97
96
90
88
87
85
85
84
83
74

6109.
1275

NOTES to Page 173: Mont hogs

1822	woollen	shirting	blankets	bed
Barnaby	5 1/2	7		
Stannard 9	4 1/4	5 2/3		
Betty Brown	5	7	1	
{Burwell				
Critta	5	7		
Davy senr.	5 1/2	7		
Davy jr.	5 1/2	7		
Fanny	5	7		
Ellen 9	4 1/4	5 2/3	1	
Jenny 11	3 3/4	5		
Indridge 19	1 3/4	2 1/3		
Doll	5	7	1	1
Dolly	5	7		1
Gill	5 1/2	7		
Isaac	5 1/2	7		
Israel	5 1/2	7	1	
James	5 1/2	7		
Critta	5	7		1
Milly 7	4 3/4	6 1/3		
Lilburn 9	4 1/4	5 2/3	1	
Matilda 11	3 3/4	5	1	
Band 15	2 3/4	3 2/3		
Lovila 18	2	2 2/3		
Nancy 19	1 3/4	2 1/3		
James Lt's	5 1/2	7	1	
Jerry	5 1/2	7	1	
Jupiter	5 1/2	7		
Amy 20	1 1/2	2		
Joe	5 1/2	7		
Edy	5	7		1
Maria 7	4 3/4	6 1/3	1	
Patsy 10	4	5 1/3		
Betsy 12	3 1/2	4 2/3	1	
Peter 15	2 3/4	3 2/3		
Isabella 19	1 3/4	2 1/3		
William 21	1 1/4	1 2/3		
Joh gardener	5 1/2	7	1	
Amey	5	7		
John Hem	5 1/2	7	1	
~~Louis~~	~~5 1/2~~	7 8	June	19.
Jenny	5	7		
41	174 3/4	231 1/3	12	4

	woollen	shirting	blankets	bed
Mary Bet's	5	7		
Mary Mos'	5	7		1
Davy	5 1/2	7		
Celia 6	5	6 2/3	1	
Tucker 10	4	5 1/3	1	
Zachoma 12	3 1/2	4 2/3		
Patsy 15	2 3/4	3 2/3		
Fosset 17	2 1/4	3		
Fontaine 19	1 3/4	2 1/3		
Nace	5 1/2	7		
Nance	5	7		
Ned	5 1/2	7		
Jenny	5	7		
Moses	5 1/2	7	1	
Sucky 6	5	6 2/3		
Peter Hem	5 1/2	7	1	
Polly Chas. 10	4	5 1/2		
Randal	5 1/2	7		
Sally Hem	5	7		
Madison	5 1/2	7		
Eston 8	4 1/2	6		
Shepherd	5 1/2	7		
Indridge	5	7	1	
Thrimston	5 1/2	7	1	
Wormly	5 1/2	7		
Ursula	5	7		
Joe	5 1/2	7		
Anne 7	4 3/4	6 1/3		
Dolly 9	4 1/4	5 1/3	1	
Cornelius 11	3 3/4	5	1	
Thomas 13	3 1/4	4 1/3		
Louisa 16	2 1/2	3 1/3		
Caroline 18	2	2 2/3		
Critta 19	1 3/4	2 1/3		
34				
Sally M	5	7		
Nancy 12	3 1/2	4 2/3		
Charlotte 16	2 1/2	3 1/3		
3				
	161 1/2	214 1/3	9	1
	174 3/4	231 1/3	12	4
	336 1/4	445 2/3	21	5

NOTES to Page 174: Slave list 1822

1823. Decemb.	woollen	shirting	blanket	bed
Barnaby	5½	7	1	
Stannard 9	4½	6		
Betty Brown	5	7		
Burwell			1	
Critta	5	7		
Davy senr.	5½	7	1	
Davy jr.	5½	7	1	
Fanny	5	7		
Ellen 9	4½	6		
Jenny 11	4	5⅓		
Indridge 19	2	2⅔		
Melinda 22	1¼	1⅓		
Doll	5	7		
~~Dolly~~ sold	5	7		
Gill		7		
Isaac	5½	7		
Israel		7		
B James	5½	7	1	
Cretia	5	7	1	
Milly 7	5	6⅔		
Lilburn 9	4½	6		
Matilda 11	4	5⅓		
Band 15	3	4		
Louisa 18	2¼	3		
Nancy 19	2	2⅔		
James L's	5½	7		
Jerry	5½	7		
Jupiter	5½	7	1	
Amy 20	1¾	2⅓		
Joe	5½	7		
Edy	5	7	1	
Maria 7	5	6⅔		
Patsy 10	4¼	5⅔		
Betsy 12	3¾	5		
Peter 15	3	4		
Isabella 19	2	2⅔	} 1	
William 21	1½	2		
John	5½	7		
Amy	5	7		1
John H.				
Jenny L.	5	7		1
41.	158½	210⅔	9	2

	woolen	shirting	blanket	bed
Mary Bets	5	7	1	
B Mary Moses'	5	7	1	
Davy	5½	7		
B Celia 6	5	7		
B Tucker 10	4¼	5⅔		
Zacharia 12	3¾	5	1	
B Patsy 15	3	4		
B Fossel 17	2½	3⅓		
B Fontaine 19	2	2⅔		
~~Moses~~	5½	7		
Nance	5	7		
Ned	5½	7	1	
Jenny	5	7	1	1
Moses	5½	7		
B Suckey 6	5	7	1	
Peter Hem.	5½	7		
Polly Cha's. 10	4¼	5⅔	1	
B Randal	5½	7	1	
Sally Hem.	5	7	1	
Madison	5½	7		
Eston	5½	7		
Shepherd	5½	7		
Indridge	5	7		1
Thrimston	5½	7		
Wormly	5½	7	1	
Ursula	5	7		1
B Joe	5½	7		
Anne 7	5	6⅔		
Dolly 9	4½	6		
Cornelius 11	4	5⅓		
Thomas 13	3½	4⅔	} 1	
Louisa 16	2¾	3⅔		
Caroline 18	2¼	3	} 1	
Critta 19	2	2⅔		
George 23. 3¼ infant. aug. 24				
Sally M.	5	7		1
Nancy 12	3¾	5		
Charlotte 16	2¾	3⅓	} 1	
3	166¼	235	13	4
	158¼	210⅔	9	2
	324½	445⅔	22	6

41

NOTES to Page 175: 1823 Decomb Woolen Shirting blankets beds

1825. Dec.	woollen	shirting	blankets	beds
Barnaby	5 1/2	7		
Stannard 9.	4 3/4	6 1/3	1	
Betty Brown	5	7	- - -	1
Burwell				
Critty	5.	7	1	1
Davy sen^r.	5 1/2	7		
Davy jun^r.	5 1/2	7		
Davy Moses's	5 1/2	7	1	
Fanny	5	7	1	1
Ellen 9	4 3/4	6 1/3		
Jenny 11	4 1/4	5 2/3		
Indridge 19.	2 1/4	3.		
Melinda	1 1/2	2.		
Doll	5	7		
Gill	5 1/2	7	1	
Israel	5 1/2	7	1	
Isaac	5 1/2	7		
James	5 1/2	7.		
Jerry	5 1/2	7.		
Amy 20	2.	2 2/3		
Jupiter	5 1/2	7		
Joe	5 1/2	7	1	
Edy	5.	7		
Maria	5	7		
Patsy 10	4 1/2	6		
Betsy 12	4	5 1/3		
Peter 15.	3 1/4	4 1/3		
Isabella 9.	2 1/4	3.		
William 24.	1 3/4	2 1/3		
John	5 1/2	7		
Aray	5	7	1.	
John Hem				
Jenny L's	5	7		
Mary Bet's	5	7		

	woollen	shirting	blankets	beds
Moses	5 1/2	7		
Nace	5 1/2	7	1	
Nance	5	7	--	1
Ned	5 1/2	7.		
Jenny	5	7	1	
Peter Hem.	5 1/2	7		
Polly Chas. 10.	4 1/2	6		
Sally Hem	5.	7	- -	1
Madison	5 1/2	7	1	
Eston.	5 1/2	7.	1	
Shepherd	5 1/2	7.	1	
Indridge	5	7		
Thrimston	5 1/2	7.		
Wormley	5 1/2	7		
Ursula.	5	7	1	
Anne	5	7	1	
Dolly 9.	5.	6 2/3		
Cornelius	4 1/4	5 2/3		
Thomas 13	3 3/4	5.		
Louisa. 16	3.	4.		
Caroline 18.	2 1/2	3 1/3		
Critta 19	2 1/4	3		
George 23.	1 1/4	1 2/3		
. . . . .	1	1 1/3		
Zacharia 12		8.		
Sally Marks	5.	7.	1	
Nancy 12	4.	5 1/3		
C Charlotte 16.	3	4.		
23. children	68 3/4	101		
21. men	135 1/2	147		
16. women	80	112		
60. Burwell J. Hem.	264 1/2	360	16	5.

NOTES to Page 176: Slave list 1825 Dec. Woolen Shirting blankets beds Sally Hem. is listed with her two remaining children below her.

NOTES to Page 177: Blank page

NOTES to Page 178: Blank page